Trinity

POLITICAL STABILITY IN
LATER VICTORIAN ENGLAND
A sociological Analysis and Interpretation

For Dr D. Russell Davies, Rosemary Mills, Gill Parry and June Eldridge, in appreciation of the patience and good-humoured co-operation in helping with the production of this book at the Design Studio, UCW Aberystwyth.

Many thanks to you all

Alice

POLITICAL STABILITY IN LATER VICTORIAN ENGLAND

A sociological Analysis and Interpretation

Alice Russell

The Book Guild Ltd
Sussex, England

The Book Guild Ltd
25 High Street
Lewes, Sussex.

First published 1992
© Alice Russell 1992
Set in Baskerville
Typesetting by Rosemary Mills
Design Studio
Registry, UCW Aberystwyth.
Printed in Great Britain by
Antony Rowe Ltd
Chippenham, Wiltshire.

A catalogue record for this book is available from the British
Library

ISBN 0 86332 695 1

Contents

PART ONE
Paternalists and their Strategies:
Leaders, Socialization and Social Control

PART TWO
Reaction: Resistance and Acquiescence

List of Tables

LATE VICTORIAN LANCASHIRE : TOWNS AND TRANSPORT

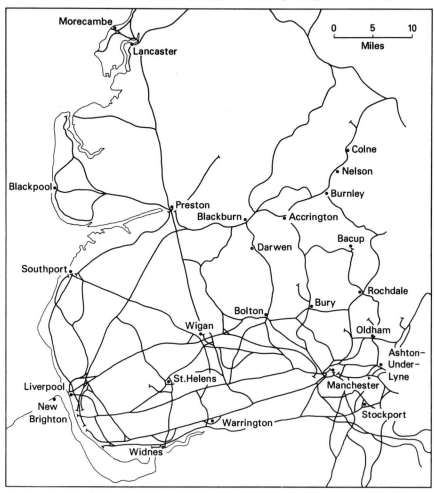

Introduction

The Debate

The origins of modern industrial society and successive stages in inter-class relationships have been the preoccupation of social historians for several decades. The nineteenth century was an evolutionary period in the development of a class-based society. Consciousness of class was taking root, and both contemporary and modern investigation focused upon the relationship between the social classes. Given changes in social structure or the stratification order, it has been the political patterns which have proved difficult to explain. In some of the most impressive work produced in the 1960s social stratification was analysed at the macro level of society as a whole. Perkin's(1) interpretation, for example, represented change as a transition from the interest groups of pre-industrial society with their vertically orientated bonds of responsibility and dependence to a modern class-based industrial society containing three major strata with horizontally structured patterns of identification and allegiance. In Thompson's(2) vastly detailed study of the making of the English working class the emergence of proletarian class consciousness was claimed to have been one of the major gains of the industrial revolution.

Arguments suggesting the creation of monolithic, solidaristic classes are persuasive, but panoramic overviews such as these tend to be rather too sweepingly dismissive of the anomalies which are to be found at the micro level of the city, the town or the village. As Foster's(3) investigation of three industrial towns located in contrasting geographical regions demonstrates, local communities were often strikingly different in terms of their degree of class consciousness, the nature of class conflict and the political response. Another problem which arises out of broad generalizations alleging the efflorescence of working-class consciousness amongst the lower orders in the early decades of the nineteenth century is that of explaining subsequent, sometimes prolonged, periods of political inactivity or political quiescence, a phenomenon which has prompted some historians(4) to locate the evolution of the working class as a permanent, settled, effectively organized force in the late nineteenth century; it was only belatedly that the institutionalized co-ordination of the economic and political roles of labour was successfully accomplished with the new working relationship between the Trades Union Congress and the embryonic Labour Party.

Other social historians, while accepting the need for attention to regional detail, have confined their micro-level investigations to comparatively short time spans with the consequence of a degree of distortion in the construction put upon inter-class relationships. This is a problem which stems, in part at least, from the fact that researchers have focused upon local communities in very different economic circumstances prevailing both generally and regionally. In Joyce's(5) otherwise path-breaking study of Blackburn and other northern towns he explains the political quiescence of newly enfranchised wage-workers in the late 1860s on the basis of paternalism. According to this line of argument paternalistic factory masters were able to cultivate communal identities which dissolved divisive class consciousness; they exercised social control over the occupational communities clustered about the mills by socializing workers in dominant ideology. Joyce's research, concentrating largely upon the cotton towns of textile Lancashire, traces the economic, social and political interaction which enabled leading employers to replicate the factory structure of authority beyond the confines of the workplace, thereby promoting a sense of mill-focused neighbourhood community; the successful reintroduction of paternalistic leadership styles during the 1850s and 1860s allegedly explains the relative social stability of the era and underlies the political conformity of the subordinate class, despite the electoral opportunities offered by the 1867 Franchise Act. The effective exercise of social control by the privileged few over the deprived many is attributed in no small degree to the former's ability to legitimate their leadership by socializing subordinates in an appropriate set of norms and values. Workers' compliance is claimed to be the product of consent rather than coercion. The argument is implicitly premised upon the dominant ideology thesis. It implies that deference was the working-class response - that in most class societies 'there is a set of beliefs which dominates all others and which, through its incorporation in the consciousness of subordinate classes, tends to inhibit the development of radical political dissent ... and to prevent the formulation of any effective opposition.'(6)

In apparent contradiction of Joyce's interpretation Dutton and King,(7) in their investigation of industrial relations in Preston during the first half of the nineteenth century, stress the limits of paternalism. Employers are represented as ruthlessly single-minded in their pursuit of profit, unwilling or unable to protect jobs or to maintain wage rates in even slight recessions, and minimalist in their approach to industrial welfare. Masters and their hired hands are depicted in oppositional terms as protagonists in the class struggle for income. Wage-workers are viewed as members of an alienated underclass with a deep-rooted sense of shared grievance; they offer a persistent, often barely controlled, proletarian challenge to the dominance of Preston's employer class, and force a series of concessions and compromises. Evidence is assembled to demonstrate prolonged, bitter, near-revolutionary confrontation between combatants locked in a state of continuous class warfare in an era punctuated by recurrent recessions. The picture is not one of social and political consensus produced by dominant ideology but of class conflict reflecting the presence of fundamentally opposed value systems.

To some extent the contradictions contained in these two last-mentioned studies are attributable to differences in prevailing economic circumstances; but they are also the outcome, in part at least, of conceptual, definitional and methodological shortcomings. The contrasting interpretations, offered by Joyce on the one hand and by Dutton and King on the other, of events and circumstances not widely separated in terms of time nor of regional location are difficult to reconcile. Both views, the one stressing the apparent pervasiveness of employers' influence at the local level of the urban industrial community, the other emphasizing the apparently effective check imposed upon employers' freedom of action by a subordinate class conscious of its own class interests, embody generalized interpretations which are too crude and too sweeping. If employers' influence was as widespread and their ability to maintain the *status quo* as profound as Joyce appears to claim, it is difficult to explain the many political, economic and legislative concessions made to the subordinate class. If, on the other hand, the confrontational, proletarian style of opposition offered by wage-workers was as extensive and as effectively organized as Dutton and King seem to suggest, it is puzzling that the institutionalized co-ordination of lower-class economic and political objectives premised on the ideology of Socialism took so long to achieve. Both views are subject to a degree of overstatement. The more balanced view would represent paternalistic employers as less pervasively influential and their workpeople as less comprehensively deferential than Joyce would have them, and it would interpret subordinates' response as less persistently oppositional and less consistently radical in thought and action than Dutton and King suggest.

The kinds of events and circumstances identified by the above-mentioned authors are clearly important, but an alternative, and in many ways preferable, approach to the investigation of the relationship between different social strata is to evaluate such events and circumstances in terms of the meaning systems or ideologies which these appear to represent. The main advantage of this approach is that it permits the construction of a more flexible and adaptable generalization capable of accommodating what are apparently dramatic changes in economic circumstances and inter-class relations during the middle and later years of the nineteenth century. It is instructive to consider, if only briefly, recent developments in sociological thought on culture and ideology.

Dominant ideology or competing meaning systems?

The recent sociological concern with the nature and influence of culture and ideology has its origins in the works of Marx and Engels.(8) There are two theories which can be traced back to these origins. The first is premised on the claim that, since each socio-economic class has a unique relationship to the means of production, this generates class-specific ideologies which reflect different material conditions and give expression to different class interests. As Engels comments in a much-quoted passage:

> The workers speak other dialects, have other thoughts and ideas, other customs and moral principles, a different religion and other politics than those of the bourgeoisie.(9)

That fundamentally dissimilar material and intellectual conditions produce different meaning systems is crucial to an understanding of the nature of social class, class conflict, class consciousness, and the political responses which these produce.

The second theory claims that in most class societies there is a set of pervasive beliefs which serve the economic and political interests of the dominant or superordinate class. These dominant values are internalized by members of the subordinate stratum. The process of internalization inhibits the formation of an effective, oppositional political force and therefore ensures the continued political superiority of those in positions of power.(10) The spread of dominant ideology is clearly dependent upon the effectiveness of the institutional framework for disseminating the normative codes constructed by the superordinate social stratum. This second theory is premised upon the argument that members of the dominant class have the means to impose their own ideology upon the rest, a process which, by discouraging the development of radical oppositional consciousness, serves to maintain the *status quo*. Dominant ideology is effectively disseminated by superordinates who own and/or control the means of material and moral production and who possess the necessary organizational ability to dominate the institutional means to legitimate their leadership. Miliband,(11) for example, drawing on Gramsci's concept of 'bourgeois hegemony' argues that, in the modern capitalist societies of the industrialized west, there is a 'process of massive indoctrination' carried out by dominant class members who have strategic influence 'by virtue of their position, for instance, as employers, to dissuade members of the subordinate class . . . from voicing unorthodox views.'(12) As Abercrombie *et al.* argue, however:

> The two beliefs are potentially in conflict with one another. The first suggests that each class forms its own system of beliefs in accordance with its own particular interests which will be basically at variance with those of other classes. The second suggests that all classes share in the system of belief imposed by the dominant class.(13)

The conflict between these two theories of ideology is not confined to Marxist thought. The contradiction recurs in Parsons's theory(14) of socialization in dominant values; in *The Social System* the problem of oppositional or deviant behaviour is simply treated as a consequence of an incomplete process of socialization. Alternatively, in Durkheimian theory deviance is interpreted in terms of the problems associated with 'boundary maintenance'. There are similar conceptual and interpretational difficulties, therefore, in both functionalist sociology and in Marxist thought:

> Functionalists are committed both to the notion that a common value system is a necessary condition of the existence of a social system, and to the theory of structural differentiation which creates pluralistic value systems. Marxists are committed to a theory of 'ruling ideas' and to the theory that each class, because of its own interests, has its own unique culture.(15)

Each of these theories has a long academically respectable prehistory in sociological thought, but more recent research appears to suggest that subordinate-class attitudes and expectations are less static than the theories imply. Hill argues that there are fluctuations in working-class consciousness between dominant and subordinate values; workers tend to adopt oppositional, combative stances in practical situations of immediate relevance, but are less militant in their attitudes when the issues are of a theoretical or abstract kind.(16) Another manifestation of this normative dualism is to be found in Mann's research which discloses that 'surges of class consciousness are continually under cut by economism....'(17)

Clarification may be assisted by closer attention to the ideologies potentially available to members of the community. Parkin identifies three major meaning systems characteristically present in western industrial societies: the *dominant*, the *subordinate* and the *radical* value systems. Each of these derives from a different social source.

The *dominant* value system(18) derives from the major institutional order. It offers a moral framework which endorses the prevailing distribution of power and privilege, opportunity and material rewards. By definition this is the ideology of the dominant class, and in so far as it is espoused by members of the subordinate class, it reflects an interpretation of the socio-economic system in either *deferential* or *aspirational terms*.

The concept of the dominant value system assumes that advantaged members of society who are to be found in formal and informal positions of power are also in control of agencies and institutions to legitimate their authority. In other words, the ideology of those who occupy dominant positions tends to become embodied in the major institutional order, to be reflected nationally in the course of legislation and locally in by-laws. Dominant values, regarded by all subgroups within the dominant class as socially, politically and morally just, may be interpreted as the perceptions and interests of relatively privileged members of society. The moral and political rules 'hold sway not because they are self-evidently "right", but because they are made to seem so by those who wield institutional power.'(19)

A major controversial theme amongst sociologists and social historians is the extent to which members of the subordinate social stratum internalize what are represented as dominant-class values. An important dimension of this debate is to be found in the interest shown in the propensity for some disprivileged members of society to support political parties which appear to perpetuate the advantages of the advantaged - working-class

Conservatives,(20) for example, whose political choice is said to be the product of deference.

Deferential endorsement by subordinates of the prevailing distribution of economic rewards, political power and social status derives from an internalization of the dominant value system. Deferentials subscribe to a moral order which legitimates their own economic, political and social subordination. The deferential view interprets the prevailing stratification order as an organic entity in which inequalities are inevitable and justifiable on the grounds that some members of the community are fit and proper persons for positions of leadership and others are not. Membership of subordinate social strata is not necessarily regarded as an indicator of inferiority since deferentials 'appear to accept the classic doctrine that all who properly fulfil their station in life contribute worthily to the common good.'(21) Deferential attitudes are most likely to be found amongst subordinates who have direct personal contact and regular social encounters with dominant class members either in the workplace, particularly where the employer regards his own role as a paternalistic one, or in relatively isolated rural communities which have only limited communications with the outside world. Access to alternative ideologies is limited; exposure to dominant ideology is extensive. From neither the world of work nor the status system of the local community does the individual learn to question the appropriateness of his exchange of deference for paternalistic guidance.

Alternatively, acquiescence in the dominant value system may indicate an aspirational interpretation of the stratification order with its associated inequalities of condition, an interpretation which emphasizes the existence of opportunities for economic advancement and upward social mobility. This view endorses the prevailing stratification order as one which is sufficiently open to permit individuals with talent and motivation to improve their socio-economic situation. As Parkin notes, '. . . whereas the deferential version of the social world accepts the class system as a fixed unchanging order, the aspirational version allows for the social exchange of personnel between classes, while accepting the necessity for classes as such.'(22) Aspirational norms are likely to be found where qualitative and quantitative advances in provision for education promote ambition by fostering competition and rewarding achievement, and where job opportunities permit the aspirations of at least a proportion to be realized.

Other theorists argue that the subordinate social stratum generates its own culture and ideology. The *subordinate* value system, sometimes termed the working-class or lower-class subculture, embodies a highly complex set of norms which defy attempts at simplistic generalization. However, sociological investigation suggests that the basic characteristic of the subordinate value system is what may be termed an 'accommodative' outlook.(23) It is an ideology which rejects both deferential endorsement of, and radical opposition to, the dominant normative order and its underpinning institutions, and which instead places emphasis upon various strategies for adaptation to the prevailing structure of inequality. As Hoggart observes: 'When people feel that they cannot do much about the main elements in their situation, feel it not necessarily with despair or disappointment . . . but simply as a fact of life, they adopt attitudes towards that situation which allow them to have a liveable life under its shadow . . . .'(24) The response may range from inertia and total apathy borne of powerlessness at one extreme to strong expressions of dissatisfaction at the other. This interpretation of the social order conceptualized in terms of social division is premised upon a power model of the structure of advantage and disadvantage and questions the morality of the prevailing distribution of rewards. Yet, as Parkin maintains, it is erroneous to 'construe the subordinate value system as an example of normative opposition to the dominant order. Least of all . . . should it be understood as exemplifying class-consciousness or political radicalism.'(25) Dahrendorf and Newton both stand accused of making misleading claims on this score.(26) Subordinate-class discontent, channelled into strong expressions of resentment towards bureaucratic officialdom and other manifestations of institutional authority, is not an indicator of political class-consciousness as conventionally defined - that is, the espousal of a radical political ideology which seeks to dismantle the institutional structure of capitalist society and to replace this and the capitalist mode of production by others based upon Socialist principles. A radical meaning system is fundamentally different from one which has as its essential characteristic accommodation to the reality of subordinate status. As Hoggart argues, adjustment to the hardships of material disadvantage, economic insecurity and humble social status may take the form of fatalistic pessimism which springs from feelings of powerlessness and reflects a reluctant but realistic acceptance of restricted opportunities to permit the restructuring of society. Since the prevailing stratification order is unchangeable, it is sensible to make the best of it.

Arguably more important, however, are accommodative

strategies based upon an 'instrumental collectivism'. Such a strategy is represented most obviously by trade unionism, a form of socio-political organization spontaneously generated amongst the subordinate class. This collectivist manifestation of the subordinate value system, a form based both on society and the local community, represents wage-workers' belief in the existence of real opportunities to achieve material improvements in standards of living within the established framework of the prevailing stratification order. Collective bargaining signifies an acceptance of existing institutional forms and of the rules governing the distribution of economic rewards. Organized labour 'directs its main efforts towards winning a greater share of resources for its members - not by challenging the existing framework of rules but by working within this framework.'(27) Collective bargaining does not seek to dismantle the prevailing stratification order nor the institutional forms which underpin it. Trade unionism may therefore be said to function as an important stabilizing agency in that, by accepting and working within the rules governing the allocation of resources, it legitimates the dominant institutional system. 'Trade union consciousness' differs from 'class consciousness' in that the latter has the potential to achieve social and political change while the former exemplifies what is arguably the defining characteristic of the subordinate value system: an 'uneasy compromise between total rejection and full endorsement of the dominant order' or what may be termed a 'negotiated version' of dominant ideology in which dominant values are neither endorsed nor dismissed but adapted or modified in the light of subordinates' social circumstances. Extensive exposure to dominant values in the context of prevailing institutional forms means that these values are not readily disavowed. Rodman argues that the underclass has two main levels of normative reference - the dominant value system and a 'negotiated' version which he terms the 'lower-class value stretch'.(28) Circumstances such as these do not in themselves generate political opposition on the part of the subordinate class to the dominant order.

Oppositional values, specifically those embodied in the *radical* normative order, are constructed by the mass political party based on the subordinate class. Party policy embodies ideals, usually Socialist or Marxist, which deny the validity of capitalist values embodied in dominant ideology; long-term policy seeks to replace capitalist institutions and the capitalist mode of production with forms based on Socialist principles. The radical interpretation of the social order differs in important respects, therefore, from the version promoted by instrumental collectivism or trade union consciousness. It differs also from that embodied in dominant ideology. In contrast to the low status attached to manual work in the scale of social honour promoted by the dominant value system, the ideals of Socialism provide members of.the subordinate class with a more favourable social identity. The radical value system 'affirms the dignity of labour and accords the worker a position of honour in the hierarchy of esteem.'(29) Once established, the radical political party performs important educational and consciousness-raising functions in disseminating information about the nature and extent of inequality and in providing an interpretation of events and circumstances which is very different from the version offered by the dominant culture.

Clearly, in an investigation of urban communities in the later nineteenth century, a great deal depends, firstly, upon the extent to which the subordinate social stratum is exposed to each of these three major meaning systems and, secondly, on factors which influence its response. Radical ideology, though available, may be met with caution. Much depends upon prevailing economic circumstances and the past performance of those in positions of leadership, but crucial also are the social sources of stability which may serve to maintain the *status quo*.

The social sources of stability

A primary task at the outset is to identify the social sources of stability. If they function effectively as social stabilizers they help to maintain the prevailing distribution of power, the institutional framework which underpins it, and the associated inequalities in the distribution of material rewards. It is generally acknowledged that some totalitarian states in the modern world attempt to resolve the problem of social control by the direct, often unsophisticated, means of repressive legislation reinforced by a draconian policing system and a formidable range of penalties for infringements. This strategy is not characteristic of democratic industrial societies in the modern world. It would not be difficult to find evidence of repressive legislation in nineteenth-century Britain, and at the local level, as we shall see, employers were often able to exploit their relative economic advantage to neutralize the power of strikers by the use of strike-breakers. Most societies have elements of coercion built into their control systems. More importantly, however, most democratic societies make attempts to persuade, to convince and to promote acquiescence without overt and persistent resort to mass intimidation and the restriction of freedoms. An important objective of a dominant social stratum is to legitimate the institutional framework, to maintain social stability by consent rather than by coercion.

The three most important social sources of stability in the nineteenth century, it is claimed, are education, religion and recreation. This is not to assert that such social mechanisms were consciously created by an irresponsible, self-seeking, dominant class with the Machiavellian aim of exploitatively controlling subordinates in order to protect a socio-political stratification order which privileged the few to the disadvantage of the many; but neither were the advantaged unaware of the stabilizing functions which these mechanisms could perform. Social control was not necessarily the primary, nor even a major, intention of those who provided such services 'from above'; but if the net result was to foster an improvement in respect for law and order, people and property, there was every justification from the viewpoint of the dominant class actively to promote the extension of appropriate facilities. The process of maintaining control by socializing lower-class members into 'appropriate' attitudes, habits of thought and patterns of behaviour is not as simple and straightforward as may be supposed. Social stability may be the intended objective but reactions may be other than those sought, and unanticipated or uncontrollable counter-influences may act as neutralizing agents.

(a) Education

There are several ways in which education may foster acquiescence. Firstly, by equipping able members of school populations with the necessary general and specific skills, particularly where these are measured in examinations and evidenced in paper qualifications, education may facilitate upward mobility by enabling youngsters from disprivileged social backgrounds to achieve higher socio-economic positions than their parental generation. Provision for elementary schooling plus the availability of more advanced vocational and technological courses, whether in day or evening classes, serve both to widen and improve the job prospects of those with the ability and motivation to succeed. Scholastic achievement, promoted by the competitive spirit and rewarded with prizes, words of praise and the listing of successful examinees in rank order, is both an end in itself and the means to skilled manual or white-collar employment. The increasing demand for clerks with the expansion of the service sector in the final quarter of the nineteenth century provided attractive employment opportunities for both girls and boys.

In practice the interchange between classes tends to be short-range and numerically modest. Sociological investigation into social and occupational mobility in twentieth-century industrial society suggests the existence of a 'social and cultural "buffer zone" between the middle class and working class proper'(30) and indicates that most mobility occurs within a comparatively narrow social span involving movement into and out of this zone rather than movement between the class extremes. In providing an escape route for able and ambitious members of the underclass, opportunities for even a modest degree of social mobility act as a safety valve to ease some of the tensions generated by inequality of condition. The opportunity to rise to a more favourable position in the prevailing stratification order promotes acquiescence in the *status quo* by offering a personal or individualist solution to low status and its attendant dissatisfactions. The means to social promotion may therefore be *one* mechanism likely to perpetuate the existing political order. For individuals with the ability to compete on the basis of the relevant meritocratic criteria it makes little sense to challenge the legitimacy of a socio-economic system which offers favourable opportunities for advancement. The individual is the more prepared to work *with* the system rather than *against* it because he or she is the less likely to experience the problems of frustrated aspirations and an associated sense of alienation.

Secondly, by an extension of this argument, a related way in which the education system assists in promoting acquiescence in the prevailing order is by encouraging those with only modest ability and limited skill potential to modify their employment expectations and social aspirations accordingly. As Parkin has observed, despite the emergence of political values and of political movements which have challenged the economic, social and ideological basis of the prevailing distribution of advantage and disadvantage, strategies of accommodation to and acceptance of low social positions continue to be a marked feature of subordinates' reactions. People who view themselves as occupants of lowly, modestly remunerated positions in society are often inclined to tailor their expectations of life to a correspondingly modest level. 'When expectations are low, the frustration caused by unsatisfied wants is the more easily avoided.'(31) This function in twentieth-century Britain has been performed by selectivity which has continued to be built into the education system since 1944. The tripartite system of grammar, technical and modern schools with recruitment based on the principles of age, aptitude and ability, succeeded by comprehensivization with an often sophisticated structure of 'setting' and 'streaming', has helped adolescents to come to terms with the reality of limited future prospects, thereby performing a 'useful and humane function in psychologically preparing future members of the underclass for the harsh realities of the world awaiting them outside the school gates . . . .'(32) The more successful the education system is in doing this, the more difficult becomes the task of radical groups in encouraging the disprivileged to challenge the socio-political order.(33)

The way in which the education system performs the function of psychological preparation is not unique to the twentieth century nor to the evolving institutional, organizational and administrative forms of the post-1944 era. In the second half of the nineteenth century a similar function was performed by the facilities for elementary schooling supplemented by day and evening classes offered by Mechanics' and similar institutes and by the narrow scholarship ladder providing financially assisted access to the grammar schools. For some, parental poverty undoubtedly blocked access to the opportunities which were available but, this apart, to the extent that the elementary schooling system fostered and tested abilities, it confronted the less able with their own limitations from an early age. The less intelligent, whose educational performance was poor or only mediocre, are unlikely to have approached the future with high expectations or inflated ambition.

Thirdly, the content of education, it is claimed, tends to reflect the ideology of the dominant class. The implicit objectives of nineteenth-century education for the masses included the cultivation of attitudes judged by its sponsors to be socially, economically and politically desirable: industriousness, conformism, willingness to comply with statutory regulations and informal codes embodying respect for authority whether in the form of law and order or of persons and property. Schooling was intended to prepare boys for future roles as sober, respectful, dutiful workers and girls for future roles as respectable, selfless, morally responsible wives and mothers orientated towards domesticity and capable of nurturing the next generation in 'right attitudes'.(34) Values were communicated by the way in which pupils were stretched or discouraged in the process of learning, by the experience of praise and blame, approbation and censure, reward and punishment. It is argued that dominant ideology is likely to have informed both the 'formal' and 'informal' curricula. The fact that for most of the nineteenth century elementary schooling for the masses was largely the product of voluntary effort on the part of middle-class patrons and religious institutions is crucial to an understanding of the kind of values, expectations and aspirations which were fostered.

This is not to argue that socialization in the ideology of compliance was a straightforward, uncomplicated process. An important qualification upon the effectiveness of efforts to inculcate a particular set of values, both before and after the move to compulsory education in the late nineteenth century, was the extent to which children were exposed to the influence of the educators. Relevant here are considerations such as the total number of years spent in school, the incidence of absenteeism, provisions permitting early leaving and the half-time system, class size, the use of pupil teachers, and the introduction of payment by results.(35) Moreover, there were counter-educational influences which affected children's attitudes and ambitions and these also may have promoted a tendency to acquiescence.

Bright pupils sometimes failed to fulfil their potential because their employment objectives were other than those achievable with good examination results. Low family income may have necessitated an early entry to the world of work; deep-rooted family tradition, which promoted a tendency for sons to follow in their fathers' footsteps, may have over-ridden other influences upon employment choices. To the extent that the individual's situation produced satisfaction and self-esteem, this worked in the same general direction as other factors promoting acquiescence.

Philosophic acceptance of the status quo is not unsurprising in circumstances where the individual lives, moves and has his being largely amongst similarly placed members of society. As Parkin argues:

> There is a well-spring of social knowledge in any underclass which derives from the personal experience of low status and which is buttressed by the knowledge that the majority of those born into this class will remain in it. Social advancement is not a realistic expectation for most and . . . this means that the normative system of the disprivileged tends to discourage or prevent the upward movement of many who do in fact possess the ability . . . to prosper . . . . Members of the working class have no realistic means of singling out potential high fliers and socializing them differently from those obviously destined for humbler positions. The dampening down of aspirations to square with adult experiences of the reward structure forms part of the social training given to everyone.(36)

Acquiescence springs not from an irrational acceptance of the socio-economic system as a closed order but from a realistic assessment of the prospective destinations of the majority of those born into the subordinate class.

(b) Religion

Religion plays a potentially important stabilizing role, particularly when, as in nineteenth-century Britain, religious institutions are also leading providers of elementary schooling for the masses. The successive waves of school building by the two great voluntary societies, the National Society and the British Society, after each of the Chartist uprisings of 1839, 1842 and 1848 argue that dominant class members viewed education in Christian truths as an effective counter to what they regarded as politically subversive tendencies.

The acceptance of religious definitions of wealth and status and the attitudes, aspirations and expectations fostered by anti-materialist ideologies are likely to promote acquiescence in the secular stratification order. The trials and tribulations associated with low status in the temporal world are viewed as essentially transient; the greater the sufferings borne with dignity and fortitude in this life, the greater the rewards in the next. For the disprivileged, religious beliefs are especially significant in that they offer an alternative framework of merit in which the order of secular priorities is dissolved or reversed; the values embodied in religious ideologies seek to effect an alignment between the mental and material conditions of life by reducing the economic and social objectives of the disprivileged to correspond to the prevailing distribution of rewards.(37) By socializing the disadvantaged into compliant attitudes religious institutions may serve as sophisticated agencies of socialization and social control since the 'manipulation of religious sanctions is generally the prerogative of those who support existing arrangements of power and privilege.'(38) Where all members of a society are united by a single faith, the political implications are formidable indeed.

In modern industrial societies, it is argued, effective normative control along these lines is less readily accomplished. This is partly due to the fact that philosophers have produced rational and scientific explanatory theories which may offer other, more immediately relevant and more convincing definitions of circumstances that are shown to be changeable for the better. Another part of the explanation rests on the spread of sectarianism and, even more importantly, the spread of religious indifference which has undermined the influence of religious ideology. The religious sects to which members of the subordinate class are attracted are often characterized by marked differences in belief and practice.

This argument may be overstated, however, particularly as it applies to British society in the late nineteenth century. To the extent that society contained practising Christians, values held in common may have been more significant than the differentiating characteristics. As far as can be ascertained, the various Christian sects collectively endorsed and actively fostered the virtues of humility, sobriety, honesty, self denial, industriousness, charity, thrift, self-discipline, respect for persons and property, a sense of duty and responsibility, and fortitude in the face of poverty and adversity. Few books dignify these virtues as does the Bible. As Child notes, the collective conscience of nineteenth-century Quaker employers was frequently troubled by the contradictions embodied, on the one hand, in the profit-orientated, acquisitive instincts of the successful entrepreneur and, on the other hand, the Biblical ideals of self denial, frugality and service to others.(39)

Religion may inhibit the spread of interest in radical politics by socializing the disadvantaged into a state of compliant resignation, but religion may function as a counterweight to political radicalism in another way. By providing an alternative focus of interest, religion diverts the time, energy and effort of the disprivileged into activities which do not seek a radical restructuring of the prevailing socio-political order.(40) Again, acquiescence is the end product.

There is little consensus amongst historians about the extent to which the relative stability of nineteenth-century British society is attributable to religious influences. Marx and Engels regretted religion as a drug which inhibited the spread of class consciousness. Both Halévy and Lecky ascribed the stability of the British political order in an era of recurrent waves of revolution in continental Europe to the spread of Methodist religion amongst the lower orders during the late eighteenth and early nineteenth centuries. Perkin interprets the stabilizing role of religion not as a damper upon consciousness of class but as an agency which produced the institutionalization of class - a process which diverted class conflict away from destructive, potentially revolutionary, confrontational violence and into channels of negotiation and conciliation leading to a 'viable class society'.(41) Certainly Andrews(42) and Wearmouth,(43) while less specific in their claims about the political implications of Methodist religion, note the importance of the Methodist organizational legacy in the growth of institutions such as trade unions, friendly societies and cooperatives, and contemporary Chartist literature explicitly acknowledges the movement's indebtedness to Methodist patterns of organization: the mass rallies, class meetings, regular subscriptions, and a local, regional and national structure of committees.

In contrast, the Marxist historian, E.J. Hobsbawm, while acknowledging that class conflict was palliated where class institutions had come into existence, nevertheless remains sceptical about claims that the relative social and political stability of the era can be explained exclusively or even primarily in terms of the mollifying influence of Methodist religion. Methodists were too few in number to have had such an overall effect; moreover, region by region, there is no convincing statistical evidence of a consistently inverse correlation between Methodism and radicalism. In point of fact, there are documentary sources which disclose the presence of practising or former Methodists amongst the leadership of radical movements.(44) It is erroneous, therefore, to assume that religion and radicalism are necessarily sharply antithetical. The extent to which socio-political stability in nineteenth-century Britain can be attributed to the influence of religion remains a controversial issue.

Recent sociological research into the socializing effect of religion in the twentieth century has also produced contradictory observations, particularly in so far as these relate to the 'counter-revolutionary thesis'.(45) Rydenfelt's investigation of two economically similar provinces in northern Sweden disclosed an inverse relationship between electoral support for Communism and a strong legacy of religious revivalism, and Blauner(46) similarly ascribed the relative indifference of white industrial workers towards radical labour movements in some of the southern states of the USA to the counter-attraction of religion.

The social groups studied by Rydenfelt and Blauner, it may be objected, were in many ways untypical in that the communities under investigation had undergone relatively rapid recent change in their lifestyles; the process of change, still incomplete at the time when the research was undertaken, involved communities which were emerging from the local traditionalism of a conservative rural existence. Considerations of this kind may account for the absence of consensus amongst sociologists about the implications of religion for social stratification. Niebuhr,(47) as Blauner, regarded religion and political radicalism as ideologies which competed for the same recruits, but Niebuhr's research suggested that, in offering practical solutions achievable in the temporal world of the 'here and now', radicalism was the more powerful magnet. Religion, therefore, did not necessarily serve as an effective counter-revolutionary force which preserved social stability since its influence could be undermined by radicalism.

Other sociologists question whether religion and radicalism should be viewed simplistically as competing ideologies; investigation indicates that members of the lower class do not regard these as mutually exclusive alternatives each providing a different set of all-purpose solutions to the multiple problems of low status. It seems convincing, as Parkin argues, that many of the disadvantaged may be drawn to religion periodically as and when there is felt to be a need for consolation; radicalism has no obvious solution for personal problems such as bereavement, loneliness and sickness.

Clearly the extent to which religion functioned effectively as a social source of stability in the nineteenth century is problematic.

(c) Recreation

The link between recreation and social stability is equally contentious. The Protestant work ethic led Victorian moralists and social reformers to exhort the subordinate class to increased industriousness, thrift, sobriety, and self-discipline during the working day. As industrialization accelerated, progressive employers were beginning to acknowledge the productivity implications of workbreaks. It was not uncommon for first and second generation factory workers with the lingering legacy of traditional, desultory work habits, to absent themselves with or without the master's consent, and for masters subsequently to regularize workbreaks to avoid the problem of wilful and unpredictable absenteeism.(48) There were, of course, some employers who continued, even in the more enlightened era of the later nineteenth century, to express a killjoy disapproval of increased leisure time for the masses as providing occasions for irresponsibly rowdy behaviour, for disturbances of the peace, for squandering family income, for drunkenness and debauchery injurious to family welfare, and even for politically subversive activities. There were still other members of the entrepreneurial class who accepted the need for increased leisure but who stressed the necessity of diverting recreational pursuits away from what were regarded as socially undesirable channels and into innocent, healthy, educative and improving ways. The shorter working week, the Saturday half-holiday and Bank Holidays were to be condoned only in so far as such occasions could be used with discretion to foster virtuous habits. During the later years of the nineteenth century the implications for the worker's productive efficiency, of physical fitness and morale were beginning to be understood. Participatory sports, for example, offered opportunities for healthy outdoor exercise and competitive achievement geared to 'fair play' and the 'rules of the game'. To this end uplifting, educative, morally improving, culturally desirable recreational facilities were provided 'from above'.(49) There were other recreational choices, however. A proliferation of commercial agencies for the sale of mass entertainment appeared in the later Victorian era. These providers were less concerned with the socialization of subordinates into a particular set of attitudes than with ensuring orderliness amongst audiences and spectators to protect the commercial viability of their enterprises.(50) Riotous behaviour, which attracted the attention of the local police and magistrates, was obviously unwelcome. There were also many subcultural forms of recreation generated independently by the working classes themselves.

Given that there was freedom of choice from a diverse assortment of recreational options available in most industrial towns of any size, both the extent to which stability was fostered and the process by which this was achieved are full of paradoxes.

Educative, healthy, recreational activities provided 'from above' may serve as a means of socialization to shape attitudes, values and aspirations. Debating societies, lectures and lantern shows, and mutual improvement societies for young men and young women were all potentially influential agencies to foster 'desirable' habits of thought and behaviour. Participation in competitive sports and team games, it is often argued, fostered a sense of 'fair play', teamwork, and disciplined conformity to the rules of the game. If harmlessly enjoyable, rational forms of recreation such as these failed positively to promote acquiescence by socializing attitudes, they may at least have served as diversions from pernicious, potentially injurious and socially undesirable pastimes. Either way, they functioned as stabilizers.

An alternative viewpoint adopted in some modern sociological investigations emphasizes the importance of leisure and recreation as means to physical relaxation and psychological release from the rigours of workplace discipline and the monotony of routinized worktasks.(51) The sense of alienation and grievance is to some extent offset and the recurrent problem of making ends meet made the more bearable by the equally recurrent prospect of small pleasures in the near future. The fact that underclass members are thereby the more predisposed to come to terms with the daily grind of physically arduous and psychologically stultifying work reduces the risk of challenge to the prevailing stratification order.

These responses are premised on the assumption that recreational facilities are provided 'from above', but as other investigations disclose, many leisure activities took independent forms generated subculturally by and for the subordinate class itself. Traditional sports and pastimes of the rural villages often maintained a migrant vestigial presence in the industrial towns of the late nineteenth century. To the extent that these provided occasions for boisterous, energetic, harmlessly enjoyable relaxation they were tolerated by those responsible for the maintenance of law and order.(52) In so far as traditional forms of amusement served as agreeable means to refresh the mind and body and to boost the morale by offering something to look forward to, the net effect was to increase the likelihood of acquiescence in the *status quo.*

Other manifestations of an independent recreational life were viewed with disfavour by members of the dominant class in that such activities flouted the definitions of moral conduct and respectable behaviour which the Victorian reformer sought to promote. Yet, contradictorily, these real or symbolic confrontations, by directing class discontent into non-political channels may have had the effect of maintaining stability. Some forms of recreation were pursued in wilful contravention of local by-laws and stretched to the full the discretionary powers of the police to suppress disturbances of the peace. The inns and taverns, particularly those in the less salubrious districts, were often the focus, not only of the more innocuous versions of lower-class leisure such as free and easy nights and pub games, but also of excessive drinking, public brawling, prostitution which offended public decency and gambling which wasted the family income of those who could ill afford such indulgence. Even so, the symbolic flouting of authority contained in the wilful adherence to what were often furtive and therefore less readily monitored and controlled forms of recreational life provided a less dislocating and less socially disruptive outlet for frustration and hostility than riot and revolution.

(d) Other sources of social stability: consensus, powerlessness, social mobility and welfarism

Potentially at least, education, religion and recreation are important social sources of stability, but there are other influences capable of promoting acquiescence. Consensus, powerlessness, social mobility and welfarism are the most obvious of these.

Consensus need not necessarily accompany *all* the avowed policies, actions and activities of those in authority; neither is it necessary that consent should be universal amongst all those affected by a particular decision, nor that a decision should correspond with preference exactly in every detail. There may be brief, recurrent periods of protest and adverse criticism interspersed with longer periods of satisfaction so that the general or predominant response is one of assent. A minority may continue to be resolutely, possibly unadventurously or myopically, opposed either to any attempt at change or to the particular means or the particular ends; there may be majority rather than universal consent. The policy line or the specific decision may fall short of what was wanted, but the discrepancy between what was sought and what was granted may be only marginal and therefore evaluatedly sufficient to justify acceptance. Alternatively, an initially negative reaction may derive from inadequate knowledge; when the relevant evidence is disclosed and the underlying reasons explained, consensus may be achieved. If interaction is to produce consensus of this kind, much depends upon the effectiveness of the means and manner of communication. These last consist not only of a network of institutions providing a forum for discussion but also of 'broadcasting centres' (formal and informal, official and unofficial) for the transmission of information via the written and spoken word. Much depends also upon trust, reliance and reputations built by decision-makers over a long period of time; people become 'known quantities' in the economic and political dimensions of life and also in the social spheres of friendships, recreational involvement, voluntary service and personal acts of kindness.

Acquiescence may alternatively stem from powerlessness, real or imagined. Opportunities to resist, to oppose or merely to express a contrary majority opinion may to all intents and purposes be non-existent. Effective agencies to promote, obstruct or direct change may be absent, inaccessible or only weakly developed; or those concerned may be unaware of the existence and potential power of mechanisms for resistance and diffident about, because inexperienced in, pressure-group strategy. Political acquiescence, therefore, may take the form of inertia or apathy amongst those who conceptualize their socio-economic situation as one of powerlessness. On the other hand, acquiescence may be an enforced condition produced by a superior strategy engineered by the pervasively powerful to suppress all forms of criticism, thereby creating a spurious harmony. Contrary initiatives, despite repeated or continuous effort, may prove futile in the face of the entrenched authority of those who monopolize the institutions of control. There is the semblance of agreement but not its actuality.

An increased propensity to acquiesce in the prevailing institutional order may be promoted by welfarism. Paternalistic attention to welfare may serve to create a degree of harmony between the social strata. In the later nineteenth century state minimalism embodied in the amended Poor Law left vast scope for voluntary welfare initiatives of all kinds and from many sources: employing enterprises, the independent charities, the churches and chapels, personal often unrecorded acts of humanitarian generosity, and the discretionary powers of town councils. The fact that the state made only limited provision in the period meant that there were numerous outlets for the expression of voluntary care and numerous wants to be met. Arguably there were needs on both sides: the need for assistance and the socio-psychological human need to be of service. A sense of community was the more effectively enhanced but, equally importantly, social integration affected the providers as well as those for whom provision was made. This is not to suggest that all welfare needs were met efficiently, nor to deny that those who received sometimes responded with ingratitude and suspicion, perhaps justifiably, given the obvious opportunities for the exploitation of the vulnerable which dependence on voluntary social welfare also created. Yet, as Patrick Joyce has shown, there was a strong sense of localism and conjecturally the wellspring of knowledge in local communities about local individuals, their family backgrounds and their reputations based on past performance, taught many lessons about who could be trusted and who could not. There are clear implications for local differences in the degree of acquiescence on this score.

There may be increased acquiescence also where there are perceived opportunities for social fluidity. Mobility, both geographical and occupational, provides an escape route for those who regard their circumstances as intolerable. In the later nineteenth century it was possible, given the transport facilities of the era, to move into, out of and between the towns, or even to emigrate overseas with, in some cases, financial assistance from the trade union. As noted earlier, the evolving education system, by no means confined to the elementary level, apprenticeship training and a well-established tradition of self-education meant that the strongly motivated, ambitious individual could achieve elevation in the world of work. At the same time structural changes in the economy and the concomitantly increased availability of job opportunities in technical, mechanical, clerical and teaching employment provided the chance for at least *some* of the more able to realize their ambitions. It was the demonstrable, perceivable existence of the escape route which was important, the knowledge that it was there for whoever wanted it or needed it. That there was movement by some individuals showed that the rest were not immutably trapped in the *status quo*. Flexibility of this kind meant that compliance was the more likely to be by choice.

Objectives

The information used in the analysis of class relations undertaken in the present study relates mainly to Burnley since an in-depth study of a typical industrial town is most likely to produce answers to the questions to be raised. Nineteenth-century Burnley was chosen as a suitable example for present purposes in that industrially, occupationally, socially and geographically it was roughly similar to the industrial towns, Blackburn and Preston, which formed the main focus of the investigations conducted by Joyce and by Dutton and King. In contrast to these two studies a slightly later period - roughly 1870 to 1895 - was chosen, a period roughly coinciding with the Great Depression, since different prevailing economic circumstances from those which provided the backdrop of the studies undertaken by the above-mentioned researchers would conjecturally enable the present writer to conclude with broad generalizations sufficiently flexible to resolve some of the contradictions discussed earlier. Dutton and King chose a period in the early nineteenth century which was subject to recurrent economic recessions; Joyce selected years which fall within an era of relative economic stability, often termed the Golden Age of Victorian Prosperity, but one which was punctuated in the North West by the 'cotton famine', 1861-5 - a regionally concentrated recession in the cotton trade which is given cursory treatment by Joyce. There is a tendency for both investigations to offer narrowly conceived era-specific conclusions about inter-class relations with blinkered disregard for the periods which precede or follow. This approach tends to produce a static rather than dynamic analysis. It is hardly surprising that Dutton and King uncovered and described little else but conflict in their article about the 'cotton tyrants' of Preston, or that Joyce disclosed an apparently pervasive calm. This book attempts to resolve some of the problems identified above.

(a) Urban leadership: élites and paternalism

The first half of the book is concerned with the identification and assessment of economic, social and political leadership, focusing mainly upon the representative case-study evidence of Burnley but with supporting or contrasting evidence from other northern industrial towns. It considers the extent to which leaders collectively comprise a local élite and inquires into the nature of leadership styles.

Chapter One discusses the structure of leadership and seeks to discover whether those in positions of authority can be said to comprise an élite. Terms need to be defined. An élite may be defined as an influential minority who, by virtue of its decision-making power, dominates or exercises extensive control over the mass. According to Meisel, an élite, whether repressive or benign, is differentiated from a group of 'top persons' in that the former displays group 'consciousness, coherence and conspiracy'. In other words, an élite is aware of its dominant position and forms a cohesive group consciously organized to maintain and further its own collective purposes. As Parry notes, one of the objectives of élite studies is to 'inquire about the technique of leadership, the relationship between the leaders and the led, and the type of people who attain positions of leadership.' The initial task is that of listing and 'weighting' the leadership roles (elective and selective) through which authority was exercised in the urban industrial context. Individual leaders are identified and, in so far as evidence is available, note is made of the occupation, religious persuasion and political preference of each individual. An assessment is made of the patterns which emerge. The chapter considers the significance of the overlapping and inter-connected patterns of multi-faceted leadership and addresses the question: can a group thus comprised of individuals who appear simultaneously in several positions of authority be represented as an élite?

This question is considered at greater length in Chapter Two which seeks to discover evidence (if such exists) of group consciousness, coherence and conspiracy. Three main thematic lines are pursued. (i) Did the leaders comprise a single, homogeneous group or a pluralistic one split decisively according to occupation, religious persuasion and political affiliation, and to what extent was group coherence reinforced by kinship ties, interlocking business partnerships, a common social life and area of residence? (ii) What was the nature of checks and balances which circumscribed the predominant group's decisions and activities? (iii) What were the leaders' collective achievements in

the period and to what extent were the relevant decisions likely
to have been the product of policies coercively imposed upon the
relatively powerless, or of policies which received majority assent?
Repressive coercion cannot be discounted (as will be shown in
subsequent chapters) but, if the main theme is one of assent and
intermittent, resolvable conflict, Burnley's social, economic and
political stability may be partially explained in terms of the general
acceptability of the leaders' policies and of the services provided
both formally and informally. Stability may, in part at least, be
the product of a degree of consensus rather than the imposition
of dominant ideology.

In Chapter Three the paternalistic style of leadership adopted
by Burnley employers is examined. As a preliminary it is necessary
to define paternalism as a form of authority, as conceptualized by
Sennett and by Newby; note is made of the unitary frame of
reference informing the paternalist's world view. Here we need
to contrast the twin faces of paternalism. The benign kindly face
is manifest in voluntary initiatives for social welfare; the stern,
repressive face in the ruthless exercise of power to suppress 'social
insubordination', not least in the sphere of industrial relations. If
the former is the more visible countenance, cooperative consent
may by the more characteristic response; if the latter, the result
may be grudging compliance in the short term but the strategic
ousting of leaders and their replacement by others at the first
opportunity. Again, there are implications for stability.

In Chapter Four we look more specifically at mechanisms
which may have enabled leaders to maintain their leadership by
socializing the mass into attitudes of compliance. A review and
assessment is necessary of the ways in which the leaders may have
attempted to mould habits of thought and behaviour via employer-
sponsored facilities for education, religion and recreation. Again,
there are potential implications for socio-political stability if leaders
are able to legitimate their leadership by successfully socializing
subordinates into dominant ideology or, as F.M.L. Thompson
has termed it, the ideology of submission.

(b) The lower class response: resistance and acquiescence

In the second half of the book attention turns more specifically to
the response to Burnley's leaders. Chapter Five is concerned with
majority and minority electoral preference in the spheres of local
and Parliamentary politics. We focus upon the gradual infiltration
of members of other socio-economic groups into positions of
leadership, the resurgence of Toryism offering an alternative

political policy, and the bid for electoral support from Socialist groups with an alternative political ideology. Yet in so far as change occurred it was neither sudden nor dramatic. The vote-casting public acquiesced in the persistent predominance of employer-led Liberalism for most of the period under review. This raises questions about the underlying causes.

Chapter Six considers whether the evidence suggests that the response may realistically be interpreted as radical or deferential. Both concepts (the radical and the deferential) are discussed - and both interpretations are rejected as inappropriate. There are frequent, occasionally violently explosive challenges to authority in the sphere of industrial relations, but persisting majority acquiescence in the political *status quo* suggests that, if a radical ideology was present, it was not widely espoused. Nor can the response be represented as one of deference.

The relative stability of the era may be partially explained in terms of leisure and recreation. The influence of these is considered in Chapter Seven. Rational, improving, educative recreation sponsored 'from above' was not the sole option, however. Other low-cost or cost-free alternatives included (i) the amenities provided by the commercial, profit-orientated sellers of entertainment; (ii) traditional, subcultural forms of recreation often (but not invariably) centred on the inns and taverns; and (iii) forms of recreation which were illegal or which gave rise to law-breaking. Leisure pursuits may collectively have contributed to the stability of the period, but for reasons other than the promotion of deference. These reasons and their implications for acquiescence are given closer attention.

Reaction to employer-sponsored religious and educational amenities is discussed in Chapter Eight. There were limits to the effectiveness of religion and education as agencies of socialization - but both may have encouraged a degree of compliance for reasons other than the imposition of dominant ideology. Again, these alternative possibilities are subjected to more detailed treatment.

In the Conclusion the influences and responses outlined in the foregoing chapters are reviewed and assessed. An alternative explanation is offered for the persistence of employers in spheres of authority in urban life beyond the confines of the workplace, and an alternative interpretation of wage-workers' reaction is suggested to those offered by Joyce and by Dutton and King.

References

1. Perkin, H.J., *Origins of Modern English Society, 1780-1880*, Routledge and Kegan Paul, 1969.

2. Thompson, E.P., *The Making of the English Working Class*, Victor Gollancz, 1963.

3. Foster, J., *Class Struggle and the Industrial Revolution: Early Industrial Capitalism in Three English Towns*, Weidenfeld and Nicolson, 1974, and by the same author, 'Nineteenth-Century Towns: A Class Dimension' in Flinn, M.W. and Smout, T.C., eds, *Essays in Social History*, Oxford University Press, 1974.

4. Thomis, M.I., *The Town Labourer and the Industrial Revolution*, Batsford, 1974, especially ch.10.

5. Joyce, P., 'The Factory Politics of Lancashire in the Later Nineteenth Century', *Historical Journal*, XVIII, 1975, pp.525-53; see also by the same author, *Work, Society and Politics: The Culture of the Factory in Later Victorian England*, Harvester, 1980.

6. Abercrombie, N. and Turner, B.S., 'The Dominant Ideology Thesis', *British Journal of Sociology*, XXIX, 1978, pp.149-70.

7. Dutton, H.I. and King, J.E., *Ten Per Cent and No Surrender: The Preston Strike, 1853-54*, Cambridge University Press, 1981; see also by the same authors, 'The Limits of Paternalism: The Cotton Tyrants of North Lancashire, 1836-54', *Social History*, VII, 1982, pp.59-74.

8. Marx, K. and Engels, F., *The German Ideology* (1845), reprinted Lawrence and Wishart, 1974.

9. Engels, F., *The Condition of the Working Class in England in 1844* (1845), reprinted Allen and Unwin, 1968, p.124.

10. See review of the thesis in Abercrombie, N. and Turner, B.S., *op. cit.* and by the same authors, *The Dominant Ideology Thesis*, Allen and Unwin, 1980.

11. Miliband, R., *The State in Capitalist Society*, Weidenfeld and Nicolson, 1969, p.182.

12. *Ibid.*, p.181.

13. Abercrombie, N. and Turner, B.S., *op. cit.*

14. Parsons, T., *The Social System*, Routledge and Kegan Paul, 1951, pp.251-5.

15. Abercrombie, N. and Turner, B.S., 'The Dominant Ideology Thesis', *British Journal of Sociology*, XXIX, 1978, pp.152-3.

16. Hill, S., *The Dockers: Class and Tradition in London*, Heinemann, 1976; see also Nichols, T. and Armstrong, P., *Workers Divided*, Fontana, 1976.

17. Mann, M., *Consciousness and Action among the Western Working Class*, Macmillan, 1973, p.68.

18. Parkin, F., *Class Inequality and Political Order*, MacGibbon and Kee, 1971, p.82.

19. *Ibid*.

20. Joyce, P., 'The Factory Politics . . .'; Nordlinger, E., *The Working Class Tories: Authority, Deference and Stable Democracy*, MacGibbon and Kee, 1967; McKenzie, R. and Silver, A., *Angels in Marble: Working Class Conservatives in Urban England*, Heinemann, 1968.

21. McKenzie, R. and Silver, A., *op. cit.*, p.249.

22. Parkin, F., *op. cit.*, p.86.

23. *Ibid.*, p.89.

24. Hoggart, R., *The Uses of Literacy*, Chatto and Windus, 1957.

25. Parkin, F., *op. cit.*, p.88.

26. *Ibid.*, p.89.

27. *Ibid.*, p.91.

28. Rodman, H., 'The Lower Class Value Stretch', *Social Forces*, XLII, 1963, pp.205-15.

29. Parkin, F., *op. cit.*, p.97.

30. *Ibid.*, p.56.

31. *Ibid.*, p.61.

32. *Ibid.*, p.63.

33. *Ibid*.

34. McCann, P., ed., *Popular Education and Socialization in the Nineteenth Century*, Methuen, 1977, identifies the objectives but argues that these were not necessarily achieved.

35. *Ibid*.

36. Parkin, F., *op. cit.*, p.67.

37. *Ibid.*, p.70.

38. *Ibid.*, p.71.

39. Child, J., 'Quaker Employers and Industrial Relations', *Sociological Review*, XII, 1964, pp.293-315.

40. Wilson, B., *Sects and Society*, Heinemann, 1961, pp.113-14.

41. Perkin, H.J., *op. cit.*, especially ch.9.

42. Andrews, J., *Methodism and Society*, Macmillan, 1972.

43. Cited *ibid.*

44. Hobsbawm, E.J., *Labouring Men*, Weidenfeld and Nicolson, 1964, ch.3, pp.23-33; Thompson, E.P., *op. cit.*, ch. 10.

45. Parkin, F., *op. cit.*, p.73.

46. Blauner, R., 'Industrialism and the Labour Response: the case of the American South', Berkeley Publications on Society and Institutions, 1958, cited in Parkin, F., *op. cit.*, p.73.

47. Cited *ibid.*, p.74.

48. Pimlott, J.A.R., *The Englishman's Holiday: A Social History*, Faber, 1947, ch. 8; Pollard, S. *The Genesis of Modern Management*, Edward Arnold, 1965, ch.5 and by the same author, 'Factory Discipline in the Industrial Revolution', *Economic History Review*, 2nd Series, XVI, 1963, pp.254-71.

49. Bailey, P., *Leisure and Class in Victorian England*, Routledge and Kegan Paul, 1978, ch. 6.

50. Thompson, F.M.L., 'Social Control in Victorian Britain', *Economic History Review*, 2nd Series, XXXIV, 1981, pp.189-208.

51. See, for example, Friedman, G., *The Anatomy of Work: The Implications of Specialization*, Heinemann, 1961.

52. Bennett, W., *The History of Burnley*, Burnley Corporation, IV, ch. 5.

PART ONE

PATERNALISTS AND THEIR STRATEGIES: LEADERS, SOCIALIZATION AND SOCIAL CONTROL

1

The Structure of Leadership
A Case Study of Burnley

Introduction

Those who occupy decision-making positions within a community are often referred to collectively as an élite. The term, élite, is one which is in common usage, but its meaning has become blurred by the way it has been stretched to fit different situations. All too often social historians simply adopt the term without pausing to elucidate its meaning, to explain how the concept is to be applied, or to discuss the wider social implications of the presence of an élite. Garrard,(1) for example, in an otherwise excellent book packed with fascinating detail about local politics in Bolton, Rochdale and Salford, utilizes the term liberally yet loosely on the apparent assumption that his readers are fully conversant with the several schools of thought on élite theory in general and with his interpretation of it in particular. The whole subject is a complex one which has been much debated since Mosca and Pareto first drew attention to the phenomenon in the late nineteenth and early twentieth centuries. At the outset it is worthwhile pausing, if only briefly, in order to give some clarification.

Élite theory

A dictionary definition, though a useful preliminary, is necessarily somewhat limited for sociological purposes; an élite is explained simply as a 'group in society considered to be superior because of the power, privileges etc. of its members' or as 'the choice part, the best'.(2) The sociological meaning goes far beyond this, however. Élite theory has been revised and refined during the twentieth century and continues to be a focus of controversy.(3)

According to the Italian theorist, Gaetano Mosca (1858-1941), whose ideas were outlined in his book, *The Ruling Class*,(4) in every

41

political regime the rulers will always be an organized minority of
people who, because of their close links and ties, are able to
dominate the unorganized majority. This minority of rulers
attempts to justify and legitimate its power on the basis of abstract
moral and legal principles - the 'political formula' - which must
be consonant with the values of the community which is governed.
Sociologists conceptualize an élite as a minority group which has
power over others and is recognized as being in some way superior.
Viewed as incumbents, those who occupy key positions in the
governing institutions of a community are collectively an élite in
the sense that they are custodians of the machinery of policy
making.(5) The assumption is that there will always be a division
between the rulers and the ruled or between those with power
and those without power, even in societies and institutions which
are nominally democratic.

An élite should not be conceptually confused with a class. The
difference between a class and an élite rests largely on the fact
that classes are defined in terms of economic position (most
obviously occupation, source and level of income, relationship to
property and the means of production, and power derived
therefrom), whereas élites may have a non-economic basis. Vilfredo
Pareto (1848-1923) distinguished between élites and non-élites,
but though he endorsed Marx's account of class struggle as an
expression of economic interests, he maintained that not all
struggles can be reduced to this same schematic form.(6) Certainly
members of an élite may all be drawn from a single class: the
landed, titled, hereditary aristocracy, for example. The whole
class is privileged in terms of its material assets, its social status
and its life style, but an aristocratic élite comprises those members
of the privileged class who monopolize decision-making positions
of authority which affect the life chances of others. Alternatively,
members of an élite may be recruited from different classes; at
the local level of political authority an elected town council may
comprise employers, professionals and blue-collar workers.

Both Mosca and Pareto were concerned with ruling élites at
top government level, but later theorists have applied the concept
to the structure of authority at other levels of decision making
and to decision-making bodies other than the institutions of
political power. Both Mosca and Pareto conceptualized a unitary
élite; both presumed that a ruling élite effectively monopolized a
nation's command posts. Likewise Michels(7) argued the
inevitability of the 'iron law of oligarchy' - but this, he maintained,
applied to any organization; in any organization an inner circle
of participants would take over and run it for their own self-

interested purposes.

Social scientists have come to use the term, élite, with reference to 'those who run things' - that is to say, certain key actors playing structured, functionally understandable roles not only in a nation's top-level governing processes but at all levels, whether central, regional or local, and in all institutional settings: political, religious, educational, industrial, commercial, recreational and so on. Whether seeking to perpetuate current patterns of life or to usher in new ones, whether paid or unpaid, élites are those people who set the style, who construct the policies and put the plans into operation. Lasswell's formulation, for example, departed from the precursory, unitary concept of élites as early as the 1930s. His formulation was radically pluralistic; élites, he argued, comprise those who rise to positions of influence in any institutional sector of society and not only in the governing institutions and ancillary processes of organized political life. At every functional stage of any decisional process in any area some participants will sequester the relevant positions of power.

There are some theorists who argue that pluralism of this kind may be more apparent than real; C. Wright Mills(8) claimed to have identified a well-integrated and partly self-perpetuating power élite in the USA in the 1960s, top groups in political, economic and military organizations being linked by ties of family, friendship and common social background. Yet, as Field and Higley(9) have argued, plural élites in practice may act as checks, balances and veto forces upon each other's activities. Military élites feud with one another, commercial élites are fragmented, industrial giants are rivals. In a custodial structure top élites do not inevitably work well together to a common purpose. The complex structure of legislatures causes them typically to have somewhat segmented, compartmentalized spheres of power. Within what may be termed the armed service élite there is rivalry and conflict between different services and branches; the apparent homogeneity of the administrative élite proves illusory under closer scrutiny.(10) In democratic societies with multi-party political systems pluralism is self-evident; whether at central or local levels of elective and selective government, there is conflict between the proponents of different party policies and different political ideologies which transcends other characteristics held in common. In such circumstances it is more instructive to inquire into which groups and which interests an élite claims to represent rather than which class its members derive from.

There appear to be two investigative approaches to the study of élites. In the traditional line of inquiry members of élites are treated as exemplars, role models, people fit to be emulated, those possessing superior talents, demonstrating qualities which set them apart and meet a crucial need. They are represented as pattern-setters, whether to preserve the existing order or to preside over its transformation into the new society. This traditional line of inquiry has not been completely abandoned, but it has been joined more recently by another approach in which élites are represented as incumbents; collectively members of élites are the influential figures to be found in governance of any sector of society, any institutional structure, any socio-geographical community. They may thus be roughly equated with influentials, spokesmen, leaders, dignitaries, key figures, decision-makers. Some social scientists hold the view that it is only when those who assume leading roles become convinced that only they are capable of carrying out the mission or function properly that a true élite emerges; self-consciously they come to think of themselves as superior by nature. In the latter approach greater attention, therefore, is paid to aspirations, expectations, objectives, ideology.

Élites are studied in two main contexts, that is, élite *characterization* work and élite *survey* work. In élite characterization work élites are identified by their mission or function; those who are seen in a custodial capacity are characterized by their performance in the institutional processes they control. In élite survey work the investigator is mainly concerned with what élites think, with qualities such as attitudes, values and the ideological perspective of élite behaviour, but he is also interested in the social backgrounds from which élites are recruited, in their social credentials, and in the opportunity structure which allows them to rise to positions of influence. The need is to identify how élite status is established, whether by reputation, position held or process participated in.

The investigator must also address the question of assessment and evaluation. Assessment of an élite's functional performance and of the wider social implications of authority in the hands of a minority is necessarily subjective. The presence of the particular élite, its activities and policy line may be applauded or regretted. As Marvick has put it:

> . . . élites are seen by many as selfish people in power, bent upon
> protecting their vested interests, contemptuous of the restraints on
> constitutional order, callous about the needs of larger publics, ready
> to manipulate opinion, to rig elections, to use force if necessary to
> retain power. A conspiratorial variant worries those who fear
> revolutionary, subversive élites: fanatical, selfless, disciplined,
> competent, and devoted to their cause, equally contemptuous of

political democracy, constitutional order, or mass contentment, willing to exploit hatred and misery, to misrepresent beliefs and facts, and to face personal degradation and social obloquy.(11)

Such an assessment may well be persuasively, even convincingly, shown to be justifiable in some situations, but there are many commentators and critics who demur at sweeping denunciations of this kind. Much depends upon whether the investigator constructs his conclusions and observations from the viewpoint of the leaders or the led; interpretations of the evidence, how the facts are represented, is a function of value judgment.

The sociologist concerned with the nature and structure of leadership in contemporary society has something of an investigative advantage over the social historian in the sense that the former's research sources are current and therefore potentially the more varied, the more available and the more accessible, whether they consist of documentary evidence, opportunities for first-hand observation in the conduct of meetings, respondents' testimony given through the medium of the formal questionnaire survey or informal conversation. Oral evidence and verbal information can be solicited, explanations can be sought, facts can be cross-checked and sources are the more amenable to different analytical and methodological approaches. The social historian of periods which pre-date living memory and living experience is limited by the nature of the source materials, their accessibility and the extent to which they have been preserved; and this projects constraints upon his or her approach to the investigation of the subject and the kinds of questions which it is feasible to ask. Given these qualifications, a combination of some of the tools of élite characterization and élite survey methods is applied in this and the following chapter to investigate the nature and structure of leadership in late-Victorian Burnley, a typical industrial town in the North West.

The initial objectives are to identify spheres of influence and to list specific decision-making positions of authority along with the individuals who occupy them. There are several questions to be addressed. Are the various specific spheres of authority dominated by separate groups largely unconnected with each other, or does one group of leaders exercise collective power across the whole spectrum of authority? Is there homogeneity or diversity in the dominant group's social composition in terms of characteristics such as occupation, gender, political preference and religious persuasion? In what sense can those who dominate the command posts at the local level of the industrial town be said to comprise an élite? We consider this last question in more detail in the next chapter so that any answer which may suggest itself here may be subject to qualification in the light of evidence examined later.

Leadership in Burnley

The first task is to identify spheres of influence and specific positions of decision-making authority. An important question to be raised here is whether those occupying positions of institutionalized power were recruited exclusively or predominantly from one socio-economic class. It is clearly necessary as a preliminary step to list the influential roles, whether formal or informal, selective or elective, which would enable the few to control much of the corporate life of the urban community. In drawing up a list of the various categories of influence both time and place are relevant, specific leadership roles being significant in the historical context of the late nineteenth century and the regional context of a rapidly growing urban centre in a major industrial locality. Having listed the relevant positions, quantitative assessment of the importance of specific individuals and particular groups can be attempted by the allocation of 'points' to each individual and the construction of a 'league table'. The presence of a large number of 'low scorers' may indicate that power is diffuse, dispersed or atomized, a small number of 'high scorers' that power is concentrated. The coincidence of a number of high scorers and lower scorers may indicate the existence of a powerful core group and a less influential peripheral group.

Firstly, we consider the economic dimension of authority. Burnley, the industrial town chosen for an in-depth case study, is an East Lancashire town set amongst others of its kind, its closest neighbours being Accrington, Bury, Blackburn, Rochdale, Nelson and Colne. In the late nineteenth century its *raison d'être* was still the cotton trade and related industries such as ironfounding and engineering, which supplied textile machinery and 'mill furnishings', and mining which supplied coal for industrial, municipal and domestic users.(12) The continuing importance of the traditional industries, especially those where technological and organizational advances were associated with increasingly large-scale factory-based production, implies that employers of the traditional entrepreneurial class were of considerable local significance for the employment and earning opportunities they generated. The investment and production decisions of those business proprietors, who were key providers of jobs and of wages to be spent at local shops, pubs and centres of entertainment, fundamentally affected the lives of many and the prosperity of the town in general. Additionally, where large numbers of wage-earners were involved, an institutional framework providing channels for negotiation between employer and employee and facilitating the process of collective bargaining suggests that the role of trade union official was an important one, since the incomes of many were dependent upon his bargaining ability. Where large numbers of men in similar employment organized themselves into trade unions led by elected officers, local masters also, a large percentage of whom in this leading textile town were engaged in the production of similar goods, joined forces in a manufacturers' association to protect their mutual interests *vis-à-vis* the wage-workers.

The Burnley Master Spinners' and Manufacturers' Association was established in the 1850s(13) and had continuous organizational identity in the period under review. In the 'Great Depression' of 1873-96, years of falling prices, shrinking profit margins and declining money wages, the roles of trade union official and of leading members of the masters' association were likely to assume a special significance. In an industrial town, given the context of the regional economy, influence and authority over others were likely to be exercised by those who appeared in the roles of employer, trade union leader, and member of the local branch of the Master Spinners' and Manufacturers' Association, all of whom exercised authority in economic decisions affecting the employment and income of comparatively large numbers.

Secondly, consideration needs to be given to the political dimension of urban authority. In the provision of basic social amenities, of pervasive significance for the environmental conditions of the community in general, by far the most influential decision-taking body was the Town Council. Burnley achieved incorporation in 1861(14) and by 1870 had long-term plans for the more efficient provision of sanitation, clean water and the 'abolition of nuisances'.(15) The decisions and plans of elected members of the Town Council clearly affected the entire borough, for there were implications not only for the quality and quantity of municipal amenities supplied for collective use, but also for the costs to be borne by the town's ratepayers. Another key area of authority affecting the urban context was the maintenance of law and order and the administration of justice. The borough established its own police force and borough bench of magistrates in the period(16) in a bid for greater independence from county authority. Members of the Town Council and of the Bench of Magistrates, therefore, occupied positions which were both influential and prestigious; policy decisions had wide repercussions upon the urban community.

Thirdly, there were influential positions in the sphere of religion. In the nineteenth century, religious institutions played a significant part in the life of the local community since their activities were not confined to the exclusively religious sphere. Those holding religious office (Anglican, Roman Catholic and Nonconformist), whether as priest, preacher, vicar, church warden, Sunday school superintendent, chapel trustee or circuit steward of the several Nonconformist sects which had established themselves in Burnley, would be likely to hold a degree of status and influence not limited to congregations of worshippers. Leaders of the churches and chapels undoubtedly commanded respect as the upholders of moral standards, and symbolically as representatives of respectability and paternalistic responsibility. The role of church or chapel leader was a potentially influential one, therefore, in the sphere of moral standards, normative values and patterns of behaviour.

Fourthly, other positions of authority in the late nineteenth century urban community were concerned with the organization of education, the administration of poor relief, and the provision of social amenities other than those made available by the Town Council. A favourite device of the Victorian era was the creation of local boards attached to a co-ordinating central body at national government level. Local School Boards and local Poor Law Unions, for example, were accountable to centrally organized agencies. The Burnley School Board(17) of nine members was formed in 1871 under the 1870 Elementary Education Act. Members of the Board were chosen by local ratepayers on the basis of triennial elections, and the accompanying pre-election publicity in the local press(18) discloses that the choice of representatives was regarded as sufficiently important to merit a not inconsiderable amount of space. There were, however, other bodies involved in the provision of educational amenities. Most of the town's elementary schools were provided under the voluntary system by the local churches and chapels on a denominational basis,(19) and in the 1870s and 1880s existing schools of this type were extended and new schools built so that church leaders and chapel dignitaries who acted as school managers(20) were also influential in determining the quantity and quality of elementary schooling. Post-elementary education in Burnley was provided most obviously by three local agencies - the Grammar School, the Mechanics' Institute and the

Church Institute(21) - and here again, individuals whose manifest interest and concern earned them positions as directors, governors and chairmen were in key positions of influence in the control of policy and the conduct of affairs within the relevant institutions. As far as education is concerned, therefore, leadership was exercised by members of the School Board, managers of the church and chapel voluntary schools, the chairman and governors of the Grammar School and the directors and trustees of the Mechanics' and Church Institutes.

In an age which pre-dates the modern welfare state, considerable importance was attached to those who were in positions of responsibility in the provision of relief for the destitute, the unemployed and the sick. The ultimate resort of the poor was the local Board of Poor Law Guardians, members of which were chosen by an electorate of local ratepayers. The Board's area of administrative responsibility, and therefore also the area of recruitment for Guardians to serve on the Board, was the Poor Law Union, an area comprising Burnley and several outlying townships including Padiham, Habergham Eaves and Worsthorne.(22) The Burnley contingent formed a fraction, albeit a sizeable one, of the total membership of the Board, but local interest was keen since the union workhouse was sited in the town itself.(23) Additional relief was provided by voluntary charity societies which, characteristically in the Victorian period, were sponsored and organized 'from above'. There were also friendly societies whose organizers and sponsors offered an escape from the stigmatizing experience of seeking pauper relief in times of distress. In connection with such rudimentary social welfare provision as the age allowed, positions of influence and authority, therefore, were held by members of the Board of Poor Law Guardians, by sponsors and organizers of sick clubs and friendly societies,(24) and philanthropists voluntarily responsible for the flow of private charity.

The influence of philanthropists was not, of course, limited to charity alone but extended to the provision of funds for projects associated with civic pride and respectable recreation such as parks, gardens and libraries(25) which would not only improve the urban environment but enhance the prestige of the donor. A particularly important project in Burnley, initiated and sponsored by local philanthropists, was the building of the Victoria Hospital in the early 1880s;(26) the Board of Hospital Governors not unnaturally contained a number of those whose donations had been particularly generous. For purposes of classification, however, the Hospital Board is treated as a separate issue area from other spheres of local philanthropy since members made policy decisions in the running of the hospital's affairs.

Finally, both of the local newspapers which served the town, the *Burnley Gazette* and the *Burnley Express*, indicate the existence of a proliferation of different sorts of clubs and societies, and it is likely that the elected officials, chairmen and committee members of these were in positions of influence and prestige amongst club members and sometimes beyond. Burnley clubs in more or less continuous existence in the period under review include sports clubs (such as the cricket, football and cycling clubs), political clubs (such as the Reform Club, the Liberal Club, the Conservative Club and the Primrose League), and also the Literary and Scientific Society, which placed emphasis on intellectual and cultural interests.(27)

In listing leadership roles relevant to the industrial town of Burnley in the late nineteenth century fifteen main areas of influence need to be taken into account; the list of roles includes those of employer, town councillor, magistrate, poor law guardian, member of the School Board, Grammar School governor, official of the Mechanics' or Church Institute, philanthropist, holder of religious office, committee member of a political club, official of a sports club, organizer or member of the Literary and Scientific Society, trade union leader, member of the Masters' Association and lastly governor of the Victoria Hospital. On the basis of these several categories, points were allocated according to the number of offices held by each individual, thus creating a 'league table' of influence and leadership.(28)

It is evident, however, that the roles represented in these several categories are not all of equal significance. Differences in the degree of influence occur not only between, but also within, categories. The potential area of responsibility of a sports club official or a church warden, for example, is considerably less in many respects than that of a town councillor or a magistrate. Within the employer category, not all employers of labour were equally important; proprietors of large firms, such as those associated with the local textile and mining industries which provided a great deal of employment and many wage packets, being of greater influence than owners of small firms which provided employment on a more limited scale. In the allocation of points, therefore, it was necessary to avoid potential distortion by 'weighting' some of the roles, and to this end, two points have been given in the case of major employers, town councillors and magistrates.

Within the Town Council, differences occurred both in the

duration and quality of service, but here it is difficult to differentiate precisely between active contributors and passive passengers, and even more so between the positively constructive and the merely voluble participant. By and large, however, long service and valuable contribution to local government led to promotion to the status of alderman or mayor. Men in these positions headed the various sub-committees where their special contribution derived from long experience and knowledge of the technicalities and procedures of municipal government. Within the Town Council category one extra point has been given to each councillor serving as alderman and a further point to those chosen as mayor; to assist clarification here two additional categories have been included in Table I for individuals who served as alderman or as mayor. In the employer and philanthropist categories, two points have been awarded arbitrarily to those who appear to be significant as large employers or particularly generous donors. No separate category of friendly society officials has been included since those societies that came to light were predominantly attached to and sponsored by institutions such as chapels, trade unions and political clubs, the implications of which are discussed in a later chapter.

The task of 'weighting' positions of influence is problematic. An alternative approach to the one adopted here would have been to weight each role to accord with the number of associated functions. In major business enterprises, for example, employers often provided rudimentary welfare services and recreational amenities for their workforces; the leaders of the churches and chapels were also actively involved in both of these spheres and also in the provision of elementary schooling. The main difficulty here lies in the fact that undoubtedly there was considerable variation quantitatively and qualitatively in the services and facilities thus made available, but to an unascertainable extent. The evidence which has been discovered is not sufficiently detailed as to permit an efficient allocation of additional points corresponding to what was offered. This is not to dismiss the significance of multi-functionalism. The multi-faceted character of leadership roles is an important phenomenon whose implications are discussed at some length in a later chapter.

Even when potential distortions have been eradicated by weighting, a quantitative approach to the task of identifying an élite within the borough community has its shortcomings. This is not to deny that such an approach has its merits in providing a hard factual basis upon which to build, but to acknowledge the limitations inherent in even the most carefully constructed statistical method of inquiry. It tends to emphasize potential rather than actual decision-making and to take no account of the influence of particular individuals or groups who have no relevant 'official' role but whose ideas and opinions, nevertheless, affect the course of events. Some attempt was made, therefore, to use supplementary, impressionistic information to qualify factual evidence and the conclusions suggested by the statistics. Regular reference, for example in the local press, the *Burnley Gazette* and the *Burnley Express*, to particular families and specific individuals implies a certain standing or prestige within the community. Obituaries and reports of marriages, funerals, baptismal ceremonies, coming-of-age celebrations and travels abroad invariably refer to families of some importance. Similarly, the presentation of prizes, cups and awards, the laying of foundation stones and the official opening of new schools, chapels and municipal buildings were often carried out by persons of influential repute.(29) Additionally, Burnley street names and the names of buildings, parks and gardens occasionally denote the prestige of philanthropists and other local 'worthies' (see Table VIII). Amongst Burnley street names(30) there occur, amongst others, Veevers Street, Hurtley Street, Thursby Road and Dugdale Road. Parks and gardens carrying the names of donors include Thursby Park, Scott Park, Towneley Park and Thornber Gardens. In other spheres there are memorials such as the Massey Pavilion in Towneley Park, the Massey Collection in the Library, the Thursby and Butterworth Wards in the Victoria Hospital and the recently-built William Thompson Recreation Centre adjacent to the Central Library. Generally such information confirms the conclusions given by the statistics and, though it may be the case that one or two people of peripheral influence have been included amongst the leaders and conversely a few have escaped the net, most of the key personalities have been successfully identified by the method adopted. What supplementary, impressionistic sources have emphasized is the status of people such as John Butterworth, John Greenwood, George Haslam and J.S. Veevers - a predominantly Anglican Conservative group of individuals who were more actively involved in local affairs than statistical sources suggest. The situation requires explanation and will be considered later.

The selection of what is a relatively long period for social analysis of this kind has its drawbacks in that some leaders disappear early either through death or through retirement due to illness or old age. Indeed, this happens with a few particularly prominent men such as James Roberts and Abram Uttley, both of whom died in the 1880s. Conversely, others in the group are comparative latecomers. Albert Carrington and the Thornber family, for example, were only influential in local affairs from the late 1880s.(31) The time scale, 1870-1914, has the effect of producing what is a rather large group of leaders, though not all of these were actively involved throughout the whole period.

Noteworthy in this connection is the extent to which group continuity was preserved by the replacement of retiring, older leaders by new men who, in terms of social class and of religious and political affiliation, conformed to pre-established patterns. There was also 'family continuity'. In the case of the Masseys, Lancasters, Thornbers, Barneses, Thompsons, Keighleys and Baldwins younger members of the family, whether brothers, nephews or sons, followed their elders into municipal government. George Barnes replaced his father, John,(32) on the latter's retirement from the Town Council; John Baldwin replaced his brother William; John Massey replaced his uncle, Lord Massey, and William Collinge replaced his father, Luke. A long period, therefore, has inherent disadvantages and it is necessary to avoid overstating the significance of men such as James Roberts, Abram Uttley and General Scarlett, who disappeared from the group in the 1870s, but whose importance in the statistical form of analysis used to assess social influence in the present exercise may appear to be considerable. A further limitation of the 'league table' method of analysis based on the number of formal, decision-making positions held by individuals is that it takes little account of the potential significance of family groups such as the Thornbers, four of whom were on the Town Council in 1903, as Mayor, an alderman and two councillors.(33) It is necessary in using a quantitative approach to the identification of leaders to make some kind of allowance subsequently in the treatment of the subject for factors such as these.

Although a long period has its analytical disadvantages it also has its merits in that, as opposed to a very short period, it is likely to disclose more readily discernible elements of change which will require explanation. In the present case to have shortened the period by beginning in 1880 would have involved the loss of the most disturbed period of industrial unrest in the town's history, while to have looked no further than 1890 would have resulted in the loss of the period which saw the emergence of Socialist political organizations. Both of these phenomena have important implications for the argument to be constructed in this study.

On the basis of quantitative and impressionistic information, a preliminary table (see Table I) of ninety-five individuals(34) who featured in not less than two categories was compiled. It is evident that this large preliminary group contains many low scorers of peripheral importance, but it forms a useful initial group from which to select the more influential. Total scores range from two to sixteen and the distribution of scores within the range suggests the presence of an active group (indicated by scores of seven or more)(35) which may *possibly* be termed the 'élite' (see Table II), and within this we note the presence of a much more pervasively involved body of individuals (indicated by scores of ten or more)(36) who appear to form a 'core' or 'nucleus' (see Table III). From the preliminary list of ninety-five, a group of fifty-four seven-plus scorers was selected and to this number were added Lady O'Hagan (score five) and W.M. Grant (score six), both of whom impressionistically appear to have been of greater significance than was indicated by their comparatively low scores. In the final count, therefore, the leadership group consisted of a body of fifty-six individuals(37) (see Table II). The nucleus of super-active ten-plus scorers contained twenty-eight individuals and to their number was added Alfred Lancaster (score nine) who, on the basis of impressionistic information, seemed to merit inclusion(38) (see Table III).

The distribution of final scores implies that in Burnley it was not the case that separate unconnected groups dominated in specific issue areas, as might have been the case had the 'élite', if such it can be termed, consisted of a large number of comparatively low-scorers. Table II shows a relatively distinctive body of high-scorers whose names recur in several positions of authority and influence. Though no single individual plays a role in all the categories considered, there occurs, nevertheless, considerable overlap of personnel in the various spheres of authority listed. Many of these roles were played concurrently, often over long periods of time. Noteworthy in this respect are the Thompsons, John Baron, John Barnes, the Keighleys, J.A. Scott, John Howorth, John Massey, George Sutcliffe and James Green(39) - all of whom figure prominently in the 'nuclear' group. Sometimes individuals appeared in some of their roles successively, serving in some spheres of authority relatively briefly. J.S. Veevers, for example, though giving a lifetime's service in the elective office of Poor Law Guardian,(40) served only a short period on the Town Council(41) and on the bench of magistrates(42) to which he was appointed late in life. Robert Handsley appeared for a few years as a Poor Law Guardian,(43) made a brief appearance on the Town Council,(44) but gave prolonged service as agent to the landed, colliery-owning Thursbys, as church warden at St

Andrew's, as director and teacher at the Church Institute and as committee member of the Burnley Conservative Club.(45)

Though some positions were held concurrently and some successively, there emerged a relatively distinctive group of leaders with considerable overlap of personnel linking up the several decision-making spheres.(46) Perhaps the Board of Guardians comes nearest to forming a separate group from the main body, partly due to the fact that the area of administration, the Burnley Union, covered not only the borough but several outlying townships, each of which elected its own representatives to the Board, so that the Burnley contingent formed only a fraction, albeit a sizeable one, of the total membership. In part also the office itself seemed less eligible in the eyes of contemporaries. Men often appeared here earlier in their careers, before moving on to the more important and prestigious offices of the Town Council and the School Board. A younger Thornber served an 'apprenticeship' on the Board of Guardians(47) before joining the elders of his family on the Town Council(48) and, characteristically, it was the ranks of the Guardians which were the first to be invaded towards the end of the period by latecomers: working men, Socialists and women.(49) Only a few of Burnley's leaders, R.J. Hurtley, H.D. Fielding and John Thompson, for example, appear to have served as Guardians(50) at the height of their careers. The activities of the Board of Guardians, however, were the object of intermittent scrutiny by influential men of Burnley and its environs who, as magistrates, attended occasional meetings in an *ex officio* capacity, especially at times of difficulty such as periods of heavy unemployment and epidemics, or at times when major issues were being discussed such as the building of a new workhouse.(51) Though less overlap of elected personnel occurred the town's authorities kept a reasonably close check on the Board's activities.

A more detailed analysis of the intricacies characterizing the web-like network of interconnection in the structure of authority in Burnley discloses the apparent pervasiveness of employer influence. In Anglican Conservative circles several of the leaders had an interest in coal-mining enterprises. Robert Handsley was agent to the landed, mine-owning Thursby family and served also as Poor Law guardian, borough magistrate, organizing official at the Church Institute, and church warden and Sunday School superintendent at St Andrew's Church. The Reverend William Thursby, his son (Colonel Sir John Thursby) and grandson (Mr J.O.S. Thursby) were also actively involved in the life of the local community. The Reverend William was a member of the board of governors of Burnley Grammar School and of the Victoria Hospital. Colonel Sir John and Mr J.O.S. Thursby were both at various times magistrates, *ex officio* Poor Law guardians and governors of the Grammar School and hospital. Many of the leaders were employers in the textile industry. In the Liberal Nonconformist camp, William Thompson, a Wesleyan, was an employer in the cotton trade along with his son, J.W. Thompson, and his brother, John. The brothers were both actively involved in municipal politics conducted through the medium of the Town Council, where at various times they served as councillors and aldermen. William also held office as mayor, borough magistrate, sponsor of the Mechanics' Institute and member of the Burnley School Board; John became a Poor Law Guardian. The family were active participants in Wesleyan chapel affairs, J.W. Thompson serving as Sunday School superintendent, lay-preacher and circuit steward. The Liberal, Methodist cotton-master, John Baron, undertook various duties as town councillor, alderman, mayor, magistrate, Poor Law guardian and member of the Burnley School Board. In a lifetime's association with Mount Street Methodist chapel he held several offices: Sunday School teacher and superintendent, circuit steward, treasurer and president of the Sunday School Union, and delegate to (and first president of) the Free Church Council.

Some of the basic characteristics of the structure of leadership in Burnley have been outlined in this chapter. The statistical analyses disclose the presence of a distinctive core group of high-scorers whose names recur, often simultaneously, in several positions of influence. The overall patterns suggest that different spheres of authority were not dominated by separate, unconnected groups; the leadership exercised was extensively interlinked and overlapping in structure. Outside the core was a peripheral group comprising persons whose range of activities and involvements was more limited. Beyond this group was a substantial number of individuals who held only one or two positions of decision-making authority. Possibly the interests of several of these were specific rather than general, or the time they were willing or able to devote to such pursuits was more restricted since many appear to have been neither extensively nor intensively assiduous in seeking office in other dimensions of authority. A salient feature of the core is the numerical predominance of employers engaged in the town's major industries.

The statistical patterns disclose a super-active group of leaders who collectively and individually appear to have been strategically well-placed to exercise wide-ranging authority over the local community; but there remains the question: can these people be said to comprise an élite? If an élite is simply defined as those who collectively occupy positions of power, the answer is an affirmative one; yet many theorists suggest that more than this is required functionally, aspirationally, ideologically and culturally before a group of top people can be termed an élite. Several questions need to be addressed. Was the group a cohesive, self-conscious minority of persons who established and maintained their dominance to self-interested and self-preserving ends? Did the group characteristically display Meisel's 'three Cs'(52) of élite behaviour: consciousness, conspiracy and coherence? Did the leaders comprise a unified or a plural élite? To what extent were their activities constrained by a network of checks, balances and veto forces? Did those who occupied the command posts abuse their authority or did they perform their duties and responsibilities with a social conscience for the common good?

References

1. Garrard, J., *Leadership and Power in Victorian Industrial Towns, 1830-1880*, Manchester University Press, 1983.

2. See, for example, the definition in *The Concise Oxford Dictionary of Current English*, Oxford University Press, 1964.

3. See, for example, the Miliband-Poulantzas Debate outlined in Abercrombie, N., Hill, S. and Turner, B.S., *Dictionary of Sociology*, Penguin, 1984, pp. 79-80, 136; Miliband, R., *The State in Capitalist Society*, Weidenfeld and Nicolson, 1969; Poulantzas, N., 'The Problems of the Capitalist State', *New Left Review*, LVII, 1969, pp. 67-78; Miliband, R., 'The Capitalist State: Reply to Nicol Poulantzas', *New Left Review*, LIX, 1970, pp. 53-60.

4. Mosca, G., (1896), *The Ruling Class*, McGraw-Hill, New York, 1939.

5. Kuper, A. and J., eds, *The Social Sciences Encyclopedia*, Routledge and Kegan Paul, 1985, pp. 243-5.

6. Ibid., p. 571; Pareto, V. (1916), *The Mind and Society: A Treatise on General Sociology*, Dover, New York, 1973.

7. Michels, R. (1911), *Political Parties: A Sociological Study of Oligarchical Tendencies in Modern Democracy*, Free Press, Glencoe, Illinois, 1958.

8. Mills, C.W., *The Power Élite*, Simon and Schuster, New York, 1956.

9. Field, G.L. and Higley, J., *The Professional Soldier*, Glencoe, Illinois, 1980.

10. Dogan, M., ed., *The Mandarins of Western Europe*, McGraw-Hill, New York, 1975.

11. Marvick, D., 'Élites' in Kuper, A. and J. eds, *op. cit.*, pp. 243-5.

12. Bennett, W., *The History of Burnley*, Burnley Corporation, 1951, IV, pp. 95-116.

13. *Ibid.*

14. *Ibid.*, p. 65.

15. *Ibid.*, pp. 65-73.

16. The Borough Police Force came into existence in 1887, *ibid.*, p. 90; the Borough Bench of Magistrates was established in 1872, *ibid.*, p. 71.

17. Young, M.E., 'The Burnley School Board, 1871-91', unpublished M.Ed. dissertation, University of Manchester, 1973.

18. See Appendix, Table IX; see also January issues of the *Burnley Gazette* and *Burnley Express*.

19. Young, M.E., *op. cit.*; Bennett, W., *op. cit.*, pp. 169-80.

20. *Ibid.*

21. Bennett, W., *op. cit.*, pp. 180-1.

22. *Minutes of the Burnley Board of Poor Law Guardians*, Lancashire County Records Office, Preston.

23. *Ibid.*

24. Bennett, W., *op. cit.*, pp. 149-68, 200-2.

25. *Ibid.*, p. 57.

26. *Ibid.*, p. 198.

27. *Ibid.*, see p. 45 for Cycling Club, p. 137 for Reform Association, p. 138 for Constitutional Club, pp. 138-9 for Liberal Club, Conservative Club and Primrose League, pp. 221-6 for cricket and football clubs and p. 202 for Literary and Scientific Society.

28. Appendix, Table 1.

29. Much information is provided in obituaries in *Burnley Gazette*; see, for example, obituary of Richard Handsley, 21 Oct. 1903; W.C. Hargreaves, 22 Oct. 1900; Abram Altham, 1 Aug. 1885; W. Lancaster, 29 Oct. 1902; W. Collinge, 23 Oct. 1897; W. Robinson, 30 Aug. 1881; J.H. Scott, 6 Nov. 1880; W.M. Grant, 18 Feb. 1888; W. Baldwin, 15 Jan. 1892; information also in accounts of 'Coming of Age' of Col. Thursby's son, 6 May 1882; marriage of a member of the Kay-Shuttleworth family, 13 Jan. 1900; attendance at prize-giving ceremonies of Mechanics' Institute, 10 Oct. 1885; Alderman Kay opens Sale of Work at Sion School, 24 Feb. 1877; Methodist Bazaar opened by Abram Altham, 20 April 1878.

30. Appendix, Table VIII.

31. Elections to Town Council reported in *Burnley Gazette*: A. Carrington, 4 Nov. 1889; Thomas Thornber, 3 Nov. 1888; Caleb and Sharp Thornber, 5 Nov. 1891; John Thornber, 3 Nov. 1900.

32. John Barnes's retirement, *Burnley Gazette*, 6 Nov. 1875; obituary of W. Baldwin and election results in *Burnley Gazette*, 13 Jan. and 6 Nov. 1892 respectively; in the same newspaper also obituary of William Collinge, 23 Oct. 1897 and election results, 5 Nov. 1883; see also article about John Massey in *Men of Burnley; Press Cuttings, 1961-3*, Burnley Central Library.

33. Town Council, *Minutes*, 1903; *Burnley Gazette*, 3 Nov. 1903.

34. Appendix, Table I.

35. *Ibid*.

36. *Ibid*.

37. Appendix, Table II.

38. Appendix, Table III.

39. Town Council *Minutes* and press reports of elections to the Town Council indicate regular re-election of some individuals and often subsequent promotion to the status of alderman; see Appendix, Table V.

40. *Minutes of Burnley Board of Poor Law Guardians*, Lancashire County Records Office, Preston.

41. Elected to Town Council in by-election 1875 (see *Burnley Gazette*, 10 April 1875) but does not appear to have stood for re-election subsequently.

42. Press reports of proceedings of Borough Magistrates' Court in the late 1890s.

43. *Minutes of Burnley Board of Poor Law Guardians*; obituary of Richard Handsley, *Burnley Gazette*, 21 Oct. 1903.

44. Obituary of Richard Handsley, *loc. cit.*

45. *Ibid.*

46. Appendix, Table I.

47. *Minutes of Burnley Board of Poor Law Guardians, loc. cit.*

48. Sharp Thornber elected to the Town Council in 1891 and John Thornber in 1900; see *Burnley Gazette*, 5 Nov. 1891 and 3 Nov. 1900.

49. David Holmes, weavers' agent and trade union officer, was elected to the School Board in 1883 (*Men of Burnley: Press Cuttings, loc. cit.*) and to the Town Council in 1889 (*Burnley Gazette*, 7 Nov. 1889). The Socialist activist, Dan Irving, was elected to the School Board in 1898, to the Board of Guardians in 1901 and to the Town Council in 1902 (Bennett, W., *op. cit.*, p. 147). Women (Lady O'Hagan, Mrs Robb and Mrs Brown) had been elected to the Board of Guardians by 1898 (see *Minutes of the Burnley Board of Poor Law Guardians*) but no women had been elected to the Town Council by 1914.

50. All were prominent members of the Board of Guardians in the 1880s; see *Minutes of the Burnley Board of Poor Law Guardians, loc. cit.*

51. *Ibid.*; James Folds, William Lomas, John Massey, William Robinson, Col. Starkie, J.H. Thursby and Sir U.J. Kay-Shuttleworth each attended intermittently in an *ex officio* capacity.

52. Meisel, J.H., *The Myth of the Ruling Class: Gaetano Mosca and the Élite*, Arbor, New York, 1962.

2

The Leaders and their Performance

Introduction

The leaders in late-Victorian Burnley have been identified. The next task is to examine in greater detail the group's characteristics, its activities as a decision-making body and the extent to which it may justifiably be termed an élite. As Parry has observed in summarization of the theories of the classical élitists:

> No mechanism for ensuring the accountability of the leaders to the public, no ideology which enshrines the principle of majority will, can prevent the élite from imposing its supremacy over the rest of society.(1)

According to this line of argument, because of their power, their ability to organize, their political expertise and their personal qualities, the members of an élite are always well-placed to exploit their positions of authority so as to preserve their collective domination. An implication of this is that the supposed élite constitutes a coherent, united, self-conscious body - attributes which appear in nearly all definitions of an élite.(2) What Meisel(3) refers to as the 'three Cs' of élite behaviour - group consciousness, coherence and conspiracy (this last term meaning a common will to action rather than secret machinations) - are clearly 'necessary features of the concept of an élite.'(4) Political élitist theories assume that members of the group act together as a body with some shared purposes. If, on the basis of the evidence, the group does not appear to act thus as a unified body, it is not so much an élite but rather a body of 'top persons'.

An élite, as conceptualized in Pareto's work, is identified by common attitudes, aspirations and objectives and by the kind of conduct in spheres of authority which these attributes produce. Pareto like Marx, though for dissimilar reasons, is ambiguous about the degree of cohesion an élite is expected to possess.

Meisel's 'three Cs' are less readily accommodated within Pareto's hypothesis. Indeed, it might be objected that Pareto's account is at times simply a description of a category of 'top persons' rather than an élite as defined by Meisel.

Meisel's approach explains the apparent unity of a supposed élite as the outcome in part of social background but in part also as the product of the very organization of the élite itself - a kind of *esprit de corps* which emanates from élite members' common situation, mutual interests and shared experience of joint action. In other words, the exercise of collective power breeds group consciousness of power. The élite's cohesiveness is regarded as one of its chief strengths; the qualities of self-consciousness, coherence and unity are viewed as mechanisms which serve to reinforce the advantaged position of the élite in its relations with other groups in society. Economic influence, wealth, social status, educational superiority all contribute to the ability to achieve power; social prestige adds weight to an élite's political activities. These advantages of what Mosca terms *positions déjà prises* tend to widen the distance between the élite and the non-élite, thereby reinforcing its social exclusiveness and contributing to the preservation of its power.

There is more to it than this, however. An élite's survival may depend also upon its capacity to adjust to pressures from outside itself, and even to admit to its ranks elements from other social interests.(5) The élite's capacity to preserve the *status quo* may, in part at least, be a function of its ability to distribute favour (what is represented by the benefactors and accepted by the recipients as concession or compromise), by its ability to adjust to the turns of economic and political fortune and, more importantly, by its ability to maintain its dominance by general consent based on satisfactory performance rather than by its monopoly control of the instruments of coercion.

Pareto differentiates between the leadership styles of those he terms 'foxes' (men of intelligence and cunning) and 'lions' (men of strength, stability and integrity). Though Pareto saw these as mutually exclusive sets of qualities, it can be argued that leaders may utilize whichever of these strategies is judged to be the more appropriate to the particular situation. It is partly a matter of force and partly a matter of persuasion or what Pareto referred to as 'gaining the consent of the governed by ruse.' In their guise as foxes, leaders seek to achieve and maintain their positions by attempting to promote consensual responses. They may seek to impose appropriate ideologies upon the masses, or to construct policies to meet immediate crises thereby satisfying the demands of the moment. Compromise, concession and pacification, however, may weaken the regime when its strategies are exposed and resisted by its more tough-minded opponents. In the lions' approach to the process of government, the pursuit of consensual acquiescence is abandoned in favour of the use of force. Opposition may be ruthlessly suppressed. The enforcement of public order rather than general satisfaction becomes a chief objective of those in authority.(6)

Most of the classical theorists acknowledge the need for élites judiciously to make concessions, particularly when it is a matter of the élite's survival; yet some theorists do not appear to recognize the potential effect of compromise on the élite's situation. The long-term outcome may be unanticipated and very different from the immediate result. The effect may be to strengthen the élite's position, or it may be to weaken it. It is equally true that refusal to compromise may produce either of these outcomes. Everything depends upon the particular situation. Yet some theorists simplistically interpret concessions not as costs, which may in the course of time serve to undermine the élite's resources for influence, but as instances of the dexterity and flexibility by which the élite retains its controlling position. Mosca's account of 'social forces' is a clear example. In his analysis leaders maintain their collective élitist position by adjusting their policies to meet the claims of new social forces which constantly arise in a society, and also by incorporating personnel from such social forces into their own lower stratum. At the same time leaders at the local level of government in the later nineteenth century, as today, operated within certain constraints. There were rules and regulations constructed by central government which had to be observed, county leaders took an interest in the state of urban law and order, powerful individual personages were sometimes able to exert an independent influence upon specific decisions, pressure groups, such as trade unions and rate-payers' associations, were capable of making their presence felt. The tactics of compromise were needed and attention had to be paid to vociferous critics and new forces. By incorporating personnel from other social interests an élite, if such it can be termed, undergoes 'molecular transformation' but still remains in authority and has continuity with its predecessors. This view is fundamentally different from one which represents an élite as a group beyond the control of the other members of society. Instead, it is a close relative of what is sometimes termed 'pluralistic élitism' or 'democratic élitism'.(7)

There appear to be four main schools of thought which seek to explain the survival of élites. Mosca(8) and his disciple,

Michels,(9) maintained that leaders owed their power to their organizational ability. In contrast, Pareto(10) emphasized the psychological make-up of both the élite and the non-élite - including considerations of factors such as ideology, attitudes, aspirations, expectations and ambitions. In an attempt to reconcile élitism with Marxism, Burnham(11) attributed an élite's power to its control of economic resources. C. Wright Mills,(12) on the other hand, explained an élite's dominance in terms of its monopolization of key institutions within a society. All of these views have a bearing on the situation.

There can, therefore, be both 'strong' and 'weak' interpretations of élitist theory. One extreme can imply the ultimate control of all stages of the decisional process - initiation, deliberation, authoritative consideration, decision and implementation.(13) Such an interpretation may also acknowledge that an élite exercises control by making entry into its ranks open to the representatives of other interest groups. This shades off into various theses of élite consensus in which several élites are 'bound together by shared beliefs on procedural and substantive matters'(14) or the much weaker variant that in organized life fewer persons issue commands than obey them. Arguably the most effective and illuminating approach to the investigation of a leading group, its characteristics, its behaviour and the extent to which it may be termed an élite, is to apply the test of Meisel's 'three Cs' - the degree to which the group is cohesive, conscious and conspiratorial. There are other relevant questions to which attention was drawn at the end of the preceding chapter. Did the leaders dominate to self-interested and self-preserving ends thereby selfishly abusing their collective authority, or did they discharge their duties fairly to the common good? Was the group unified or pluralistic, homogeneous or heterogeneous? To what extent were the leaders' activities constrained by a network of checks and balances and characterized by concession and compromise?

The extent to which Burnley's group of leaders displayed these characteristics in the later nineteenth century can usefully be assessed with reference to the group's occupational, religious and political composition and by reviewing its achievements during the era. There are three main strands. Firstly, some insight into the potential effectiveness of the group in the sphere of political leadership exercised through the Town Council may be gained by ascertaining whether members comprised a single, united, homogeneous group. It is also instructive to consider whether the group's coherence was reinforced by intermarriage, kinship ties, interlocking business partnerships and a common social life in membership of the same clubs and common residence in the more salubrious districts of the town. In the light of statistical evidence we return to the question: do the leaders comprise an élite or a group of top persons? Secondly, some attempt needs to be made to identify and to assess the implications of the checks and balances which constrained the scope of leaders' collective activities. For example, were policies applied in a relatively modified or unmodified form, and to what extent were they obstructed or resisted by the presence of countervailing forces? Thirdly, it is necessary to address the question: how dynamic and enterprising did the leaders prove to be as a group in action? It is relevant here to ascertain what the leaders achieved, whether major policies introduced by them were the product of coercion or consent, and whether the policies applied can be interpreted in terms of concession and compromise.

Characteristics of the dominant group

A useful starting point is to determine the extent to which the leaders' collective self-consciousness as a functionally distinguishable group within the urban community of Burnley was enhanced by factors such as business partnerships, kinship ties, intermarriage, common areas of residence and a similar life style. Evidence suggests that, though there were *some* connections of this kind, they were not extensive. One of the most obvious examples of a longstanding business partnership in the textile trade is the cotton weaving enterprise linking the Collinge and Lancaster families.(15) Representatives of both families, but particularly the Collinges, were elected to the Town Council as members of the Liberal faction, and both families were prominent in the leadership of the Wesleyan community as Sunday School teachers and circuit stewards.(16) Business, religious and also kinship ties connected the Fielding and Barnes families.(17) H.D. Fielding and John Barnes were brothers-in-law, both acted as circuit stewards at the Wesleyan Westgate Chapel (where the Collinges and Lancasters were also prominent) and were partners in a cotton spinning and manufacturing concern where they were later joined by John Barnes's son, George. H.D. Fielding and John Barnes each served as alderman and mayor, and on his retirement from the Town Council John Barnes was replaced by his son George. The Lancaster, Collinge, Barnes and Fielding families were socially connected in the Wesleyan chapel community with other leaders: Adam Dugdale, John Howorth, John Butterworth, William Nowell, the Thompsons and B. Moore who was for many years associated with the *Burnley Gazette*, the mouthpiece of local Liberalism.(18)

Other kinship and business ties contributed little to the group's cohesion. Abram Altham, for example, married a Miss Oddie from Brierfield; William Lancaster married Alice Standing of Forton in the Fylde; W.C. Hargreaves married the daughter of William Jackson,(19) cotton manufacturer, and subsequently joined the firm of William Jackson, Sons & Co. none of whom appear in the league tables of leaders. C.J. Massey, son of John Massey, a Liberal Congregationalist, married Miss Howarth of Clitheroe and later severed his connection with the Congregational community to join Trinity Anglican Church. One of his sisters married Robert Handsley, agent to the Thursbys, churchwarden of St Andrew's Church, and a leading Tory Anglican.(20) All the indicators disclose that, in so far as the group was coherent or cohesive, this was not strongly reinforced by kinship ties, intermarriage or business partnerships.

There is much more evidence of a shared life style manifest in exclusive residential areas(21) and membership of social clubs. Group consciousness and coherence amongst the town's leading families were more decisively enhanced by what appears to have been a collective preference for housing in particular districts and by association with at least two social clubs, the Cricket Club and the Literary and Scientific Club.

Within the town itself, a neighbourhood of suitably imposing residences, much favoured amongst the well-to-do, was a central area comprising the lower end of Manchester Road, Carlton Road, Hargreaves Street and Palatine Square. Along Manchester Road, for example, lived R.J. Hurtley (Sunny Bank), William Lupton, William Parkinson (Clevelands), John Baron, Adam Dugdale and James Greenwood (Cumberland Place). In Palatine Square lived the Keighleys, the Moores, William Dickinson and the Grants. In Carlton Road lived William Lancaster, William Nowell, the Rawlinsons and Dr Brumwell, while Henry Bulcock lived in Hargreaves Street. However, several wealthy families forsook the town proper and built palatial dwellings on the rural outskirts of the borough, a particularly favoured locality being the area comprising Burnley Wood, Reedley Hallows and Colne Road to the north east of the town. In Burnley Wood, for example, lived John Howorth (Spring Bank), William Lomas (Park View), James Roberts (Tarleton House), J.H. Scott (Oak Hill), the Thompsons (Oak Bank), James Cooper (Mosley Villa) and the

Fieldings (Woodside). Along Colne Road lived Caleb Thornber (Holme View), the Armisteads, the Burrows family (Osborne Grove), Robert Handsley (Reedley Lodge), W.C. Hargreaves (Bankfield Villa) and Abram Altham whose residence, 'Oakleigh, Colne Road' was described in his obituary as 'a superb mansion in Reedley Hallows.'(22) Another exclusive suburb to the east of the town was the Todmorden Road area lying towards the Towneley estates. Here lived the Kays (Towneley Villa), the Folds family (Fir Grove), the Butterworths (Oakbank) and the Collinges (Park House).

Recreationally, the Cricket Club, whose early committee members such as James Folds, James Greenwood, Miles Veevers and Joshua and W. Rawlinson were also regular players, served, in the earlier years at least, both as a sports club for the town's leaders and as a social club to which selectively they could bring their friends. Annual subscriptions of five shillings per head conjecturally kept out the rabble, but a more positive indication of social exclusiveness lies in the resolution that 'no person be allowed to dine with members of the club unless introduced by four *bona fide* members.' After matches, the players and their friends often adjourned to 'The Bull' for a beef-steak supper.(23)

Apart from the annual celebrations, such as the hospital ball, which press accounts show were conspicuously attended by the leaders and their families,(24) the most significant focus of regular social interaction was the Literary and Scientific Club.(25) It was exclusive both in its fee-paying membership and more specifically perhaps in the intellectual nature of its activities. Though invited speakers appeared there quite frequently, it was more usual for members to entertain each other by preparing and reading papers(26) on an astonishingly wide range of subjects. Certainly the club provided an excellent forum where members could demonstrate their intellectual accomplishments and capabilities. The list of members reads like a roll-call of the town's leaders, with very rare exceptions, and includes many of those of lesser influence and authority such as Dr Dean, Dr Brumwell, George Slater and J.S. Horn. No lower-class participants have been identified amongst the membership. If such there were, they were very few in number. Unlike the Church and Mechanics' Institutes, the chapel football and cricket clubs and the improvement societies spawned by churches and chapels of the various sects, the Literary and Scientific Club was not a sponsored mission to the masses but a socially exclusive club where many of the town's leading families met on a group-conscious, social and recreational basis.

The leaders numbered conspicuously amongst those who read papers. The Thompsons, for example, talked on their wide-ranging travels in and beyond Europe. Dr Coultate discussed Burnley place names and the natural sciences. John Howorth spoke about 'explorations' and Alfred Lancaster about 'mechanical models' which he also demonstrated. Thomas Nowell lectured on the composer, Haydn; W.M. Grant gave a series of papers on the life and works of Oliver Goldsmith. The impressive range of subjects covered - including literature, music, history, art, travel, statistics and a wide variety of sciences - argues that members were articulate, self-confident, well-educated and well-informed. Social interaction was enhanced by the fact that club activities were not confined to lectures, but included regular 'conversational evenings', musical soirées, annual dinners and frequent excursions (every month or so) to places of interest usually connected with the subject matter of a recently read or forthcoming paper. Amongst a great many examples which could be cited were trips to Skipton Castle, Bolton Abbey and Woods, Downham and Pendle, Malham, Hardcastle Crags, Kirby Lonsdale and Casterton Woods, Ribchester, Stratford upon Avon, Warwick, Grange and Cartmel, Oxford and Blenheim. On occasions Lady O'Hagan held a reception for the club at Towneley Hall.(27) The club had its own library which contained an impressive collection of books, both fiction and non-fiction, and took several scholarly journals such as the *Transactions of the Field Naturalist and Archaeological Society* and the *Transactions of the Lancashire and Cheshire Record Society*.(28)

The club was in continuous existence from 1873 to 1912 and, although it is impossible to calculate the level of attendance at meetings, the increasing number of membership subscriptions listed in the club's records strongly suggests rising popularity during the 1880s and early 1890s. The impression given is that the club provided an added social, intellectual and recreational dimension to the leaders' group identity, and along with distinctive residence areas and some less clearly ascertainable kinship and business ties, served to reinforce a sense of collective self-awareness of superordinate status.

The leaders emerge as a self-conscious group, but they cannot be represented as a 'unified élite', homogeneous in terms of occupation, political affiliation and religious preference. Judged on the basis of these characteristics they come closer to what some theorists conceptualize as a 'pluralistic élite' - one which was split along lines of social class, religious denomination and political persuasion.(29) Individuals were drawn from the landed gentry, employers (not all of whom were engaged in the same industry), shopkeepers and professionals, and there was even one subordinate-class member. Nevertheless, it was what Perkin has termed the 'entrepreneurial middle class' which was numerically predominant, and within this employer group it was proprietors of relatively large firms in the traditional industries of the area (cotton, ironfounding and engineering) who formed by far the most significant proportion. Proprietors of cotton spinning and weaving firms, of cotton-waste processing and dealing firms, and of combined ironfounding and engineering firms mainly specializing in loom production, collectively formed 64.3 per cent of the leadership (see Table II). Within this group were men involved in the running of family firms (such as Masseys, Thompsons, Kays and Whitakers) and others involved in business partnerships such as 'Collinge and Lancaster', 'Temple and Sutcliffe' and 'Barnes and Fielding'.

With the coming of limited liability and the joint stock form of organization, many proprietors still retained direct links in the earlier part of the period both with employing enterprises and the town. In the case of Altham and Co. Ltd, for example, Jesse L. Altham followed his father Abram into the Town Council as director of the limited company(30) which had grown out of the family tea packing and merchanting firm formerly run by his father. W.C. Hargreaves, a main partner in the firm Jackson, Sons and Co. Ltd, held several offices(31) in the town. J.M. Grey and E. Whitehead, both directors of limited liability companies, appeared as aldermen on the Town Council in the early years of the twentieth century.(32)

Employers in the town's major industries dominated the main areas of the town's affairs via the Town Council and the Borough Bench of Magistrates, and they appeared also on the School Board and the Board of Guardians. As Table II shows, this large employer group was supported by a smaller number of men drawn from the professions (a doctor, a banker, three solicitors and a school proprietor), and by a few shopkeepers. The landed group, composed of members of the Kay-Shuttleworth family of Gawthorpe, the Townley-Parkers of Royle, Lady O'Hagan of the Towneley estates, and the landed, mine-owning Thursby and Scarlett families (related by marriage), form 14.4 per cent of the leadership. They dominated mainly in the areas of philanthropy and on selective bodies, such as the Hospital Board and the Board of Grammar School Governors, to which recruitment in part at least was a reflection of wealth and social status. They were not found, with two exceptions, competing for election to the Town Council, the School Board or the Board of Guardians. In their capacity as JPs they appeared at the more influential county level rather than on the Borough Bench of Magistrates.(33) As members of the county leadership and, in the case of the Kay-Shuttleworths also of the national leadership at central government level, they were less directly concerned with the regular administration of borough affairs. Interconnections of this kind linked the three levels of authority: municipal, county and national. As we shall see, personnel involved in the two higher levels of leadership could reinforce or constrain the actions of the municipal leaders. The former moved in closely, for example, in times of crisis - Sir U.J. Kay-Shuttleworth arrived with troops to assist in the restoration of law and order in Burnley on the occasion of the town riots of 1878, travelling from the other end of the country in order to do so.(34) The Thursbys tended to become more actively involved on the occasion of general elections when the borough chose its MP; at such times they were prominent in political rallies and meetings, especially when General Scarlett, their relative by marriage, stood as a Parliamentary candidate in 1868, and when J.O.S. Thursby stood in 1887.(35) Landed personnel were prominent also when the scheme to build a town hospital was under discussion; indeed the scope of the original plan of providing a small cottage hospital was considerably enlarged when landed concern and interest were translated into offers of land for a site from the Thursbys and of substantial cash donations from others.

The exceptions to this pattern are Lady O'Hagan and Canon Townley-Parker. Lady O'Hagan's influence in the early days was confined to philanthropy and social welfare causes such as care for the blind, but the later years of the period witnessed her involvement in election to the School Board and the Board of Guardians. In many ways, however, her active participation on these two Boards can be viewed as an extension of her former work in philanthropy and her interest in social welfare, particularly that of children. Press reports show she lectured as a 'Progressive' on several occasions to various groups in the town on the aims and objectives of education.(36) She continued to display little active interest, however, in the activities of the Town Council or in the political campaigns which preceded general elections. Canon Townley-Parker, as incumbent at St Peter's, was in many ways more closely associated with the town than the rest. He was not involved as a candidate in contested elections for municipal government and, like Lady O'Hagan, he confined his attention to specific areas. In his case, these were the Church Institute and the School Board(37) where the related religious and educational issues were paramount and a logical extension of his authority as incumbent of the town's largest parish.

Burnley's group of leaders contains only one subordinate-class member - weavers' agent, David Holmes. Although other working men infiltrated very gradually into local elective office towards the end of the period, only David Holmes was of any major significance judged on the basis of the number of leading positions he attained. In addition to his role as trade union official he became a Poor Law guardian, a member of the School Board, a town councillor and, more belatedly, a borough magistrate.(38) By the late 1890s, however, his increasingly extensive involvement in regional and national trade union affairs, plus a prolonged union-sponsored trip to America, led to his withdrawal from many areas of municipal authority.

Socially, therefore, though the group of leaders contained individuals from different social strata, it was numerically dominated by members of the entrepreneurial middle class involved in the town's traditional industries, and these employers, along with a lesser number from substrata within that section of society conventionally termed the 'middle class', dominated in the decision-making processes of municipal government. Landed leaders were less pervasively involved; as members of county and/ or national government their direct participation was limited to specific spheres and issues within the borough. In the nuclear group of super-active individuals the proportional split was even more unequal; as Table III shows, 82.7 per cent of the membership consisted of employers of the entrepreneurial middle class, 10.2 per cent were professionals and 6.9 per cent were landed. Here again, the involvement of the Thursbys in local office was of a more peripheral nature than that of the rest of the group.(39) The Thursbys are the only landed members of the nuclear group; their inclusion is in large part attributable to the family's association with the Anglican Church in Burnley and to their role as employers of labour in the Thursby-owned coal mines.

Burnley's leaders were split also along religious lines (see Table II). The main groupings represent Anglicanism, Roman Catholicism and Nonconformism, but there were sectarian subdivisions which fragmented Nonconformism and the Anglicans were split into 'high' and 'low' church factions. Unfortunately, the religious affiliation of 17.9 per cent of the leaders has not been discovered and this introduces a not inconsiderable degree of distortion into statistical analyses. The available information, nevertheless, is sufficient to permit some broad generalizations.

As Table II shows, the Roman Catholics, comprising 3.6 per cent of the whole, were by far the smallest group, and amongst these Lady O'Hagan was the most influential judged on the number of positions attained. The Anglicans had a larger proportional share; they formed 23.2 per cent of the leaders (see Table II), but this is reduced to 17.2 per cent of the nucleus (see Table III). A large body of Nonconformist members formed 55.3 per cent of the leaders and an overwhelming 72.3 per cent of the nucleus. However, compared with the Congregationalist predominance in Darwen for a slightly earlier period disclosed by Doyle's research, Burnley Nonconformism was more fragmented. Burnley's leaders, as noted in Tables I and II, contained representatives of the Baptist, United Methodist, Wesleyan and Congregational sects. The most significant of these were the Wesleyans who formed 51.6 per cent of the Nonconformists and 28.6 per cent of the whole group (see Table II). In the nuclear group they formed 47.6 per cent of the Nonconformists and 34.5 per cent of the total group (see Table III). As far as religion is concerned, therefore, cohesiveness was not, on the face of it, strongly enhanced. Heterogeneity rather than homogeneity was the salient characteristic.

The statistics overstate the political influence of the Anglicans in Burnley. As noted earlier, several were landed individuals who, as members of a county leadership, had limited direct involvement in the administration of municipal affairs via the Town Council. This leaves a relatively small group centring on St Peter's, St Matthew's and St Andrew's Churches and the Church Institute - the Folds family, John Greenwood, Robert Handsley, William Robinson, the Grants, James Roberts and Canon Townley-Parker. Of these only William Robinson appears in the nuclear group. Peripherally involved were the Slaters, Haslams, Grimshaws, Pritchards and Dr Butler of the Grammar School.

Nonconformism was, therefore, dominant in the key areas of local government, especially in the Town Council. The heterogeneity of Burnley Nonconformism has already been noted but it is possible to overstate the significance of the cleavage. Given their doctrinal differences, all the chapels emphasized similar Christian ideals and in a practical sense encouraged mutual aid and self-improvement. Recreationally, chapel football and cricket teams played each other and their supporters mingled socially. Additionally, the cause of temperance was strenuously supported by all the chapels(40) and all undertook pastoral care and a similar range of welfare services for their congregations. The impression given is that the chapels enjoyed relatively amicable co-existence and the Baptist, Wesleyan, United Methodist and Congregationalist chapel elders, who figure prominently in the leadership and nuclear groups, may well have experienced 'group consciousness' as exponents of similar chapel ethics which transcended sectarian differences. The very fact that leaders represented a number of different sects undoubtedly had the effect of extending and reinforcing the leaders' collective ability to maintain their positions of authority through the creation of a broadly-based network of communication rather than one narrowly based upon a single sect within what was a large and growing town.

The Church of England in Burnley did not present a united front; but whereas amongst the Nonconformists fragmentation appears to have been a source of strength, the Anglican rupture was both divisive and weakening. The Church of England was split into 'high' and 'low' church factions and, according to Bennett, mutual recrimination and hostility persisted between the two. At St Peter's Canon Townley-Parker had replaced the 'cold dull style of evangelicalism' with a 'more ornate choral form of service' and had introduced practices associated locally with Roman Catholicism, such as 'lighted candles on the altar, stoles, birettas and surplices, the practices of crossing, bowing and kissing the Gospel book . . . prostrating before the Elements . . . and standing on the West side of the altar.' St James's and St Matthew's Churches followed St Peter's lead, to the dissatisfaction of some of the parishioners. By 1889 opposition to 'high church' practices crystallized in the formation of the Burnley Protestant Association. By 1892 the issue of auricular confession resulted in indignant public meetings by the 'low church' faction - and reactionary rallies by the supporters of 'high church' ceremonial. The outcome was the secession in 1892 from St Peter's of the 'low church' proponents led by one of the church wardens.(41)

To the extent that the leaders' ability to retain their positions of authority was dependent upon allegiance constructed via the religious institutions, Nonconformism was advantaged. Whereas Nonconformists, who were numerically by far the largest group within the leadership, came together in relatively amicable co-existence which served to unite the community and spread the leaders' influence, leading Anglicans were associated predominantly with St Peter's, St Andrew's and St Matthew's, and appear in the main to have represented the 'high church' party. In consequence their network of communication and spheres of influence were the more limited.

The leadership was split also along political lines. For most of the period the great divide was between the two traditional parties, the Liberals and the Conservatives. Liberalism was overwhelmingly predominant in both the leadership and the nuclear groups (see Tables II and III); it formed 73.2 per cent of the former and 82.8 per cent of the latter. In contrast the Conservatives formed only 25.0 per cent of the leadership and a mere 17.2 per cent of the nuclear group.(42) As Table II shows, the main body of Conservative leadership comprised a small group of landed people - members of the related Thursby and Scarlett families supported by their neighbours, the Townley-Parkers. The whole group, given the presence of Canon Townley-Parker and the Reverend William Thursby, was closely connected with the Anglican Church. Other Conservative leaders were also connected with the Anglican Churches and with their educational and recreational activities, particularly those of the Church Institute - an Anglican-sponsored, Tory rival to the Mechanics'.(43) Some of the Anglican clergy associated with the Conservative party, such as Reverend Winfield and Reverend Owen, taught at the Church Institute while Robert Handsley, a key organizer of the Conservative Club connected with the Church Institute, was agent to the mine-owning Thursbys, church warden of St Andrew's and long-serving official in the organization of the Institute's educational work. Associated with the Church Institute also was the Conservative Working Men's Benevolent Society sponsored by local Anglican Tory leaders. There were similar connections in the case of other Conservative leaders. W.M. Grant had close ties with St Peter's Church and the Church Institute; John Greenwood was church warden at St Peter's and headed the Conservative Club.(44) In Burnley, therefore, there is a not entirely unexpected positive correlation between the local Tory faction and the Church of England with its attendant institutions.

Occasional exceptions to the rule do occur, of course. The most obvious one is the cotton manufacturer, George Sutcliffe, the only Tory of any long-term significance in the Town Council to become first an alderman and subsequently mayor in a largely Liberal Council. Significantly enough, he was a Wesleyan. On the other hand the banker, William Robinson, prominent member of the Liberal faction, was an Anglican married to the daughter of an Anglican clergyman.

A corresponding correlation between Liberalism and Nonconformism is disclosed in Table II, but here the leadership was composed largely of employers in the town's major industries particularly cotton. They dominated the lay leadership of the chapels plus their associated schools, clubs and recreational activities, and they were associated with the Mechanics' Institute.(46) Particularly prominent were the Keighleys and Scotts in engineering, the Masseys in textiles and brewing, and the Collinges, Lancasters, Thompsons, Barons, Kays and Howarths in the cotton trade.

The evidence examined so far suggests that Burnley's leaders can more realistically be termed a group of 'top persons' rather than an élite. Certainly they were conscious of their leading roles and of their status, reinforced as this was by a distinctive life style; but the emphasis, as we shall see, was on responsible service rather than self-interest in the exercise of authority. The Liberals' predominance is attributable in no small measure to the fact that their direct, personal contact and communication with the rest of the local community via employing enterprises and the chapels were more extensive than those of the Conservatives. The social and residential distance between the Conservatives and the people of the town was wider; collectively and individually the Liberals were less remote. The latter were familiar, well-known figures. Respect and trust was founded upon reputations for reliability and predictability built over many years.

The nature of checks and balances

Burnley's leaders in their several multi-faceted and interconnected decision-making capacities within the local community were not entirely unconstrained in the exercise of authority. They functioned within a framework of checks and balances of various kinds which circumscribed their activities, their decisions and the implementation of their policies. In the period under consideration, such checks appear to fall into three main categories. Firstly, there were the checks on specific issues imposed by particular individuals or groups of individuals with a vested interest in the outcome of policy deliberations and with sufficient influence to offer effective resistance. Secondly, there were basic, general checks such as public opinion and the apparatus of national legislation. The latter affected such bodies as the local School Board and Board of Guardians, both of which were accountable in various ways to centrally-based governmental authority. Thirdly, there were the checks encountered within elective bodies, such as the Town Council, the School Board and the Board of Guardians, by the presence of an organized faction of opposed opinion which was potentially capable of obstructing or modifying plans and decisions. In the case of the School Board, for example, one of the main concerns in the triennial elections was denominational representation and the Board contained potentially opposed forces grouped along religious lines.(47) In the case of the Town Council, the key electoral issues were political and the Council at all times contained both Conservative and Liberal representatives and more belatedly Socialists and Independents. These were present in unequal proportions, but by persuasion and rational argument it was possible for the minority faction to exert some influence upon the aims of the majority.

Firstly, in the sphere of checks upon specific decisions, by influential individuals or groups of individuals, the two most obvious examples occur in the 1870s. In 1870 the Borough Council attempted to press forward with plans, already much discussed in the Council Chamber, to extend the borough boundaries and the geographical area of administrative responsibility to include the outlying districts of Habergham Eaves, Lowerhouse, Ightenhill and Brierhill. Influential local landowners, however, anxious to obstruct borough encroachment, raised objections. Canon Townley-Parker of Royle objected to the prospective destruction of the amenities of his estates by urban pollution. The Towneleys of Towneley Hall objected to the threatened encroachment upon their deer park. The Dugdales, employer-landowners of Lowerhouse - at that time a factory colony largely detached from the town -were strongly opposed to borough incursion, and the colony's inhabitants (many employed by the Dugdales) supported the objection on the grounds that corporation gas, water and cemetery facilities would cost more in rates to be paid to the town than similar services already supplied to them privately by Dugdales. The combined resistance of wealthy landed families with county and central government connections proved formidable. The original scheme, therefore, was much modified and the 1871 Extension Act (at a cost of £72,830) increased the area of the borough by only 600 acres from 1,131 to 1,731 acres. For the time being, at least, further borough extension was abandoned and it was not until 1889 that plans were resumed with any degree of success.(48)

Another example is to be found in the plan for a new town sewerage scheme. In one sense this took the form of a spur rather than a check; in another sense it was a check upon complacency. An efficient sewerage system was one of the town's most urgent requirements and subsequently proved to be a major improvement. The decision to act, however, did not stem exclusively from Town Council initiative. Action was precipitated by the influential landowners of Royle, the Townley-Parkers, whose environment was allegedly befouled by nauseous smells from the Calder due to pollution by the town's effluence discharged directly into the river. The persistence of the nuisance, despite repeated complaints to the appropriate authority, led to stronger measures. Canon Townley-Parker obtained an injunction restraining the Corporation from discharging untreated sewage into the Calder to the detriment of his estates. Plans were subsequently drawn up by the Council for the complete re-sewering of the town, to include intercepting main sewers, street sewers and house drains. Canon Townley-Parker's refusal to allow the town's sewage-disposal works to be located near Royle is not altogether unexpected; he did, however, offer to sell the Corporation, at an independently fixed price, a more distant site at Duckpits. The offer was accepted, though it necessarily increased the cost of the scheme to the disadvantage of the ratepayers. The completion of the project was delayed by technical difficulties, and there were further objections from landowners when the pollution problem recurred in the late 1880s.(49) However, what is significant here is that, although the Corporation would undoubtedly have provided a comprehensive sewerage scheme sooner or later along with other urban improvements, its decision to act as and when it did appears to have been provoked entirely by exogenous forces. Significant also is the source of pressure. It was landed members of county society who were capable of exerting effective influence, singly or in comparatively small numbers, as and when their vested interests were threatened.

Secondly, there are the basic general checks exerted from above by a government-imposed framework of legislation, and from below by public opinion from an electorate capable of expressing its dissatisfaction with a particular course of action by voting the opposition on to the Town Council at the next opportunity.

Much nineteenth-century legislation relating to local government was of the permissive rather than mandatory kind, leaving individual boroughs considerable scope for local initiative and enterprise in the provision and organization of basic amenities. However, both education and relief of the poor were subject to basic codes, and local Boards were in many respects accountable to a government department. Much of the time of the Burnley Guardians, for example, was devoted to the straightforward month-by-month task of regular administration, the appointment of medical officers, inspection of accounts, receipt of revenues and disbursement of relief benefits. The minute books for the union, however, indicate an ever-present awareness of the Board's accountability to a higher authority. Monotonously regular correspondence was carried on both with the relevant government department and with other unions in the district; advice and consent were sought on countless small matters and written accounts were given detailing the appointment of medical officers, workhouse overseers, vaccination programmes, steps to find work for local paupers, and so on.(50)

The School Board, similarly through its secretary, Joshua Rawlinson, corresponded regularly with the Education Department set up under the 1870 Act; it gave accounts of the extent of school accommodation available in the area, of school attendance figures and inspections made by School Visitors. The 1870 Act and the creation of a government department precipitated feverish activity in the building of new schools and the extension of existing accommodation by Burnley's leaders, not however (until the 1890s) in their role as School Board, but in their role as church and chapel managers of voluntary denominational schools. In Burnley, as in other towns, many decisions on educational provision were prompted by legislation imposed from above by leaders at a higher level of authority, but such decisions were given specific local interpretation within what the law allowed and required.(51) More than twenty years elapsed in fact before Burnley's leaders on the School Board built their first Board Schools; but by that time, as church and chapel dignitaries and managers of denominational schools, they had vastly extended the town's school accommodation for elementary education.

In their role as employers of labour and payers of wages also, the leaders were increasingly subject to the constraints of a framework of legislation imposed from above. A proliferation of Factory Acts and an increasingly effective inspectorate served to control the length of the working day, to limit juvenile employment and to establish safety regulations and required standards of lighting and sanitation in the workplace. The fact that Burnley had a resident factory inspector, appointed in 1861,(52) undoubtedly encouraged greater compliance with the law. Prosecutions for infringements of the Factory Acts appear regularly in the local press, and magistrates, some of whom were themselves employers, imposed fines, reputedly 'without fear or favour', for breaches of the law. In the 1850s some of the Burnley mills were notorious for running over time. George Slater, for example, was fined the maximum penalty of £100 plus costs of nearly £50 in 1859 for running fifteen minutes over time. Heavy penalties and adverse publicity in the local press ensured that fewer offences of this kind were committed after 1860. There continued to be prosecutions for other infringements, however: unwhitewashed walls, failure to provide guards on dangerous machinery, allowing sweeping around and the oiling of moving machines, and employing juveniles who had not produced the required 'age certificate'. An illuminating example in the cotton trade concerns a Burnley employer who paid a portion of a weaver's wage with a piece of faulty cloth that the weaver was alleged to have woven. When the case was brought before the magistrates the verdict went in favour of the employer. However, the weaver appealed to a higher court on the grounds of infringement of the Truck Acts - his appeal was successful. In another case a female operative went to law with a claim against her employer for damages for wrongful dismissal. Investigation disclosed that the woman had been allowed 'three or four days' off from her work at the factory because she was 'sick and unfit'; subsequently she had been dismissed at the end of the week because at the end of the 'four days' she had neither returned to work nor sent a 'sick weaver' to take her place temporarily. The woman's claim was successful as the four days of sickness absence permitted by her employer had been followed by a weekend day not normally worked at the factory.(53)

An interesting example of the way in which the course of local decisions was affected by a higher authority occurs in the mining industry. In 1881 the colliery-owning Thursbys proposed the formation of the Burnley Miners' Relief Society for the relief of their miners in periods of sickness and recovery from accidents, and for the relief of the widows and children of men killed in the mines. Miners joining the company-sponsored friendly society, to which the company subscribed 25 per cent of total employee subscriptions, forfeited their rights to compensation for accident as granted under the Employers' Liability Act of 1880. The Society, says Bennett, flourished till 1896 when the Workmen's Compensation Act rescinded the right of masters and workers to 'opt out' by making independent arrangements for claims for compensation. Further restrictions followed and the Society was eventually abandoned.(54)

In addition to constraints 'from above', there were limitations imposed 'from below' in the need, as far as the Town Council, School Board and Board of Guardians were concerned, to satisfy an electorate with the power to reject the proponents of an unpopular policy and to vote others into office. While on the one hand municipal parsimony might provoke opposition in the face of inadequate and inefficient sewerage, gas and other basic urban amenities, prodigal spending, as in Darwen,(55) might precipitate reaction on the part of the rate-paying electorate worst hit by the burden of soaring Corporation debt and increases in the rates. In Burnley the Nonconformist employer-led Liberal faction, which dominated the Town Council for most of the period under discussion, managed by and large to steer clear of the Scylla and Charybdis of parsimony and profligacy and thereby to retain its hold on municipal affairs.

Public opinion, nevertheless, occasionally rose to check a specific plan within a policy package which otherwise proved acceptable. In 1881, for example, the Burnley Tram Company, at that time a privately run concern, acquired steam-driven vehicles, ran them through the town in defiance of the local police and magistrates, and was threatened with the revocation of its licence for failure to comply with by-laws. The company was forced to put in thirty horse-drawn vehicles to maintain the local service. The immediate response was public indignation at the return to a less efficient transport service and the cavalier attitudes of those in authority. At a public meeting in the Mechanics' Institute the police and magistrates came in for strong criticism and it was subsequently agreed to widen Church Street the better to accommodate the community's preference for steam-tram passenger transport services.(56) Similarly, the pressure of public opinion vetoed an unpopularly expensive plan in 1881 to increase the town's water supply by the creation of a new reservoir. After some costly mistakes had been made and unanticipated geological problems had created further time-consuming impediments, the Council decided to cut its losses and to begin with an altogether new excavation site in the Robin Hood and Thursden area. However, opinion at the public meeting called to sanction the promotion of the necessary Parliamentary legislation was so hostile in the aftermath of the heavy costs involved in the earlier abortive scheme, that action was postponed until 1883 when an alternative more acceptable because less costly project sited at Cant Clough was devised.(57)

Thirdly, given the division of the leaders into different factions (the one mainly Anglican and Conservative and the other largely Nonconformist and Liberal), there were powers which could be exercised by an effectively organized opposition to modify the activities of the numerically larger group. On the Town Council the political split was predominant; on the School Board the religious division was paramount.

The extent to which the power of an organized opposition within specific areas of authority was actually and effectively exercised depended upon the degree to which the policies of the different factions diverged and upon the relative voting strength of each. In elections to the School Board throughout the 1870s and 1880s the leaders contrived to keep a mutually acceptable balance between the various interests. The Board, consisting of nine members in these years, usually contained one Roman Catholic representative, four Anglicans and four Nonconformists.(58) Given one or two clashes of personality usually involving the outspoken Father Dillon, different factions within the Board worked together in relative harmony for most of the period since they had more or less identical policy objectives.(59) The Board was created to offset whatever inadequacies there were in elementary school accommodation made available by the churches and chapels; for most of the period members of the Board were unanimous in their aim to keep education in the hands of the respective religious institutions. Many of these extended and improved their school premises to this end. More than twenty years elapsed before the first Board Schools were built in the early 1890s. Until the end of the 1880s there was consensus on the School Board on this major area of local education policy. It was not until the end of the 1880s, when other personnel appeared on the Board and when circumstances had changed, that there was any divergence of policy. We return later to consider the nature of the challenge and reaction to it.

On the Town Council, where political matters were uppermost, the situation was different. Here Conservative and Liberal policies were opposed. The Liberals adhered to a policy which favoured vigorous municipal enterprise, the extension of the Corporation's powers not only geographically in widening the borough boundaries, but also administratively in the widespread municipal provision and control of urban amenities such as gas, water and sewerage facilities, the ownership and/or control of markets, abattoirs and cemeteries, and the maintenance of municipal firefighting and transport facilities. Municipal building plans included a town hall, library, public baths, the Burnley Borough Magistrates' Court and police cells. It was a programme involving heavy spending on large-scale projects, and, as such, necessitated large-scale borrowing and debt repayment on the part of the Corporation.(60) There were, of course, implications for the rate-payers. The Tory policy, on the other hand, was one of 'economy'. The Party's representatives advocated a reduction in the rates and the pruning of what it saw as extravagant and over-ambitious plans.(61)

Throughout the period, the Liberals had a majority, sometimes a *large* majority, on the Town Council and therefore the extent to which the Tories were able to organize themselves into an effective countervailing force and to act as a check to modify proposed plans at the discussion stage was very modest, especially in the earlier years of the period. The Tories, with persistently small representation seldom amounting to more than nine or ten councillors, decided towards the end of the 1870s to abdicate from Town Council affairs altogether and for several years the Tory Association refused to contest municipal elections, leaving the Liberals in a position of virtual monopoly.(62) For some time, a total Council of thirty-two members contained only two Conservatives, James Cooper and George Sutcliffe, and these also would have withdrawn from the sphere of municipal government if their re-election had not been actively sought by the Liberals in 1879.(63) At election time that year the *Gazette* stated, 'The Burnley Tories are still in the sulks . . . and under the weight of despair which seized them two years ago . . . . For years, the Liberals were willing to let them have two seats out of eight, but they would not accept the offer. The result is their annihilation.'(64) Another issue of the same paper continued:

> The Tories, in a moment of disappointed rage . . . threw up every seat and refused to contest a single ward, giving up even St Peter's, their greatest stronghold . . . . They left the town in the hands of the Liberals without check on power or control . . . . They have had seats offered without contest but they have refused to accept them . . . . Mr Handsley, Mr Butterworth, Mr John Greenwood and Mr Folds . . . were too high and mighty to accept a sure seat even in St Peter's.(65)

It was in October 1877, after a run of poor Conservative performances at the polls, that they resolved to secede from municipal government, and in that year contestants, Adam Dugdale and George Haslam, withdrew their nominations at the bidding of the Conservative Committee headed at that time by Mr John Greenwood. Bills posted in the town, their message reprinted in the local press, announced:

> To the Conservatives of Burnley,
> Ladies and Gentlemen,
> I have the honour to inform you that at a meeting of your Executive Committee held on Tuesday, it was unanimously resolved not to contest any of the wards in the forthcoming municipal election. The chief reasons which induced the committee to adopt this course were that the Conservatives, although the heaviest ratepayers in the town, are in such a minority in the Town Council, having 8 out of

32 seats, as practically to have no influence, and that the rates of the town under the management of Liberals have increased to such an extent (namely from 1/- to nearly 4/- in the £) as to press most onerously on the ratepayers, especially the working class. Finding that the gentlemen of the Conservative side were unwilling under such circumstances to enter the Town Council or to submit to the annoyance and abuse of contested elections . . . the committee have decided to withdraw from all further municipal contests until such time as the ratepayers generally desire to have representatives in the Town Council who will endeavour to manage the business of the town in a more economic and efficient manner . . . .

I am your obedient servant,
John Greenwood (Chairman)
23rd October 1877.(66)

To the extent that the Liberals' policy in municipal government was checked or balanced by countervailing forces, this was not the net result of an effective Tory opposition within the Town Council.

The leaders' achievements

The Liberals appear to have had little difficulty in maintaining their majority leadership on the Town Council. The greater part of the electorate repeatedly chose to reject the Conservative alternative at the polls. Part of the explanation for the long Liberal predominance may lie in the fact that, in general, the Liberals were demonstrably capable, responsible leaders and that Burnley's voting population approved of their policies and the execution of them. As we have seen, plans and proposals were not always accepted uncritically, but the leaders were not heedless of contrary opinion. They were prepared to communicate their ideas, to make information available, to discuss the difficulties - and to make concessions and compromises.

This raises the questions: what did the Liberals achieve in the sphere of urban improvement, and how dynamic and enterprising did they prove to be as a group in action? Their record appears to be a commendable one. After intermittent activity and periods of dilatory incompetence by successive Improvement Commissions in the earlier years of the century, the Liberal Nonconformist employer-led majority party, which virtually monopolized the borough's affairs during most of the period under discussion,(67) showed itself to be well-endowed with initiative and the spirit of enterprise. The last three decades of the nineteenth century were years of vigorous activity. Although in Burnley, as elsewhere, mistakes were made, some of which were costly,(68) nevertheless within the limits upon efficiency imposed by the state of contemporary scientific knowledge and technology, the town appears to have been provided with wide-ranging urban amenities in a reasonably efficient manner(69) which did not burden the rate-payers with excessively heavy financial obligations.

The leaders' aims were threefold. Firstly, they aimed to provide essential services such as clean water supply, gas, sewerage, paving, street lighting, controlled markets, a fire brigade and transport services. For administrative efficiency as well as civic pride, they also planned a new Town Hall to incorporate public baths, a borough police court and a police station. Secondly, they aimed to maintain law and order and to control nuisances such as smoke pollution and the obstruction of thoroughfares. Thirdly, they planned to extend the borough boundaries the better to accommodate population growth and the necessary extension of housing and related amenities.

In the sphere of amenities, perhaps the two most urgent services needed by any town are clean water supply and sewage-disposal facilities. In the period concerned technological and topographical difficulties encountered in new undertakings of this kind in the Burnley district were compounded by steadily rising demand as the town's population grew.

Two reservoirs inherited from the pre-1870 period were already in use, one acquired from the Improvement Commission and the other initiated by the Town Council in the 1860s, but the supply proved to be erratic. In the 1870s, therefore, the Town Council petitioned Parliament for borrowing powers and in 1879 a Government Commission granted the Council permission to borrow the necessary investment funds to extend the water supply. A new reservoir was begun at Thursden but a Government Inspector declared that the whole scheme was 'impracticable' and the Council was forced to abandon the project. An apparently more suitable site closer to the town was found at Cant Clough, and Parliamentary assent was acquired by an Act of 1883. However, progress was delayed by technological difficulties arising from topographical and geological features and the scheme took eight years to complete, instead of the estimated three, at a final cost of £150,000 instead of the £60,000 originally estimated. Nevertheless, with alterations to the old reservoirs and the subsequent somewhat belated addition of the new Cant Clough project, the town was adequately provided with water. The cost of the scheme provoked some hostility but the fact that the contemporary press contains few complaints about the failure of supply seems to indicate that the service provided was, at least, acceptably efficient,(70) and that the cost to ratepayers was not excessively burdensome.

Another key area of municipal enterprise was the adoption and completion of a planned sewerage scheme. In the early 1870s plans were drawn up and work begun on the costly task of laying intercepting main sewers, street sewers and house drains. A main problem, however, was the method of disposal. Calcination treatment proved only partially successful and a whole series of different methods were tried before a reasonably efficient service was finally attained.(71)

The Corporation's record in the provision of gas was less chequered by mishaps. An existing gas works was acquired by the pre-1870 Town Council from the Improvement Commissioners but little was done at that time to improve the service further. After 1871, however, the Council pursued a much more vigorous policy. It laid larger mains, established mechanical stoking devices and telescopic gas holders and encouraged enlightened public interest and approval by holding regular gas exhibitions in St James's Hall. Large-scale production, increasingly efficient technology and additional modifications initiated by the gas engineer brought the price of gas down to 3s. and then to 2s. 2d. per 1000 cubic feet in the period, a price which could be matched by few other towns in the area. Between 1855 and 1885 production increased fivefold and from the 1880s, the sale of gas was showing a steady profit. In addition to gas, the Corporation determined upon municipal provision of electricity. In 1890 the Burnley Electric Lighting Order granted the monopoly of manufacturing and selling electricity in the borough to the Borough Council, and generation began in 1893.(72)

Control of the markets had been acquired in 1865 and a Market Inspector, appointed the same year, introduced a number of improvements. By 1879 municipal abattoirs had been erected which to a large extent dealt with the problem of disposing of butchers' refuse. From 1884 market dues were also bringing in a regular profit.

Corporation initiative in the provision of fire-fighting services began in 1864, but here again it was not until the 1870s that a decisive, innovative policy was pursued. A modern steam engine was bought in 1874 and by 1881 a new fire station had been erected, with telephone communications connecting the centre to eight parts of the town where ladders were kept to improve the speed and efficiency of the service. The Burnley fire station, according to Bennett, was 'one of the most up-to-date in England.' In addition to the more spectacular projects, the work of providing street paving and lighting went on steadily throughout the period as urban growth proceeded.

Major areas of control for which the Corporation assumed responsibility were the suppression of nuisances and the maintenance of law and order. Agitation by aldermen and a number of councillors in 1872 led to the establishment of the Burnley Borough Bench of Magistrates, and some years later a new borough court house was attached to the resplendent new town hall. In the same year, the Burnley Borough Police Force was established so that by the close of the 1880s the town was no longer entirely dependent upon the county for such services.(73)

Plans to extend the borough boundaries, and therefore also the geographical area under the leaders' control, met with some opposition and proceeded more slowly. The 1861 Act of Incorporation created four electoral wards within a borough area of 1,131 acres. The Borough Extension Act of 1871 increased the area to 1,731 acres subdivided into eight electoral wards, and this was followed in 1889 by a further Act which substantially increased the size of the borough to 4,015 acres. Under the County Councils Act of 1888, Burnley received the status of County Borough, which gave the Council control of highways and bridges, the power to issue 'all manner of licences', to supervise technical education and to administer such Acts as the Contagious Diseases Act and Adulteration of Food Act.(74)

The record of achievements could be extended, but arguably the evidence elaborated here is sufficient to show that the leaders were vigorous, enterprising and responsible. Although their ambitious plans did not always run smoothly, their extensive activities in the provision of basic amenities and the establishment of a Borough Police Force and Borough Bench Magistrates meant that in the context of the period the town was well provided with satisfactorily efficient services. Satisfactory service forms part of the explanation for persisting acquiescence in the leadership of those in positions of authority, but leadership style is equally significant. Another part of the explanation may lie in the fact that the style of leadership was paternalistic.

References

1. Parry, G., *Political Élites*, Allen and Unwin, 1969, pp. 31-2.
2. *Ibid*.

3. Meisel, J.H., *The Myth of the Ruling Class: Gaetano Mosca and the Élite*, Arbor, New York, 1962.

4. Parry, G., *op. cit.*, p. 32.

5. *Ibid.*

6. *Ibid.*, p. 47 summarizes this aspect of Pareto's theory.

7. *Ibid.*, p. 138.

8. Mosca, G. (1896), *The Ruling Class*, McGraw Hill, New York, 1931.

9. Michels, R. (1911), *Political Parties: A Sociological Study of the Oligarchical Tendencies in Modern Democracy*, Free Press, Glencoe, Illinois, 1958.

10. Pareto, V. (1916), *The Mind and Society: A Treatise on General Sociology*, reprinted in translation, Dover, New York, 1973.

11. Burnham, J., *The Managerial Revolution: What is Happening in the World?*, Day, New York, 1942.

12. Mills, C.W., *The Power Élite*, Simon and Schuster, New York, 1956.

13. Parry, G., *op. cit.*, pp. 138-9.

14. *Ibid.*

15. Obituary of William Collinge in *Burnley Gazette*, 23 Oct. 1897; obituary of William Lancaster in *Burnley Express*, 29 Oct. 1902.

16. Appendix, Table VII.

17. *Men of Burnley: Press Cuttings, 1961-3*, loc. cit.

18. See Appendix, Tables III, V, VII.

19. Abram Altham's obituary in *Burnley Gazette*, 1 Aug. 1885; William Lancaster's obituary in *Burnley Express*, 29 Oct. 1902; W.C. Hargreaves's obituary in *Burnley Gazette*, 22 Dec. 1900.

20. *Men of Burnley: Press Cuttings, 1961-3, loc. cit.*; Richard Handsley's obituary in *Burnley Gazette*, 21 Oct. 1903.

21. Addresses given in *Barratt's Directory of Burnley*, 1872 and in *Worrall's Directory of Burnley*, 1896; some information also in obituaries, noted above, in *Burnley Gazette* and *Burnley Express*.

22. Abram Altham's obituary, *loc. cit.*

23. Kneeshaw, J., *Burnley in the Nineteenth Century*, Burnley, 1921.

24. See, for example, issues of *Burnley Gazette* for 11 Feb. 1888 and 6 Feb. 1892.

25. Bennett, W., *History of Burnley*, Burnley Corporation, 1951, IV, p. 203.

26. Details of membership, subscription rates and club activities in *Transactions of the Burnley Literary and Scientific Club*, Burnley Central Library; membership fee was 10s. 0d. per annum for most of the period under review; lists of the club's officers were recorded annually.

27. *Burnley Gazette*, 9 Jan. 1895.

28. *Transactions of the Burnley Literary and Scientific Club, loc. cit.*

29. Appendix, Table II.

30. Jesse Altham was elected to the Town Council in 1897; see *Burnley Gazette*, 5 Nov. 1897.

31. Obituary of W.C. Hargreaves, *Burnley Gazette*, 22 Dec. 1900.

32. Appendix, Table V.

33. Appendix, Tables I and II; Lady O'Hagan was elected to the School Board and Board of Guardians, Canon Townley-Parker to the School Board; regular accounts of proceedings of Borough Magistrates' Court and of County Magistrates' Court appear in *Burnley Gazette* and *Burnley Express*.

34. *Burnley Gazette*, 25 May 1878.

35. Bennett, W., *op. cit.*, pp. 197-8.

36. *Burnley Gazette*, 5 Nov. 1898.

37. *Men of Burnley: Press Cuttings, 1961-3, loc. cit.*; Young, M.E., 'The Burnley School Board, 1871-91', M.Ed. dissertation, Manchester University, 1973.

38. Appendix, Table II; Bennett, W., *op. cit.*, p. 128.

39. Appendix, Tables II and III.

40. Bennett, W., *op. cit.*, pp. 154-5; obituary of Abram Altham in *Burnley Gazette*, 1 Aug. 1885.

41. Bennett, W., *op. cit.*, p. 158.

42. Appendix, Tables II and III.

43. Bennett, W., *op. cit.*, pp. 182-4, 205-7; *Men of Burnley: Press Cuttings, 1961-3, loc. cit.*

44. Bennett, W., *op. cit.*, p. 138; obituary of W.M. Grant in *Burnley Gazette*, 18 Feb. 1888; Greenwood's letter to the electorate in *Burnley Express*, 25 Oct. 1877.

45. Obituary of W. Robinson in *Burnley Gazette*, 30 Oct. 1881.

46. Appendix, Table II.

47. Appendix, Table IX.

48. Bennett, W., *op. cit.*, pp. 68-9.

49. *Ibid.*, p. 70.

50. *Minutes of the Burnley Board of Poor Law Guardians, loc. cit.*

51. Young, M.E., *op. cit.*; Bennett, W., op. cit., p. 174.

52. Bennett, W., *op. cit.*, p. 104.

53. *Ibid.*, pp. 103-4; report in *Burnley Gazette*, 4 Dec. 1886 shows that thirty cases of irregularities under the Factory Acts were adjudicated in the Borough Court.

54. Bennett, W., *op. cit.*, p. 112.

55. Doyle, M.B., 'Social Control in Over Darwen, 1839-78', M.A. dissertation, Lancaster University, 1972.

56. *Men of Burnley: Press Cuttings, 1961-3* contains reference to the incident in an article about Peter Rylands whose intervention eased tension.

57. Bennett, W., *op. cit.*, p. 80.

58. Appendix, Table IX.

59. Young, M.E., *op. cit.*

60. Bennett, W., *op. cit.*, pp. 79-95.

61. See Greenwood's letter in *Burnley Gazette*, 25 Oct. 1877; see also *Burnley Express*, Special Election Issue, 30 Oct. 1884.

62. *Burnley Gazette*, 25 Oct. 1877.

63. Cooper and Sutcliffe were nominated for re-election to the Town Council in 1879; see *Burnley Gazette*, 25 Oct. 1879; see review of the issues involved in the editorial column of this issue.

64. *Burnley Gazette*, 25 Oct. 1877.

65. *Burnley Gazette*, 1 Nov. 1884.

66. Greenwood's letter, *ibid.*, 25 Oct. 1877.

67. Appendix, Tables IV and V.
68. *Burnley Gazette*, 1 Nov. 1884.
69. Bennett, W., *op. cit.*, pp. 63-94.
70. Details of the project *ibid.*, pp. 79-81.
71. *Ibid.*, pp. 70-1.
72. *Ibid.*, pp. 81-2.
73. *Ibid.*, pp. 86-7, 90-2.
74. *Ibid.*, pp. 68-9, 73-4.

3

The Benign and Repressive Faces of Paternalism

Introduction

There is a good deal of evidence to show that in the later decades of the nineteenth century the prevailing socio-economic structure in Burnley and other northern industrial towns was such that townsfolk were exposed to many direct and indirect influences from above. These certainly had the inherent capacity to stimulate vertically orientated loyalties which were capable of producing acquiescence. The interlocking and overlapping framework of decision-making roles played by the leaders provided potentially effective linkages for the exercise of authority by the minority over the majority. The fact that many of the positions of authority were subject to public election, notably those on the Town Council, the School Board and the Board of Guardians, suggests that efforts to forge and maintain vertical bonds were not altogether ineffectual. The leadership style, Joyce has argued, was essentially paternalistic.

Voluntary compliance was always preferable. Paternalists recognized, whether consciously or intuitively, that coercion alone was likely to maintain the *status quo* neither serenely nor indefinitely. Enlightened employers were well aware that workers who identified *with* them and with the employing enterprise were in the long run more reliable and more efficient than a workforce whose response was one of grudging consent under the threat of sanctions. This line of reasoning can be extended to the relationship between the leaders and the masses beyond the workplace.

Dutton and King(1) question the extent to which leadership in northern industrial towns could be described as paternalistic. These authors maintain that the activities of leading employers in Preston were self-interestedly exploitative rather than paternalistic. The concept of paternalism requires closer scrutiny.

Paternalism as a form of authority: the two faces

Paternalism is a term which is extensively used by historians, but the concept of paternalism tends to be a matter of vague inference and assumption rather than definition. Dutton and King, for example, dispensing with the inconvenience of the need to define terms, offer a great deal of impeccably detailed evidence of what they claim is 'entirely unpaternal' employer activity: the cavalier imposition of short-time working, payment of wage-rates below the prevailing average and the maintenance of harsh, often punitive, factory discipline.(2) The implication is that paternalism is synonymous with kindliness and benevolence. This kindly, caring, charitable facet is indeed an important, but by no means sole, defining characteristic. It served, as Joyce(3) effectively demonstrates, an essential purpose in creating goodwill and encouraging sentiments of loyalty among subordinates; but paternalistic strategies were wider than this.(4) The limited definition overlooks the other face of paternalism. Many writers, as Roberts argues, have defined the term too narrowly.

The exercise of paternalism involves inherently contradictory impulses contained in the need, on the one hand, to observe hierarchical differentiation from subordinates and, on the other, to foster a sense of identification and unity of purpose. The contradictions are manifest in the co-existence of conflicting characteristics: distance and familiarity, power and obligation, ruthlessness and compassion, oppression and benevolence, punishment and protection. Paternalism, it must be emphasized, is essentially a form of authority. The attributes of paternalistic leadership, according to Sennett, include not only assurance and superior judgment but also the 'ability of impose discipline' and the 'capacity to inspire fear'.(5) The image of the boss, with profit-orientated motives and responsibility for the control of often large numbers in his 'family', is superimposed upon the image of the father. This immediately places constraints upon the kindlier, more benevolent aspects of the paternalist's leadership style.

Clarification may be assisted by attention to the paternalist's concept of society and of his own function within it. The nineteenth-century paternalist(6) comprehended society as a hierarchical entity in which superordinates undertook decision-making leadership functions which involved duties and responsibilities to subordinates. The paternalist's right to assume leadership over others derived from a firm conviction on his part that he possessed the superior intellectual qualities, experience and expertise to guide others and that others, because of their lesser, even defective capacities, stood in need of such guidance. His was a unitary concept of society where, ideally, harmony prevailed, where 'each individual had his function, his place, his protectors, his duties, his reciprocal obligations and his strong ties of dependency.'(7) Order and discipline were to be regulated in the light of standards and objectives unilaterally set by him. But there was always the risk of transgression. Some of the moral and intellectual tendencies of subordinates could give rise to the kind of activities that threatened to subvert the harmonious stability and structured unity of the paternalist's ideal world. Where kindlier means of encouraging voluntary compliance failed, or were judged inappropriate, sterner strategies were utilized to exact obedience; superintendence and control could be severely, even brutally, authoritarian. Ideological justification drew upon familial practice. Just as the wise and tolerant father would from time to time chastise the dependent child who wilfully flouted or disrespectfully questioned his rightful authority, so the paternalistic employer would check 'deviant' behaviour by resort to harsh, possibly punitive, means to restore order and stability. The typical paternalist of the early Victorian period, Roberts(8) reminds us, believed in capital punishment, severe game laws, summary justice for delinquents, strict laws governing the duties of servants, and the imprisonment of seditious writers.

This is not to imply that such authority was unconstrained. In nineteenth-century Britain the paternalist did not have the absolute power of an autocrat or a despot. As we have seen, an evolving network of legislation relating to employment, public health, education, the franchise and so on, was extending the citizenship rights of the masses. Though the activities of those in positions of authority in the industrial towns of the North West were circumscribed by a progressively more complex framework of constitutional constraints, it would be erroneous to claim that the regulations embodied in factory and mining legislation were never covertly, or even overtly, violated. In practice, there were some 'paternalists' who abused their power or scorned the codified standards of the era. The salient point to be made here, however, is that there were many forms of coercion which neither constitutional law nor the tenets of paternalism precluded. During the second half of the nineteenth century, as will be shown, those in positions of authority in Burnley utilized both kindness and coercion, incentives and punitive deterrents in attempts to maintain the kind of order and stability which they viewed as essential to the common good. This raises the question to be addressed in a later chapter, of whether the collective response of subordinates can be represented as one of deference.

The benign, kindly face of paternalistic leadership is manifest in voluntary initiatives for social welfare; the stern repressive face in the ruthless exercise of power to suppress what was viewed as social insubordination, most obviously in the sphere of industrial relations. If the former is the more visible countenance, cooperative consent is likely to be the more characteristic response; if the latter is the more frequently exposed visage, the response will be alienation masked by grudging compliance - followed in all probability by the strategic ousting of leaders and their replacement by others at the first opportunity, should such opportunity arise. Clearly, there are implications for the socio-political *status quo*.

The leadership styles of paternalists were often markedly different. As Joyce(9) demonstrates, the relaxed and expansive style of the Blackburn cotton master, Harry Hornby (popularly known as 'th'owd Game Cock') with his reputation for 'spirit' and 'pluck' ran counter to the strenuous and restrictive, abstinent and evangelizing style of Ashton's Hugh Mason. More important than idiosyncratic personality in the paternalist's ability to maintain his leadership, however, was his dexterity in constructing channels of communication with subordinates via personal contact inside and outside the workplace. Equally important was his persistence in ensuring that the channels remained unblocked. Means of communication provided opportunities for the leaders and the lower classes to discuss, to explain, to justify a line of action and, possibly more importantly, to get to know each other better. Highly significant, also, is the fact that the paternalist's ability to legitimate, and therefore also to retain, his position of authority depended upon a reputation built up over many years. This enabled the individual to construct confidence bridges premised upon trustworthiness and predictability. Some of his decisions and actions may not have been to the liking of subordinates, but the intermittent, exceptional incidence of suppression and exploitation may be countenanced where the prevailing theme is perceived to be one of well-intentioned, responsible and even humanitarian stewardship. Where the collective actions of a group of 'paternalistic' leaders are viewed as predominantly self-seeking, exploitative and irresponsible, and authority over others to be persistently misconducted, their claims to legitimate leadership are the more likely to be disputed.

The benign face of paternalism

The benign, caring face of nineteenth-century paternalism is nowhere better illustrated than in the sphere of voluntary initiatives for social welfare.(10) Such initiatives epitomized the benevolence and responsibility of paternalism. Welfarism in Burnley took two main forms. Firstly, there were special efforts of an essentially temporary nature undertaken in circumstances of crisis; secondly, there were other more permanent welfare structures to assist those who were persistently disprivileged either because they were low-income earners or because they suffered some physical disability or personal misfortune. Minimalist state provision offered by the much-amended Poor Law of the latter half of the nineteenth century left ample scope for voluntary effort of both temporary and permanent kinds.

There are numerous, well-documented manifestations of voluntary action undertaken to ameliorate distress during recurrent periods of general economic crisis and during recessions in particular trades. An illuminating example of the paternalistic exercise of welfarism in circumstances such as these is to be found in Burnley during the 'cotton famine'(11) of the early 1860s. According to one estimate, roughly a quarter of some twelve thousand cotton operatives in Burnley and Habergham Eaves were unemployed in 1862 and the remainder were working a three-day week; when distress was at its worst between October 1862 and January 1863 as many as nine thousand weavers were reportedly without work. Much suffering was endured. The *Burnley Advertizer* noted:

> ... the miserable condition of our operatives ... the haggard looks and wretched appearance of those who may be met with at every corner, or wandering away in unwilling idleness ... the painful story of the inside of the dwellings of these poor men, the wan and sorrowful aspect of the anxious wife and mother, the ragged and shoeless children, the terrible appearance of the table where not half enough of the coarsest and weakest food was placed, the diminished furniture and the empty drawers in the chest.(12)

Press reports claimed that there were many who collapsed from exhaustion, fatigue and undernourishment while waiting in the long queues which gathered outside the Guardians' Relief Office in Curzon Street.

There was a ready response from Burnley's leaders to press appeals to 'remember the poor operatives'. The response in the main was one which was led 'from above', taking the form of direct relief in cash and kind, job creation initiatives and activities organized to fill the idle hours of the unemployed. Soup was provided at Mount Pleasant Chapel, meal was distributed at the Temperance Hall in Keighley Green, and bread was given out at St Paul's Church. The clergy, at the instigation of the Reverend A.T. Parker, opened a Clergy Relief Fund. Much of the relief work appears to have been associated with the churches and chapels, but there were other efforts. In July 1862 the Mayor formed a Town Committee of Relief for the distribution of money, food tickets and basic commodities. Initially the cash relief, given weekly, amounted to 1s. 6d. per head, but this was subsequently increased to 1s. 9d. and then to 2s. 0d.

There were also attempts to combat the problem of enforced idleness by providing the workless with other activities to fill their time. For example, day schools and evening schools offering instruction in reading and writing were opened. More important in a practical sense were the efforts, rudimentary though they were, to create temporary opportunities for paid employment not only for men but also for women in an area with a strong tradition of female employment outside the home. Sewing schools were set up in Keighley Green and at the Mechanics' Institute where girls and women were employed at 1s. 9d. per week to make army shirts and other items of clothing; work for male operatives was found in road repair, in various municipal undertakings, on drainage schemes at Royle and on similar projects at some of the outlying farms. Retraining facilities were offered for those who might wish to transfer to another trade or to become self-employed. The Burnley Industrial School for men and boys was started, with payment as an incentive to attend. Further to ease the pressure upon family income at a time when many of the distressed refused to apply for relief available under the Poor Law, the cost (2d. per week) for children attending the denominational elementary schools was defrayed by the Guardians.

During 1862, in November alone, as many as 17,500 people were given assistance at Burnley's local welfare centres: the Guardians' Relief Office in Curzon Street and the Relief Offices opened by the Mayor's Town Committee. But assistance was not confined to local effort. As Bennett notes, the Lancashire Committee for Relief, to which the Burnley Town Committee became affiliated, and the Lord Mayor of London's Relief Fund provided grants; even small villages and towns in the colonies sent donations to ameliorate distress in Burnley.(13)

These intermittent but recurrent welfare expedients must be set against the backdrop of less dramatic though more permanent forms of voluntary welfarism.(14) Again, these were constructed and sponsored by 'top persons' or by institutions and organizations largely dominated by them. Churches and chapels, employing enterprises, voluntary educational institutions, individual philanthropists, the Town Council, the charity societies and so on all made their contribution to the social welfare of the community. In some cases it was the male benefactor who predominated, other spheres fell more naturally to the ladies, but there were still others in which men and women worked together.

Most of the churches and chapels in Burnley appear to have sponsored their own benevolent societies, sick societies and town missions which distributed money, food, clothing and other necessities to the sick and distressed. The Conservative Working Men's Sick and Burial Club to which General Scarlett, a relative of the Thursbys, donated a thousand pounds, was spawned by the Constitutional Club associated with the Church Institute. The United Methodists had their own Methodist Friendly Society and Sick Club; Keighley Green chapel had its Wesleyan Sunday School Sick Club.

Practical assistance to provide a rudimentary form of income maintenance was important in the context of the era, but an equally important aspect of the welfare work undertaken by the religious institutions was pastoral care. The Wesleyan Methodist sect had paid missioners who organized the work of the Town Mission, paid house-to-house visits and held cottage prayer meetings as well as helping the sick and giving relief to the poor. It would be unjust to treat the practical assistance given by the chapels dismissively but it would be equally erroneous to overlook the importance of psychological wellbeing enhanced by regular visits which reduced a sense of isolation and alienation. Bonds of trust and confidence were forged in this dimension of welfare work. Where there was personal contact, the distressed were at least assured that others cared about them. Those who visited the less fortunate in their own homes witnessed at first hand the latter's standard-of-living problems and tried to compensate by informal, sympathetic counselling, or a little conversation over a cup of tea. Such actions went some way in dissolving social barriers in the sense that communication was promoted, and people grew to know, understand and trust each other better.

There were other manifestations of the welfare role undertaken by Burnley's religious bodies. Voluntary welfare provision was made for the deaf and dumb in 1889 at the instigation of prominent members of the Burnley Rural Deanery. The society which came into being was controlled by a joint committee of representatives from both Burnley and Blackburn. The two towns made equal contributions for the maintenance of a salaried missioner charged with the task of spiritual and social care for those in need. In 1895 the original society split into two sections to cater for the specific problems of deafness and dumbness separately, though the two bodies continued to share the services of the same missioner. At the outset meetings were held in St James's School but the premises proved to be somewhat comfortless and Canon Winfield, the society's president, invited members to hold their social gatherings in his vestry. For deaf and dumb people who had difficulty in following conventional church services Canon Winfield regularly held special services, including Holy Communion. By the end of the century the society had become firmly established, but it was becoming increasingly clear that there was a need for a more satisfactory meeting place. In 1900 a move was made to Brown Street, and six years later a more permanent, centrally located home was found in the Church Institute. The transfer enabled the society to establish a small church, to hold evening social meetings more frequently, and to extend the range of its recreational activities to include the formation of a billiards club.

Important aspects of welfare work were undertaken by the ladies. The Ladies' Relief Committee for the care of women in childbirth was formed as early as 1820 and continued its welfare activities for many decades, but several new charities were formed in the later nineteenth century. Lady O'Hagan (Alice Towneley) founded a Deaf and Dumb Society to teach lip-reading specifically to Roman Catholics. There was other provision for the blind. In November 1882 a Society for Home Teaching and Help to the Blind was founded. Interest in its work, as well as very generous financial assistance, was given by the ladies of the Towneley and Kay-Shuttleworth families, and also by Canon Townley-Parker and the Thursbys. The society appointed a teacher, opened a school at Fulledge, attended to the general welfare of the sightless, established a club room and in 1890 started its first workshop for the blind in Eastwood Street.

The ladies of the town and district came to the fore also in providing assistance to young girls whose special personal circumstances, deriving from a variety of misfortunes - homelessness, unsatisfactory home conditions, poverty, loneliness - exposed them to moral and physical danger. In 1883 Lady Kay-Shuttleworth and Mrs John Brown, wife of a local doctor, co-ordinated and placed on a sounder organizational footing the informal but random aid given formerly. In that year they founded a Home for Friendless Girls. There was much rescue work to be done in this sphere, the increasing number of appeals for assistance necessitating a succession of moves to larger premises. The first home, situated in Padiham Road, soon proved to be too small to house those in need of care; a large house was taken in Todmorden Road, and subsequently a more permanent settlement was established at No. 60 Bank Parade. Here two deaconesses were given responsibility for the management of the home's affairs, including also evening educational classes and the provision of a small library.

A similar home for friendless girls was established in 1888 at Fulledge House by Burnley's Roman Catholic community. The society, the Congregation of our Lady Mother of Good Council, owed much to the efforts of Alice O'Hagan who paid for alterations to the building and took a keen interest in the work being undertaken. The girls were encouraged to regain their self-respect by helping themselves and each other; all were required to assist with laundry work, sewing and other household tasks. In promoting social and practical domestic skills, the experience of living in the home helped not only in the formation of friendships but also in the rehabilitation of the girls in preparation for their return to the outside world.

The ladies were also involved in voluntary effort in organizations devoted to the welfare of children. A Burnley branch of the Society for the Prevention of Cruelty to Children was formed in 1888 and, once again, Lady O'Hagan played a major role in the work of bringing many cases of extreme cruelty before the magistrates. But Lady O'Hagan's concern for the young was not confined to rescue work; in the mid-1890s she maintained at her own expense two trained midwives who dealt with roughly two hundred maternity cases per annum in the three-year period, 1893-6.

The provision of medicine and medical care was one of the major achievements of voluntary welfarism in Burnley. Here, as in other spheres of social welfare, provision did not come exclusively from above. Certainly members of the superordinate social stratum were prominent in initiating, organizing and financing the projects which were undertaken, but the disprivileged were not merely passive recipients of such aid, nor were the medical services, thus provided, intended for the exclusive use of the poor. Initiative may have come from above, but the town's community in general shared in the services made

available. Voluntary fund-raising efforts of this kind undoubtedly
promoted a sense of community which bonded members of the
different social strata; moreover, the successful completion of a
major project served symbolically as a focus of shared civic pride.

An illuminating project of this kind is to be found in Burnley's
Victoria Hospital. A precursory plan, formulated by Mr S. Howard,
for the building of a hospital near Holy Trinity Church proved
abortive. Some time later the Reverend Robert Giles, vicar of St
Matthew's, attempted to generate enthusiasm for the erection of
a hospital to serve the whole town, but this plan also came to
nothing. Subsequently, on October 21 1882, the Reverend Giles
called a meeting of leading parishioners to discuss the possibility
of founding a cottage hospital to serve his own parish. At the
meeting Dr Brown cogently argued the necessity of enlarging the
scheme and of appealing to the Mayor to investigate the whole
issue. By this time the hesitancy of the preceding years had
evaporated, to be replaced by more widespread enthusiasm for
the proposal. At a public meeting called by the Mayor a committee
was formed with John Butterworth as chairman, Joshua Rawlinson
as honorary secretary and N.P. Grey as honorary treasurer. The
need for new, purpose-built premises, urged by the town's doctors,
was accepted and the decision was followed by a series of fund-
raising efforts.

Amongst the most generous benefactors were Abram Altham
(£1,725), the Reverend William Thursby, John Butterworth and
Miss Barnes (£1,000 each), Sir Ughtred Kay-Shuttleworth, Thomas
Brooks, J.T. Dugdale, Messrs Tunstill, W. Ecroyd, B. Thornber
and J. Graham (£500 each). Additionally, Reverend William
Thursby gave three acres of land as a site for the hospital and a
few years later Lord Shuttleworth endowed a cancer research
clinic. But donations did not come exclusively from members of
the superordinate social stratum. The operatives in the cotton
spinning and weaving trade raised over £1,000, and it was the
generosity of townsfolk in general, both rich and poor, which met
the cost of modern equipment and extensions to the building
(including the addition of a children's ward); almost every
institution and society in the district gave contributions, made
subscriptions and arranged collections in aid of the hospital. In
Bennett's words:

> The Victoria Hospital . . . represented the greatest voluntary united
> effort that Burnley had ever made. Political, social and religious
> differences were laid aside to bring about this much-needed reform,
> so that when HRH Prince Albert opened the building on October

13 1886, the whole town gave itself over to celebrating the occasion. Streets were decorated with flags, streamers and flowers, three electric lights of 6,000 candle power surmounted the archway in Manchester Road, a medal was struck, and a holiday was given in mills and workshops that all might share in the rejoicing . . . .(15)

Perhaps the most direct means of cultivating a corporate identity and sentiments of goodwill were the rudimentary welfare arrangements made by employers for their workers in large employing enterprises. At their most meagre, they consisted of sick clubs; at their most comprehensive they represented company-based mini-welfare states. Some of the components featured as the gifts of welfare paternalism; others, reflecting the philosophy of the era, were based upon the principles of self help. The employer-sponsored but largely self-financing sick clubs are the most obvious manifestations of what may be termed the minimalist approach to welfare. Yet in another sense the sick club was of major significance in that it provided some security against one of the most troublesome of the problems experienced by the operative's family: loss of earnings during periods of sickness absence.

In the Burnley district, at the instigation of the landed, mine-owning Thursbys, the Burnley Miners' Relief Society(16) was founded in 1881. The objective was to provide assistance for miners who were unfit to work due to sickness or pit accidents and to assist the widows and dependent children of men who lost their lives in the mines. Joint contributions from employer and employee were important in that they emphasized combined effort and shared responsibility. Adult miners paid 3d. per week, boys below the age of sixteen contributed 1d. per week and the company subscribed a sum equal to 25 per cent of total contributions from colliers. In the same year the Towneley Miners' Relief Society(17) was set up and run on similar lines to the scheme operated at the Thursby mining enterprises. Work in coalmining was arguably the most hazardous of all the employment options available in the district.

In Burnley forms of paternalistic welfare fostered by social leaders beyond the factory gates, particularly welfare services made available through the religious institutions, appear to have been more significant in a practical sense than those provided within the employing enterprise. There were, of course, more comprehensive forms of company-sponsored welfare elsewhere. Arrangements made by the Quaker Crosfields(18) at their soap and chemical plant in Warrington went far beyond the sick club.

The Crosfields made extraordinary efforts to promote a sense of community by attention to welfare. In the later nineteenth century the company, though expanding, was still run on lines which enabled the employing partners to become acquainted with their workpeople on a personal, face-to-face basis; their welfare concern was pastoral as much as practical. John Crosfield's obituary(19) claims the workpeople employed at the family firm were not simply 'hands'; he is reputed to have known most of them by name, conversing with them freely and providing the gift of retirement pensions for those who had grown grey in the firm's service. A contributory sick club, managed by the firm's cashier, was in operation by 1868. Likewise an illuminated address, presented in 1892 to Arthur Crosfield by the employees, acknowledged his 'warm interest in the welfare of the workmen' and his personal 'efforts to promote harmonious feeling.'(20) Medical and dental services supplemented the contributory sick club. These piecemeal welfare provisions at Crosfield's were the precursors of the more comprehensive welfare scheme which evolved during the closing decades of the century.

Again, there is the emphasis upon community; the unitary concept of the employment relationship between the employer and his workforce is at the root of claims made by John Crosfield, a model of nineteenth-century welfare paternalism, that the 'interests of employers and employees are indissolubly bound together' and that the additional financial outlay for the firm sprang not only from essentially philanthropic motives but also from the expectation of ample returns in 'services more cheerfully and more efficiently performed.'(21) Paid holidays, for example, were 'gifts', not 'negotiated rights'; the availability of the gift was stringently conditional upon the expectation of satisfactory attendance and punctuality. The conditions may have been unilaterally designed by the employer but there is little to suggest that the workforce judged these to be unfair. The gains were reciprocal.

The repressive face of paternalism

Nineteenth-century leaders were not blind to the economic and socio-political advantages which ensued when goodwill prevailed in the workplace and in the wider community of the town, but when the spirit of cooperation and reciprocity failed, or when authority was flouted, the paternalist was capable of resorting to harsher strategies to restore order and stability. Such strategies could be ruthlessly suppressive on occasions. In Ashton,(22) for example, a benevolent employer-dominated group of leaders set the pace in philanthropic initiatives and voluntary welfarism, but the benign face of paternalistic authority was averted when operatives' dissatisfaction with wage rates erupted in the weavers' strike which began in December 1886. Overlookers, exercising authority delegated by employers, utilized intimidation and threats of dismissal to enforce a return to work. There was a similar reaction on the part of the formerly kindly paternalists in Accrington(23) in response to the region-wide weavers' strike of 1878 when disorder spread throughout most of the major towns of textile Lancashire.(24) Attempts to restore industrial discipline and to contain civil disorder by the use of repressive policing, sometimes reinforced by the presence of the militia, were not unusual during a period characterized by economic uncertainty, the spread of industrial unionism and progressively more assertive union attitudes. In practice paternalism does not appear to have precluded the intermittent resort to draconian strategies in attempts to recreate the organic unity, founded though it was on a spurious symbiosis of unequals, which characterized the paternalist's ideal world.

It is equally clear that the paternalist's concept of fairness and justice was sometimes markedly different from that of subordinates, and that in certain conjunctural circumstances the paternalist was strategically well-placed self-interestedly to impose his will upon groups with little power to offer effective resistance. Paternalists' objectives cannot be construed consistently and undeviatingly in terms of altruism or even of the utilitarian ideal of the greatest good for the greatest number.

Past experience of employers' power and the kind of reprisals that they could take, sometimes functioned as major constraints upon operatives' willingness to resist. For example, support for the weavers' strike of 1859-60 in Padiham and Burnley was patchy, fear of dismissal being the main deterrent. The concessions demanded by workfolk on strike included the adoption of the Blackburn 'List' (thought to have been 12 per cent higher than the average rates paid in Burnley and district), and recognition of the local branch of the weavers' union for collective bargaining purposes. In Padiham four out of ten mills worked all through the strike and a significant proportion of the rest were only partially affected because many operatives refused to join the strikers. On this occasion the spread of industrial action in nearby Barrowford was effectively checked by the masters' federation when weavers were required under the threat of dismissal to sign

'The Document' agreeing not to join a trade union and to refrain from inciting others to strike.(25) This example apparently served as a warning to the rest and the strikers gradually drifted back to work.

Masters were often able to 'turn the tables' on workers by converting a strike into a lock-out with the assistance of strike-breakers, often brought into the town from distant localities. Strike-breaking was difficult to counter, and there were limits to unions' financial resources to support strikers and their families for any length of time. The cotton and coal industries were major regional generators of employment and the implications of a recession affecting either of these trades put employers in a strong position to act unilaterally to control industrial relations at such times. Moreover, operatives' solidarity was often weakened if strikes were prolonged; cost-of-living considerations and attention to family welfare tended in time to override any personal commitment to the ideology of collectivism. A strike at Colne seeking to enforce the adoption of a uniform 'List' had spread to Accrington, Blackburn and Burnley early in 1861 but, despite collections and levies on looms in most of the major towns of Lancashire in support of industrial action, the defeat of the eleven-months-long walk-out was hastened by strike-breakers brought in from Coventry.(26)

The failure of strikes was not always solely attributable to the repressive strategies devised by employers for, clearly, there were cash limits to union funds which constrained the potential duration of resistance. Also, consensus amongst members of the workforce was sometimes elusive. There were some who were not drawn into the union movement; there were some unionists who disagreed with union policy and refused to support a strike; others feared victimization, and still others with family responsibilities were deterred by inadequate levels of strike pay. In such circumstances employers were able to exploit the actual or potential fragmentation of the opposition. During the 1872-3 weavers' strike, which lasted from February 1872 to October 1873, the Burnley branch of the union appointed an 'agent' to 'police' districts where operatives were too timid to come out on strike. The intention was to provide some sort of protection,(27) but such rudimentary arrangements as these inspired minimal confidence amongst those who feared future reprisals. The effectiveness of the walkout at one of the mills was undermined by lack of support from non-unionists who continued to work.

Efforts to protect workers by legitimate means usually made use of the evolving citizenship rights embodied in legislation relating to employment. A major responsibility shouldered by officers of the Burnley branch of the weavers' union was to ensure that employers observed the standard rate of pay set out in the 'List' and to take up cases where infringement had occurred. Redress was important because random infringement invited emulation by other employers, and there was the risk of the unilateral down-rating of the 'List' itself by the local masters' federation. But there were many other individual dissatisfactions which were difficult to resolve by an operative acting alone. It was one of the duties undertaken by union officers to collect information about grievances, to conduct thorough investigations into the circumstances surrounding complaints and, if there appeared to be a genuine case of violation of a worker's rights, to fight for redress in the magistrates' courts. Frequently recurring grievances included the imposition of what, from the operative's viewpoint, were unjust fines imposed for various minor misdemeanours, which led to resented deductions from weekly pay. Such cases were fought both on cost-of-living grounds and on legal precedent. Many of the cases taken up by the unions involved alleged infringement of the Truck Acts, which illegalized the substitution of kind for cash in take-home pay. There were also numerous cases of dismissal for what trade union opinion regarded as inadmissible reasons: minor instances of faulty work, refusal to work overtime when required, and absence from work due to sickness. Some of the verdicts relating to cases brought by the unions went against the operatives; the recorded comment, made by a judge in a case tried in Colne in 1891, that cases supported by the weavers' union were to be viewed in the light of 'benefit-actions which served a good and useful purpose,' can have provided cold comfort for the suspiciously large number of unsuccessful plaintiffs. One of the grievances recorded most often concerned alleged inaccuracy in the measurement of cloth produced by weavers which consequently reduced the individual's cash earnings. It was not until 1891 that the volume of complaints on this score was dramatically reduced after the introduction of a statutory requirement for employers to attach to each warp a ticket itemizing all the relevant information needed to calculate the list price to the operative who wove the particular piece. The unions, in point of fact, were prominent in campaigns to improve employment rights. The weavers' union, for example, conducted a systematic and ultimately successful attack upon the 'slate system' and 'driving' in the early 1890s.(28)

Victimization, intimidation, summary dismissal for what appear to have been relatively minor transgressions and the general unilateral reduction of wages by masters are all manifestations of the less benign face of paternalism. David Holmes,(29) long-time leader of the Burnley branch of the weavers' union, was himself victimized during the 1878 weavers' strike; during the period of his dismissal, and until the return of more propitious times, he became a hawker in Burnley and district, using the basement of the Weavers' Institute to stable his pony. Many miners who lived in company-provided cottages were in an even more vulnerable position; dismissal involved not only the loss of earnings of the main, possibly sole, family breadwinner but, equally seriously, it led to the eviction of the family from its home. This was a major hazard in the many pit villages scattered throughout the Lancashire coalfield, particularly where there was extensive dependence for employment upon the one industry; but it was also a problem in the growing industrial conurbations where employers' associations often kept blacklists of reputed 'miscreants' whom they would not knowingly re-employ. Added to these problems was the stress-laden indignity of replacement by strike-breakers. During the 1867 miners' strike at the Cliviger pits on the outskirts of Burnley there were major disturbances when the company attempted to evict strikers from its pit cottages in order to accommodate strike-breakers.(30) The strike-breakers took their leave early in 1868, by which time the damage had been done; the exhaustion of union funds and the disintegration of the local branch of the Miners' Association resulted in a return to work with what amounted to a 25 per cent pay cut. Victimization continued, however, even after coal prices started to recover in 1872. Optimistic expectations, which proved ill-founded in retrospect, led to the formation in that year of the Burnley branch of the Amalgamated Miners' Association.(31) Deputations were sent to each pit owner requesting an increase in pay rates. Higher wages were conceded at most of the collieries but at the Bank Hall pit all the members of the deputation were summarily dismissed and in July 1873 local colliery owners issued a collective statement of their future intention to employ only non-union men.

Symptomatic of periodic breakdowns in the ability of Burnley's employers to maintain control by peaceable means and a consequent need, as they saw it, to resort to sterner strategies, were recurrent strikes in the cotton and coal trades during the 1870s and 1880s. The details of two major industrial relations confrontations in Burnley - one in the cotton textile trade and the other in the coal industry - are worth detailing for what they reveal about the tactics used by otherwise benign paternalistic employers to maintain discipline.

The textile depression in question first became apparent in 1875. During the following two years several cotton masters in Burnley were compelled to reduce wages due to shortage of orders, diminishing profits and uncertain business prospects. The recovery of the industry from the 'cotton famine' of the early 1860s had been followed in 1873 by an agreement amongst masters to construct a Burnley 'List' to be recognized and observed by all. Adherence to the agreed rates was jeopardized in 1875, however, by a textile recession which gave rise to talk of impending wage reductions. Precipitate action by one or two employers encouraged emulation by others and provoked protest amongst the operatives. An attempted 10 per cent wage reduction at Watson's Danehouse Mill caused a walk-out and a potentially explosive situation developed when strike-breakers were brought in from Stockport. The police were summoned to restore order and to disperse a crowd of some two thousand operatives who had converged on the Old Hall Mill intent upon venting their fury upon employers' property. There were several injuries in the clash between millhands and the forces of law and order.(32)

The situation had deteriorated dramatically by March 1878. The most serious of a succession of disturbances were the riots of that year.(33) A resolution to introduce a district-wide wage-cut of 10 per cent in the textile trade was published on 23 March 1878 by the North East Lancashire Master Spinners' and Manufacturers' Association.(34) In Burnley notices posted at most of the larger mills led to a mass meeting of operatives in the market place.(35) Speakers fulminated against the unilateral action taken by employers and against their intransigence in refusing to discuss alternative means of accommodating the financial difficulties masters would have to face during the recession. The weavers' union had indicated its willingness to accept short-time working until the state of trade had recovered; this solution was preferable since it maintained the wage rates set out in the 'List' and therefore avoided the struggle to restore them in the future when trade recovered. The masters persisted in their refusal to entertain any offer to enter into discussion on the matter.(36) In Burnley the strike spread and the strikers became the more embittered. Resolutions to resist cuts to wage rates were taken at numerous meetings held in Burnley and the other major cotton towns of textile Lancashire. The union had struggled for many years for the standardization of rates at the level prevailing in 1873 and was not predisposed to countenance a reversal without strong protest.

The rejection of appeals to masters to maintain wage rates and to accommodate the problem of slack trade by short-time working led to the breakdown of public order in Burnley. During the first two or three weeks of April 1878 sporadic looting and stone-throwing occurred, reflecting increasing social tension in the town. On May 13th a large crowd gathered in Standish Street intent on rescuing several weavers being escorted to the railway station at the start of their journey to the court of assize in Preston. The crowd got out of control and it was difficult for the town's police force to contain the violence. The following day, May 14th, a meeting of masters' and workers' representatives in Manchester, called to negotiate a compromise, was widely expected to produce an agreement satisfactory to the operatives. There were optimistic rumours throughout Burnley and district of the imminence of a favourable settlement.(37)

Expectations were soon dashed, however. At 3.30pm on May 15th a vast throng had assembled in the market place to hear the official statement by David Holmes. His announcement, that the negotiations had failed, was greeted with bitter disappointment and much resentment by a crowd which had been anticipating a very different kind of declaration. In spite of appeals by union officers, that the strikers should persist resolutely with disciplined industrial action and that the crowd should now disperse in an orderly manner, anger and frustration were unleashed, erupting into riot. A large mob marched through the streets and converged upon the Mechanics' Institute where they shouted threats and abuse at members of the Exchange who were meeting there. The rabble then proceeded in great disorder to John Kay's mills in Rawlinson Street and Parliament Street where, a press report states, 'bricks and stones were soon flying through the air in all directions with a special inclination to policemen's helmets.' These symbolic gestures of defiant disrespect for, and rejection of, established authority were accompanied by much jeering and cheering amongst the crowd. The thirty-one police constables were powerless to stop the rioters who packed several streets close to the mills. Here the crowd, bent on destruction, 'threw bricks and stones and drove in windows with large pieces of wood.' Meanwhile a section of the mob proceeded to smash in windows and doors at Kay's warehouse and, after scattering cops of yarn about the street, set fire to the building and obstructed the attempts of the fire brigade to intervene by cutting the hoses and jostling the fire officers.(38)

The town clerk read out the Riot Act in Springfield Road but his efforts proved futile and he was forced to retire with cuts and bruises inflicted by stones thrown from the rabble. Severe disorder continued and, in an effort to disperse the mob and clear the streets, the police resorted to the use of batons, with the result that there were several injuries. At 10.00pm that day the rioters converged on Towneley Villa, Mr Kay's home, where windows were smashed and property damaged. The following day, May 16th, a small crowd reassembled at Kay's mills but heavy rain interrupted attempts to resume the previous day's vandalism. The respite was only brief, however. When rain ceased in the evening the crowd gathered once more in the town centre and again the Riot Act was read by the town clerk, on this occasion from the comparative safety of a window on the first floor of the Thorn Hotel. The action, provocative under the circumstances, inflamed the mood of the throng, a large section of which made its way through the streets and attempted to destroy Whitaker's Whittlefield Mill. The arsonists were interrupted and, robbed of victory here, proceeded to the homes of Mr Kay and Joshua Rawlinson, secretary of the local Masters' Federation. Both men, along with their families, had judiciously taken refuge elsewhere in anticipation of trouble. The following day there was further damage to property owned by employers, Andrew Ogle and Mr Walmesley.(39) During the evening the crowd gathered again and this time ransacked the house of J.H. Whitaker and, after completely wrecking the ground floor, brought the remaining furniture, including a piano - symbol of Victorian bourgeois status - out into the street where it was smashed and burned. The local police, many of them injured, were jostled and hampered in their attempts to restore public order.(40)

The first reaction of Burnley's leaders to the eruption of violence was to attempt to reassert their authority via local agencies for keeping the peace. The town's police force was called into action and the symbolic reading of the Riot Act underlined the punitive treatment which recalcitrants could expect at the hands of borough magistrates. When these measures proved ineffective, reinforcements were summoned from further afield. In response to urgent appeals for assistance from Burnley's Town Council, troops were despatched from Manchester and Leeds. Before long the town's resources to counter 'social insubordination' were reinforced by the presence of 'eighty-seven cavalrymen, one hundred and thirty policemen, one hundred and fifty infantrymen of the Fifteenth Brigade Depot and one hundred and fifty-two of the Eighty-Fourth Regiment of Foot, along with one hundred and forty special constables.'(41) By the weekend the rioting had subsided but there was a significant closing-in by the local landed gentry on the side of law and order in the borough. 'Colonel Thursby, one of the senior county magistrates, has arrived in Burnley and will stay during the continuation of the strike,' it was stated in the *Gazette*, and a report in the same edition of that newspaper announced that the previous day 'Sir U.J. Kay-Shuttleworth, Bart, M.P., had come down from London . . . and since then had applied for an additional troop of cavalry with a view to being in readiness for any disturbance in the locality.'(42) Also, infantrymen were to be 'brought down from the barracks to the centre of the town each evening to be ready for any emergency, and cavalry patrols were to be sent out each night in different directions . . . during the continuance of the strike.' Saturday night's patrols that week were headed by leaders of county society - Colonel Thursby, Major Starkie and Sir U.J. Kay-Shuttleworth - whose ownership of land and property beyond the boundaries of the town gave them a personal interest in containing the disturbance on their doorstep.(43) The collective highly visible presence of influential landed personnel in support of borough authorities undoubtedly provided considerable reassurance for harassed employers, the Town Council and the police.

The mob violence subsided almost as suddenly as it had arisen. The strike continued for several more weeks but support became progressively weaker, a reflection perhaps of the gradual realization amongst the operatives of the futility of their efforts in the face both of the economic limits of paternalism and of the strength of reinforcements which the paternalists could muster. By the end of June there was a slow drift back to the mills - at a 10 per cent reduction in the wage rate.(44) By the end of 1879 further reductions meant that rates were 20 to 25 per cent below those set out in the original 'Lists'.(45) Industrial unrest continued at several mills and wages fluctuated in successive waves of strikes which occurred in 1883, 1884, 1887 and 1892.(46)

The second case-study example of the less benign face of paternalism is provided by the coal industry. The persistence of industrial relations conflict in mining in Burnley and district, erupting into a series of bitter, sometimes prolonged, strikes during the last four decades of the nineteenth century, defies attempts to represent the miners' response to authority as one of deference; clearly, there were recurrent situations when the compliance of miners was non-existent or when it sprang from sentiments of a different order. The colliery owners were uniquely placed to command cooperation by the adoption of what appear to have been ruthlessly coercive means in circumstances which left miners with few options but to return to work on the employer's terms.

After 1872, when coal prices began to rise, the miners formed the Burnley branch of the Amalgamated Miners' Association and sent deputations to the coal owners seeking an increase in pay. At most pits higher wages were granted. This initial success, the spread of unionism in the industry and further rises in the price of coal led to another claim for a general pay increase. Consensus amongst the miners was elusive, however, and undoubtedly fragmentation weakened the will and the ability to resist when the strike, which began in July 1873, became a lockout.(47)

The miners were divided on the details of the pay claim. While some wanted payment by 'weight', others preferred payment by 'measure' and the whole issue was further complicated by an inability to decide upon other items to be fought for. In the event, the strike of mid-1873 was less a response to the employers' refusal to concede higher pay than a reaction to their attempt to stifle unionism out of existence in the local mining industry. During the preceding twelve months the numerical strength of the Burnley branch of the union had grown from 250 to 700 and this number leapt when miners from the Church district acquired membership. In order to contain what the coal owners regarded as an increasingly troublesome threat to their ability to control industrial relations, they issued a statement of their intention to employ only non-union men. The ensuing strike, involving a walk-out by 1,200 men and boys, virtually brought production in the Burnley mines to a standstill. Before long industrial action spread to Padiham. Solidarity was maintained at first by the provision of strike pay of 12s. 6d. to 16s. a week plus 1s. 3d. for each dependent child. The implications of cash limits to the union's ability to provide an income replacement sufficient for family maintenance for a prolonged period of time became only too painfully apparent when colliery owners brought into the Burnley district some 400 miners and their families from as far afield as Devon and Cornwall.(48) The strike became a lockout. The Cornish miners, engaged to work on a two-year contract at 7s. a day, were housed initially in an iron building converted for temporary use as family living quarters, but they were soon transferred to cottages in Brunshaw in an area near the Griffin Inn, known subsequently as 'Little Cornwall'. Charges of 'conspiracy' against union leaders who attempted to dissuade the strike-breakers from taking local men's jobs reveal the real vulnerability of labour, despite improvements in legislation relating to employment. In point of fact, no fines were imposed, but the verdict of 'guilty' to the charges against them highlighted the risk involved in any further 'interference' of this kind. The strike dragged on until August 1874 when, after holding out for more than a year, the miners admitted defeat and the union branch was dissolved. The recession of that year, which cut profits for the colliery owners, led to a 15 per cent wage reduction, the introduction of short-time working for some and dismissal for others. It is ironic testimony to the less benign face of paternalism that, although most pits in the district worked only half-time, many miners were prosecuted for absenteeism.(49)

Implications of paternalism's two faces

Burnley's leaders displayed both the benign and harsh faces of paternalism in the later nineteenth century. The benevolent, compassionate face was manifest in attention to the welfare of the town's less fortunate inhabitants, the severe, authoritarian face in the suppression of what they regarded as social insubordination. That there was greater emphasis upon welfarism without rather than within the workplace ensured a broader distribution of voluntary services and therefore also wider influence amongst the community at large. Access to welfare was general rather than selective - gratitude, or at least grudging respect, for the volunteer providers was the more widespread.

Certainly there is evidence of severity and even of ruthless suppression; a few of the paternalists behaved exploitatively, persistently so in some cases; some otherwise caring leaders resorted infrequently *in extremis* to draconian means to maintain order. Peaceful co-existence was recurrently shattered when there was divergence in the concepts of fairness and justice held by the leaders and the lower classes, but in so far as major confrontations occurred, they tended in the main to crystallize in the sphere of industrial relations. Yet the reactions of wage-workers and their dependents to the experience of unemployment were rather different during the two most dramatic periods of economic crisis: the 'cotton famine' of the early 1860s and the textile recession of the late 1870s. During the former, relatively few castigated the employers, for the interruption in imports of raw cotton from overseas was viewed as a circumstance beyond the employers' collective control. Indeed, the cotton masters appear to have made strenuous efforts to maintain the viability of their enterprises, to protect as many jobs as possible, and to attend to the welfare of the many casualties who became involuntarily unemployed through no fault of their own. Subordinates' general response seems to have been one of stoical, mostly law-abiding, philosophical fortitude in the face of adversity.

The response in the late 1870s, when employers were regarded as at least partially responsible for the state of trade, was rather different; operatives, their grievance sharpened by a sense of injustice and goaded by the employers' cavalier rejection of the union's offer to discuss an alternative solution, resorted to street riots and the destruction of property. Yet even on this occasion, and despite the provocation involved, collective bargaining by riot was neither urged nor condoned by the responsible majority of union leaders. Violent confrontation such as this occurred only intermittently, however. There were, admittedly, recurrent strikes in both cotton and coal, but these were interspersed with longer periods of calm when both sides co-existed in relative peace.

The salient point to be made here is that opposition in the workplace does not appear to have been projected on to the relationship between the leaders and the led elsewhere. There was no wholesale rejection of employers in their roles as town councillors. The kindly, caring face of paternalism appears to have been the more pervasively and consistently visible of the two countenances. Arguably this is one of the factors underlying the stability of the socio-political order. More may be involved than this, however. Stability may have been reinforced by the leaders' ability to construct mechanisms for socialization and social control.

References

1. Dutton, H.I. and King, J.E., 'The Limits of Paternalism: The Cotton Tyrants of North Lancashire, 1836-54', *Social History*, VII, 1982, pp. 59-74.

2. *Ibid.*, p. 60.

3. Joyce, P., 'The Factory Politics of Lancashire in the Later-Nineteenth Century', *Historical Journal*, XVIII, 1975, pp. 525-53; see also Joyce, P., *Work, Society and Politics: The Culture of the Factory in Later Victorian England*, Harvester, 1980.

4. Roberts, D., *Paternalism in Early Victorian England*, Croom Helm, 1979, p. 5; Newby, H., *Property, Paternalism and Power: Class and Control in Rural England*, Hutchinson, 1978, p. 29.

5. Sennett, R., *Authority*, Secker and Warburg, 1980, chs 1 and 2; see also Roberts, D., *op. cit.*, ch. 1.

6. Roberts, D., *op. cit.*, chs 1 and 2.

7. *Ibid.*, p. 3; see also Newby, H., *op. cit.* pp. 26-31 and ch. 8;

Newby, H., *The Deferential Worker*, Allen Lane, 1977, ch. 1; Newby, H., 'Paternalism and Capitalism', in Scase, R., ed., *Industrial Society: Class Cleavage and Control*, Allen and Unwin, 1977, pp. 59-73.

8. Roberts, D., *op. cit.*, chs 1 and 2.

9. Joyce, P., 'The Factory Politics ...'

10. For a factual account of some of these initiatives in Burnley see Bennett, W., *The History of Burnley*, Burnley Corporation, 1951, IV, pp. 120-1, 197-210.

11. *Ibid.*, pp. 120-2, 212-18; Margaret Jones, postgraduate researcher at Lancaster University (Independent Studies) is investigating voluntary initiatives as an aspect of her study of the effect of the 'cotton famine' in Burnley.

12. Quoted in Bennett, W., *op. cit.*, p. 121.

13. Many details reported in the *Burnley Advertizer*, especially issues published during the later years of the 'cotton famine'; Bennett, W., *op. cit.*, pp. 120-5.

14. Bennett, W., *op. cit.*, chs 11 and 14; see also *Men of Burnley:Press Cuttings, 1961-3, loc. cit.*

15. Bennett, W., *op. cit.*, p. 198.

16. *Ibid.*, p. 112.

17. *Ibid.*

18. Musson, A.E., *Enterprise in Soap and Chemicals: Crosfields of Warrington, 1815-1965*, Manchester University Press, 1965, ch. 10; Windsor, D., *The Quaker Enterprise: Friends in Business*, Muller, 1980, ch. 5.

19. 'Social Gathering of Employees of Messrs J. Crosfield and Sons: Presentation to and Speech by Mr A.H. Crosfield', reprint of extended article in *Warrington Examiner*, John Walker and Co., 1892.

20. *Ibid.*; Musson, A.E., *op. cit.*, ch. 5.

21. *Ibid.*

22. Hall, A.H., 'Social Control and the Working Class Challenge in Ashton-under-Lyne, 1880-1914', M.A. dissertation, University of Lancaster, 1975.

23. Wale, D.A., 'Politics and Society in Accrington, 1880-1939', M.A. dissertation, University of Lancaster, 1976.

24. Royal Commission on the Depression of Trade and Industry, Parliamentary Papers, 1886, XXII, *Minutes of Evidence*: Evidence of Joshua Rawlinson; see also *Accrington Times* and *Accrington Guardian*, issues for 1878 and 1879.

25. Bennett, W., *op. cit.*, pp. 118-19.

26. *Ibid*.

27. *Ibid*., pp. 122-5; numerous references also in Burnley's local newspapers, see, for example, *Burnley Gazette*, Feb. 1872 to Oct. 1873.

28. Recurrent references in *Burnley Gazette* and *Burnley Express* issues for the late 1880s and the 1890s; for overview see Bennett, W., *op. cit.*, pp. 125-30.

29. See Holmes's obituary and press articles on his career in *Men of Burnley: Press Cuttings, 1961-3*; *Men of Burnley: Press Cuttings, 1963-5*; *Burnley Notabilities, Press Cuttings, 1971*, Local History Collection, Burnley Central Library.

30. Bennett, W., *op. cit.*, pp. 130-3.

31. *Ibid*.

32. *Ibid*., pp. 122-3.

33. *Ibid*., p. 122.

34. *Burnley Gazette*, 23 Mar. 1878.

35. *Ibid*.

36. *Burnley Gazette*, 4 May 1878.

37. Account summarizes lengthy press reports, *ibid*., 18 and 25 May 1878; see also Bennett, W., *op. cit.*, pp. 122-5.

38. *Ibid*.

39. *Ibid*.

40. *Ibid*.

41. *Burnley Gazette*, 18 May 1878.

42. *Ibid*.

43. *Ibid*.

44. Bennett, W., *op. cit.*, p. 124; see also subscription lists to the Mayor's Relief Fund in *Burnley Gazette*, 8 June 1878 and published letters of thanks to the various charities from the union in *Burnley Gazette*, 25 May 1878.

45. Bennett, W., *op. cit.*, p. 124.

46. Kneeshaw, J., *Burnley in the Nineteenth Century*, Burnley, 1921, p. 87.

47. Bennett, W., *op. cit.*, pp. 130-3.

48. *Ibid.*

49. *Ibid.*

4

Paternalism
Socialization and Social Control

Introduction

The inter-connecting and overlapping character of the multi-functional roles performed by Burnley's leaders has been identified. This focuses attention on the processes by which they achieved and maintained their leadership status. Many of the decision-making positions they occupied were elective or selective, with the implication that successful contestants, however chosen, exercised a sufficient degree of influence whereby they could mobilize the support of others by commanding the willing acquiescence of fellow townsfolk or the grudging compliance of a sufficiently large section of the local population to ensure success.

The persistent presence of employers of labour in Burnley's group of top persons and of a disproportionately large number of wage-workers in the socio-economic composition of the urban community suggests that, whatever the state of industrial relations and of the local economy, acquiescence *was* secured, particularly in so far as authority was exercised through the agency of an elected Town Council. Tables II and III show that 61.1 per cent of the leaders and 79.2 per cent of the nuclear group were employers in the towns's major industries: the Masseys, Barneses, Barons, Fieldings, Collinges, Thompsons and Lancasters in textiles, for example, and the Keighleys and Scotts in engineering. The support given by wage-workers may, of course, simply reflect a shrewd and rational assessment of the fact that men with sufficient business acumen and managerial expertise to run successful companies(1) were best fitted for the task of taking decisions in the conduct of municipal affairs. Potentially at least, successful businessmen were by definition men who were capable of sound judgment, accustomed to assessing probable risks in times of uncertainty, and sensitive to the need for a degree of financial caution where municipal expenditure upon urban amenities had

117

cost implications of rate-payers. Direct intimidation by the threat of summary dismissal of operatives who voted the 'wrong way' may be discounted as a *major* instrument of social control after the introduction of the secret ballot in 1872. Thereafter, the emphasis was the more likely to have been upon the carrot rather than the stick as a means of political persuasion. Logically, consent rather than coercion was paramount. This returns us to the *means* of persuasion. In chapter three we considered the implications of voluntary welfarism as an inducement to acquiescence; here we turn more specifically to the process of socialization as a means of maintaining social control.

Political and socio-economic instability, possibly taking the form of riot or even revolution, may be triggered by a perceived and experienced disparity in the distribution of material rewards where the degree of inequality is judged to be intolerable and unchangeable by other means, and where opportunities for real material improvement are blocked. Those in the relatively advantaged social stratum are faced with the problem of maintaining their hegemony, a problem which is compounded by the fact that members of the superordinate stratum are, in general, numerically fewer than those in the subordinate strata. The privileged must necessarily discover the means to cultivate acquiescence amongst the disprivileged.

It is a self-evident truth that those who enjoy what they regard as legitimate power over others will use their authority to self-preserving ends. It is equally clear, as noted earlier, that maintaining the *status quo* can be accomplished by means of either coercion or consent, the former involving repressive, often punitive, control mechanisms, the latter cultivating voluntary compliance. These are not mutually exclusive categories, of course. As we have seen, the paternalists in Burnley used a combination of each according to situation and circumstance. It may be the case that the prevailing structure of leadership was strengthened and perpetuated by the ability of 'top persons' to socialize subordinates in dominant ideology, thereby producing Gramsci's 'bourgeois hegemony'.(2) Precise definition of the terms, socialization and social control, is problematic but necessary, nonetheless, to assist clarification.

Sociologists use the term, socialization, with reference to the process by which members of communities learn to conform to social norms, a process that 'makes possible an enduring society and the transmission of its culture between generations.'(3) It has been argued that within a community a particularly powerful group with its own group-specific norms and values may succeed in imposing its own ideology upon the rest. This emerges as the 'dominant ideology' which, from the standpoint of those outside the power group, may be interpreted as the 'ideology of submission'.(4) Subordinates are persuaded of the need to conform to the meaning system which characterizes the world view of the superordinate social stratum, in the sense that they endorse their own low socio-economic status by internalizing a particular set of values, attitudes, aspirations and expectations. Their collective self-perceived identity is affected, indeed determined, by the perceptions of superordinates.

Socialization may be defined, therefore, as the internalization of social norms; social norms become internal to the individual and become self-imposed constraints upon social behaviour. The process affects personality because the individual feels the need to conform. It may best be understood as the product of social interaction, given that people desire to enhance their own self-image by gaining approbation and acceptance in the eyes of others. In this case individuals become socialized as they guide their own actions to accord with the expectations of others.(5) It is where the expectations of the superordinate stratum govern conformity by their effect not only upon individual personality but on the collective self-perceived identity that socialization becomes an instrument of social control. The normative code of the dominant minority receives general acceptance.

Norms are prescriptions(6) which serve as common guidelines for social action. There is a general tendency for human behaviour to display certain regularities which are the product of adherence to common expectations or norms; human action in this sense may be described as 'rule governed'. Since the term refers to social expectations about 'correct' or 'proper' behaviour, norms imply the presence of legitimacy, consent and prescription. Conformity is promoted when norms are acquired by internalization; subordinates are socialized into habits of thought and behaviour required of them by superordinates. These concepts are central to some of the theories of social order.

Durkheim(7) saw social norms as regulating people's behaviour by means of institutionalized values which the individual internalized. Religion played a significant role in this process. In 1912, in *The Elementary Forms of Religious Life*, he suggested that primitive religions embodied the idea of society, and that sacred objects were so because they symbolized the community. Religious culture consisted of the collective values which comprised a society's unity. Religious ceremonies served to reinforce collective values and reaffirm 'community' among individuals. Religious practices were best understood, therefore, as contributing to social stability by encouraging and reinforcing social integration. There is a body of modern sociological thought(8) which, following Durkheim, defines religion in terms of its social functions; religion is a system of beliefs and rituals relating to the sacred which binds people together into social groups. In consequence, it has a socially incorporating function. The idea recurs in the work of Gramsci. In his version of Marxism, Gramsci(9) argued that domination could not be represented merely in terms of economic determinism. It required political force of some kind, but, much more importantly, it needed an *ideological* apparatus in order to secure the *consent* of the dominated. Religious institutions were a part of the apparatus capable of promoting endorsement of the dominant group's leadership.

This returns us to the concept of social control. Sociologists and social historians apply the concept of social control, defined somewhat vaguely as the 'capacity of a small group to . . . generate conformity to its own standards,' to relationships between the major social strata. One body of sociological thought, usually referred to as the 'compulsion approach', emphasizes the role of coercion and repression in maintaining social order, enforcement being most obviously applied through the agency of the police, the armed services and the judicial system; deviance is discouraged by a range of often draconian deterrents: imprisonments, fines, capital punishment and so on. Marx and Weber are perhaps the most noteworthy exponents of 'compulsion theory', though admittedly neither goes so far as to deny the contributory role of cultural values. However, it has been convincingly demonstrated that, paradoxically, attempts to increase forms of coercive control by, for example, more extensive police surveillance, tend to amplify deviance rather than to diminish it. The implication is that effective social control depends more on the stability of social groups, community relations and shared values than on coercion.

The role of shared values in preserving social order is emphasized in the 'cultural approach'; Durkheim and Talcott Parsons are probably the most influential exponents of 'value consensus'. This does, of course, raise the problem of what is meant by consensus and how it is achieved - a problem to which we return later. It may be argued that, to some extent, consensual values were beginning to be embodied in the formal codification of evolving standards of fairness and justice in the later nineteenth century as, for example, in by-laws and in national legislation progressively less self-interestedly designed by a powerful minority to entirely selfish ends. It was, after all, a governmental body of superordinates of one kind or another who constructed a progressively more complex framework of factory and mining legislation to improve working conditions and who made a start upon establishing standards of public health. There is little to indicate that there was majority disagreement with the principles embodied in these reforms.

The majority of sociologists, however, argue that social control is achieved through a combination of compliance, coercion and commitment to social values.(10) As we have seen, the paternalists in Burnley were certainly capable of resorting to force to check what they regarded as manifestations of civil disobedience when friction in industrial relations erupted into riots in the streets. But successful social leadership in Burnley and in other northern industrial towns was not founded upon force alone. Indeed, force appears to have been used *in extremis*, possibly as a panic measure. More important in Burnley were measures, whether manipulatively designed or less consciously constructed, to win the hearts and minds of subordinates. In this chapter we focus upon efforts to win compliance by the process of socialization. The potentially effective agencies of socialization - religion, education and recreation - were discussed earlier and protracted repetition is unnecessary at this juncture. By these mechanisms the leaders attempted to guide others into what they regarded as socially desirable habits of thought and behaviour. Whether their efforts produced Gramsci's 'bourgeois hegemony' or the organic unity of the paternalist's ideal world is a question which we address later. To the extent that the inter-linked religious, educational and recreational agencies sponsored 'from above' functioned as effective media for the transmission of superordinates' normative code, they *may* have encouraged subordinates to endorse the prevailing stratification order plus its attendant disparities of power, status and material rewards.

Socialization: religion, education and recreation

In stratified societies religion is alleged to have a stabilizing effect upon society.(11) This is not to claim that the perpetuation of the prevailing socio-political order is the primary objective of those who involve themselves in the teaching of Christian truths, whether in the nineteenth century or today, but Christian values and ideals may have had this effect as a by-product of Christian virtues: moral respectability, care and compassion for the less fortunate, suffering borne with dignity and fortitude, family responsibility, honesty, sobriety, love of one's neighbour, being content with, or making the best of, one's lot in the temporal life of the present. This last-mentioned virtue is of major importance for acquiescence. Moreover, as Parkin(12) notes, amongst members of the lower social stratum religious beliefs are of particular significance in that they present the disprivileged with an alternative rank order in which the scale of secular priorities is dissolved or reversed. Where religious belief promotes a reconceptualization of values in the temporal life it may act as a counter to political radicalism and reinforce the stability of the social order by encouraging an acceptance of what are perceived as divinely ordained but essentially transitory inequalities. The greater the suffering in the here and now, the richer the rewards in the life hereafter. Few books dignify poverty as does the Bible. Yet the Protestant work ethic and the Methodist emphasis of the virtues of thrift, industry and self-reliance imply approbation for effort and advancement. It is this dual message of hope and reassurance, of aspiration and resignation, which underlies the importance of religion as a potentially influential source of social stability.

This line of argument may also be applied to education, given the nineteenth-century link between religious and educational institutions. The related agencies for both were largely sponsored or extensively influenced by members of the superordinate class. Education was informed by the values of Christianity and by dominant ideology. The objectives of its providers included moral character training to produce obedience, orderliness and disciplined behaviour as well as numeracy and literacy. Those who sponsored the voluntary elementary schools were in many ways uniquely placed to impose their own ideology and what they judged to be an appropriate code of conduct upon school populations at a stage in intellectual development when the mind is most impressionable. *Compulsory* elementary education in the later nineteenth century ensured that exposure to the message of the providers was virtually inescapable for the majority of children from disprivileged home backgrounds, at least during the required period of schooling.

In the industrial towns of the era many of the leisure amenities for wage-workers and their families were also sponsored 'from above'; employing enterprises, the churches and the chapels were important centres of recreational activity, and town councils and philanthropists led in the provision of leisure amenities such as parks, libraries, museums and swimming baths. The kind of recreation actively fostered was fully intended to be healthy, improving, educative, respectable and, above all, 'rational'; the providers consciously aimed to encourage the masses to relinquish what were viewed as debauched and morally damaging leisure pursuits. The total recreational package with its 'brand image' and diverse contents was thus value-laden, not value-free.

The tenets of the Christian faith may have promoted acquiescence in persuading the disprivileged to come to terms with their secular lot, but the implications of religion for the preservation of social order went beyond this in the nineteenth century. Clearly, the socialization of lower-status groups in dominant ideology depends upon the existence of opportunities which enable superordinates to disseminate the appropriate set of values, expectations and aspirations. The relevant ideals were variously embodied in the kind of religion, education and recreation the leaders actively sponsored and broadcast through the transmitting stations of the institutions they controlled; but the message is likely to have been the more effectively communicated in so far as the messengers' presence was highly visible, their voices audible, the opportunities for personal contact numerous, and their personalities charismatic. As we have seen, in the lay-leadership of religious institutions many of Burnley's most influential employers were closely associated with the clergy and with the organization of church and chapel affairs. This was a form of dutiful service to the community, but it also meant that the leaders were directly involved with members of congregations not only as lay-preachers, Sunday school superintendents and so on, but as fellow-worshippers and as co-workers in the collective effort of fund-raising.

Certainly social leaders of ample means were prominent amongst those who contributed in cash and in kind for the building, extension and maintenance of the fabric of churches, chapels and their voluntary schools. Amongst the Anglicans in Burnley and district(13) Sir James Kay-Shuttleworth gave one thousand pounds and the site to build All Saints' Church and Sunday school; the Reverend William Thursby and his relative by marriage, General Scarlett, provided the site for St Paul's as did Canon Townley-Parker for St Stephen's; the Reverend William Thursby gave one thousand pounds and Sir James Kay-Shuttleworth four hundred pounds for building work on St Matthew's; the site for St John's was given jointly by the Reverend William Thursby and his relative, Lady Scarlett, and the tower and reredos were built with money donated by the Thursby family.

The wealthy, however, were not the sole benefactors. The three thousand pounds needed to build the new chancel at St

Peter's, dedicated on 3 December 1872 to the memory of General Scarlett, was raised by subscriptions(14) that ranged from individual donations of five hundred pounds to the pennies of the Sunday school scholars. As Bennett notes, the division of the ancient chapelry of Burnley into separate independent parishes during the nineteenth century was not accomplished without financial difficulty. There were wealthy donors who volunteered land and money for the erection of many of the new parish churches, but the maintenance of the fabric and the building of additional premises for schools was costly. In consequence, it was necessary for Anglican clergy and congregations collectively to devote considerable time and effort to fund-raising by means of bazaars, sales of work, concerts and gift schemes. There were similar initiatives amongst the Nonconformist sects to build and maintain their own premises. The Masseys donated the site and subscribed a large part of the funds for the building of Westgate Congregational Chapel. Substantial sums were made available by the Keighleys, Thornbers and Barons for the financial support of Methodist chapels and Sunday schools, and by the Lancasters, Collinges and Dugdales in support of Wesleyan chapels and schools. The multitudinous announcements and advertisements in the local press of collections and fund-raising events are ample testimony to the fact that fund-raising involved the not-so-wealthy as well as the wealthy.

Such events served more than mere cash-collecting purposes; the experience was a participatory one which went beyond the aim of raising funds. Activities of this kind provided occasions for members of congregations, whether rich or poor, to work together for a common goal, the shared activity reinforcing a sense of community. They permitted opportunities for personal contact between the leaders and the led, promoted a sense of shared pride in the achievement of the objective, and a closer identification with the particular institution premised not least on the experience of shared sponsorship.

As responsible chapel elders, trustees and circuit stewards, employers symbolized paternalistic respectability. The dual nature of their role as co-worker and leader gave ample scope to promote personal loyalty founded upon both formal and informal social interaction; the leaders could thus communicate their values and ideals, and inspire emulation by their example as men of moral conscience. Undoubtedly the faith of the believer and a sense of Christian duty motivated employers and other top persons to undertake leading roles in the religious sphere. Committee work and the many other duties involved for office-holders, with the inevitable requirement of regular evening and weekend attendance, was certainly time-consuming, occasionally inconvenient and intermittently thankless, yet most appear to have taken their responsibilities seriously.

To quote but a few examples of the many employers who held some kind of religious office in Burnley: the Thompson family(15) provided Wesleyan Sunday School teachers, J.W. Thompson holding office as Sunday school superintendent, lay preacher and circuit steward; John Massey(16) was a leading member of the Congregationalist community as Sunday school superintendent, Sunday school teacher and chapel trustee; John Baron(17) in his lifetime held several posts including those of Sunday school teacher and superintendent, circuit steward, treasurer and president of the Sunday School Union, and also delegate and first president of the Free Church Council; W.C. Hargreaves(18) was a Sunday school teacher and superintendent at the Baptist Sion Street Chapel; John Barnes, Adam Dugdale, John Howarth, William Lancaster, John Butterworth, H.D. Fielding and William Nowell all at various times undertook the duties of Wesleyan circuit steward. In Anglican circles Robert Handsley(19) and John Greenwood(20) served both as church wardens and Sunday school supervisors at St Andrew's and St Peter's Churches respectively, and both were actively involved in the fund-raising initiatives of the parishes they served.

The spread of religious influence in Burnley, reflected in the building of centres of worship, kept pace with urban expansion,(21) as Table X shows. For the various sects the second half of the nineteenth century was one of vigorous life and growth, well illustrated by the fact that over thirty new buildings were erected to accommodate some sixteen thousand people. In the case of the Nonconformist sects, advance was based upon open-air gatherings and meetings in rented rooms and private houses, followed later by the provision of purpose-built premises.

The presence of many Christian sects in Burnley offered a variegated choice to accommodate differences in Christian preference. Equally importantly, though a significant number of the leaders were Wesleyan Methodists, there were many who belonged to other sects so that their collective influence in the religious dimension was widespread. Moreover, social contact was not confined to Sunday services conducted at the chapels and churches; religion was taken to the people in regular visits by the clergy and lay leaders to the homes of the sick and distressed where prayers were said and words of comfort given.(22)

Much religious teaching was done in the Sunday schools. From the middle of the nineteenth century the Sunday schools in Burnley,(23) as elsewhere, gradually abandoned the task of giving basic instruction in literacy and numeracy and, as more voluntary day schools were opened, began to concentrate more specifically on Bible study. Testimony to the vigour of the Sunday school movement is contained in the formation of Sunday school unions. Two were formed in Burnley, one by the Wesleyans as early as 1859 and the other at a slightly later date as a joint venture by other Nonconformist sects. Both organizers and teachers involved in the two unions approached their duties with a strong sense of responsibility. There were regular meetings to discuss past progress and future objectives; teachers presented statistical evidence and commentaries on attendance at their Sunday schools, reviewed teaching methods and approaches to organization, exchanged ideas, and pooled suggestions to improve and widen the scope of their activities. The role of the Sunday schools was regarded as social as well as educational; tea-treats, family picnics and day trips to the seaside in summer were an integral part of the recreational side of their work and these social activities undoubtedly served to increase membership and to promote regular attendance.

The success of the Sunday schools in maintaining and increasing attendance testifies to the commitment of the Sunday school teachers. The 1867 report(24) of the union representing Gannow, Ebenezer, Mount Pleasant, Mount Pisgah, Salem, Westgate and the Salford Band of Hope School in Burnley indicates that teaching roles were not undertaken frivolously; the document noted that all teachers spent time in the preparation of lessons, followed a systematic course of study and encouraged their scholars to do homework which usually took the form of Bible reading. In an era when Burnley was becoming progressively more populous the Sunday school unions widened their network. The 1867 census gives the following statistics:

	Sunday Schools	Scholars	Teachers
Wesleyan	2	867	120
Baptist	3	953	103
Congregationalist	3	1353	98
Primitive Methodist	1	510	116
United Methodist	1	744	96
Church of England	9	2646	199
Mission Schools combined	n.a.	8000 (approx.)	800 (approx.)

Many more chapels were built during the next two decades and

the associated extension of Sunday school work led to a substantial
increase in the numbers of scholars. In 1860, the centenary year
of the Sunday school movement, there were some 560 teachers
responsible for roughly 4,000 scholars; by 1887 the total number
of those involved variously as scholars, teachers and helpers in
the activities of the Sunday schools (all denominations combined)
was estimated to be somewhere in the region of 20,000.(25)

In addition to their function as centres of worship, chapels
and churches in northern industrial towns led the voluntary
movement to provide day schools for elementary education.
Burnley appears to have been well-supplied with such schools.
The 1854 *Directory* for Mid-Lancashire states: 'Perhaps no town in
Lancashire is better supplied with public educational institutions
than Burnley, every church and chapel in the town having either
a day school or Sunday School in connection with it.'(26) As a
crude statistical indicator of the precocious success of voluntary
education in Burnley, a local report for 1861, before elementary
schooling became compulsory, claims that almost seven out of
every ten people in the town could write, and it seems probable
that a higher proportion than this had gained some proficiency
in reading, usually the first of the 'three Rs' to be attempted. Up
to the mid-1890s the main duty of providing day schools for
elementary education was undertaken by the religious bodies.(27)
By 1871 Anglican voluntary schools included St Peter's founded
in 1827, Habergham opened in 1832, Back Lane and Lane Head
both dating from 1835, Sandygate from 1839, Pickup Croft and
St Paul's both opened in 1848, St Stephen's in operation from
1865 and St Andrew's opened the following year. The main wave
of Nonconformist building of elementary day schools occurred
somewhat later. By 1871 the largest of these included the Wesleyan
schools in Red Lion Street founded in 1851 and Fulledge in
1863, the Primitive Methodist school in Hammerton Street opened
in 1870, the Congregational schools attached to the Bethesda and
Salem chapels, the former dating from 1851 and the latter from
1863. The Roman Catholic churches provided their own
denominational schools, and the chapels of the smaller
Nonconformist sects often doubled as schoolrooms where it was
impractical from the viewpoint of numbers and finance to provide
separate purpose-built premises. From 1870 the growth in the
number of schools accompanied the spread of church and chapel
building.

The sects in Burnley, and elsewhere, made special efforts to
provide Ragged Schools, sometimes termed Mission Schools.(28)
These were made available in the most deprived parts of the

town to cater for the education of the children of the very poor. As early as 1857 the Band of Hope School was opened in a back-to-back cottage in Royle Road and attracted such large numbers that an adjacent cottage and two others in Vernon Street were leased to accommodate some three hundred children. Another such school was opened at Fulledge in 1855 with an average subsequent attendance of roughly two hundred scholars. Others included the Bethesda Ragged School opened in 1868 with teaching conducted in the Temperance Hall at Keighley Green until alternative premises were built in Salford in 1872, and also three Wesleyan Ragged Schools opened at Wood Top in 1881, in Red Lion Street in 1885 and at Lane Bridge in 1865. These schools were essentially rescue operations for those viewed as most in need of the civilizing influence of education.

The major part of the cost of building and maintaining the elementary day schools in Burnley and elsewhere was met by voluntary subscriptions, donations and collections, by modest parental fees, and by fundraising initiatives. From the 1830s there was also financial assistance from central government.

Extraordinary efforts by leading philanthropists brought some schools into being. Crosfield initiative and money were behind much of the school building in the Bank Quay area of Warrington.(29) In Burnley the Kay-Shuttleworths built Habergham School with some financial assistance from the Dugdales; they paid for the cost of extensions necessitated by increasing numbers of scholars, and continued to provide funds for maintenance purposes until the school was finally handed over to the School Board in the 1890s.(30) State funds(31) for voluntary education were made available to inspected schools to assist with the cost of equipment and extensions to premises; up to 1861 there were additional annual grants related to numbers on roll and attendance. After 1861, following changes in education policy which affected the conditions upon which government funds were to be made available, a maximum sum of 12s. per capita of the numbers on roll was granted to inspected schools, the maximum comprising 8s. for the scholar's performance at the annual examination conducted by government-appointed school inspectors and 4s. for satisfactory attendance. The 'payment-by-results' system, as this was termed, demanded proficiency in the designated subjects and a minimum number of two hundred attendances during the school year. By 1870, at a time when there was much activity to enlarge existing schools or to build new premises, the total government grant to the Burnley district amounted to almost three thousand pounds.

State subvention, however, despite the undoubted rigours of government inspection and the regulations governing the distribution of funds, did not dramatically reshape the education system; nor did it sever the pre-established link between the providers and the recipients of elementary education in the voluntary schools. Indeed, one of the objectives of the architects of national education policy was to promote and protect the activities of the two great voluntary societies, the National Society and the British Society, under whose auspices many church and chapel schools came into existence. State intervention, in condoning the kind of education being offered by the proliferating network of voluntary denominational schools, had the entirely intentional effect of endorsing the values embodied in both the 'formal' and 'informal' curricula. Potentially at least, the evolving education system offered scope for the providers to socialize school populations in what the former regarded as an appropriate set of values. This argument may appear the more persuasive because the influence of elementary education affected individuals at a particularly impressionable stage in their intellectual development and because it was conjecturally the more pervasive after schooling was made compulsory and, more belatedly, 'free'.

It may be argued, of course, that schools built by local School Boards after 1870 resulted in the loss of direct personal contact with less devout families who drifted beyond the influence of denominational education and its local sponsors, and that where new Board schools compensated for a perceived insufficiency in the supply of voluntary schools direct contact had not existed in the first place. New Board schools(32) in Burnley, however, did not make an appearance until the 1890s. These new non-denominational schools included those at Abel Street opened in 1891, Burnley Wood in 1892, Stoneyholme in 1896, Rosegrove in 1898, Coal Clough in 1900 and Heasandford in 1903. Existing voluntary schools handed over to the Burnley School Board included those at Accrington Road in 1893, Claremont and Ebenezer both in 1894, and Westgate Congregational in 1895.

Change there was, but it was belated. The introduction of non-denominational education cannot be convincingly represented as a new departure nor as a clean break with past practice, since some of Burnley's top persons, including members of the clergy, successfully contested for election to the School Board. If there was much continuity both of practice and of personnel, there was continuity also in another sense. Though the flurry of School Board activity in the 1890s occurred during a decade when the traditional leaders were withdrawing from positions of authority in the town, the withdrawal was an essentially gradual one. Change in education was neither sudden nor dramatic for the transition was presided over by a group of top persons whose own socio-economic composition was itself subject to an essentially gradual transformation. Moreover, the clergy continued to secure representation on the School Board. Arguably, therefore, the surrender of voluntary schools to the School Board had minimal effect upon personnel, practice and curriculum content which continued much as they had done before. The main changes were those of administration and source of finance rather than what was done and by whom in the classroom; and there were many voluntary denominational schools which were *not* handed over to the School Board.

The 1870 Education Act was premised on the assumption that the work of the local School Board was to build around and to supplement the existing voluntary structure. It is unlikely that any other legislative strategy would have succeeded in securing the assent of the established church, strongly represented as it was in the House of Commons and House of Lords. In consequence, during the later decades of the nineteenth century the inter-related, multi-purpose religious and educational institutions continued to function, potentially at least, as strategically significant transmitting stations to broadcast the attitudes, standards and values which superordinates judged to be appropriate. On the face of it at least, the structure was conducive to the socialization of children and adolescents - many of them the offspring of subordinates and therefore the next generation of factory hands - in habits of industry, discipline, respect for authority, obedience, thrift and sobriety.

In the realms of formal schooling, post-elementary education accessible to the lower classes in Burnley was supplied by the town's two institutes - the Burnley Mechanics' Institute and the Church Institute. Advertisements and reports in the local press suggest that the activities of these two agencies generated an interest which went beyond the sphere of the formally educational. Not only did the institutes offer advanced courses of study and opportunities to obtain qualifications leading to occupational and social advancement, but their concerns extended to the spheres of informal political education and the provision of recreational amenities. Here again, sponsorship by the town's leaders and the institutes' religious and political links rendered them potentially influential agencies for the dissemination of the paternalists' normative code, especially as several of the more prominent sponsors were also actively involved over many years in the work of the institutes. As H.J. Perkin has pointed out:

> These institutions became part of a middle-class mission to the working class in general, not confined to technical instruction but extending to moral and political education . . . controlled and supported by middle-class managers and money . . . and involved in the self-conscious dissemination of the entrepreneurial ideal.(33)

In Burnley the Mechanics' Institute was associated with Nonconformism and Liberalism, the Church Institute with Anglicanism and Toryism. The Mechanics' was originally a small organization brought into being by working men for the benefit of their fellows, but growing interest led to the opening of larger premises in 1855 and what amounted to a takeover by some of the town's leaders. Sir James Phillips Kay-Shuttleworth, first Secretary of what became the Board of Education, perceived that the education offered by the Burnley Mechanics' Institute and other such institutes in the area suffered from dependence on 'teachers exhausted by six hours of instruction in day schools, on the voluntary exertions of ministers and other professional gentlemen, or on the aid of men with very humble qualifications.'(34) He therefore urged in 1856 the creation of the East Lancashire Union of Institutes in order to improve and extend adult education by maintaining the co-ordination of the work of all the institutes within a ten-mile radius of Burnley. The town's two institutes thus became linked with those in Padiham, Lomeshaye, Bacup, Stacksteads, Haslingden, Crawshawbooth in the 1850s, and with others during the following decade. By 1871 the Union comprised twenty institutes plus local evening classes held in more modest premises. The advantages of the scheme promoted by Sir James Phillips Kay-Shuttleworth included the appointment of a well-paid, well-qualified Organizing Master who selected teachers, arranged classes in all the affiliated centres, and himself taught chemistry, physics and physiology to higher grades. Many of the teachers giving instruction in less advanced evening courses were the most proficient of the students who attended advanced daytime classes. In 1872 the East Lancashire Union of Institutes was absorbed into the Lancashire and Cheshire Union of Institutes and in 1880 the Burnley Mechanics' became affiliated with the City and Guilds of London Institute.

Though initially founded by working men the Mechanics' rapidly acquired sponsors and patrons from amongst Burnley's leading townsmen. Influential at the Burnley Mechanics' Institute were Dr Coultate and several leading industrialists including the

Masseys, the Keighleys, J.H. Scott, James Kay, William Thompson and Abram Altham, while at the Church Institute much voluntary unpaid teaching was done by the Grants who owned a local private school, by Dr Verity of All Saints' and by Dr Butler of the Grammar School. Listed amongst those who bought shares in the Church Institute building fund to pay for the site and fabric of the building were General Scarlett, the Reverend William Thursby, Sir James Phillips Kay-Shuttleworth and Colonel Starkie.(35) In 1880 Alderman Scott, director and vice-president of the Mechanics', built a new Art School at his own expense to function as part of the institute, and a few years later Alderman Altham personally paid off a two hundred pound debt which the institute had incurred.

Local educational opportunities went beyond Burnley's network of elementary schools and what was provided under the auspices of the town's two institutes. There were less formal agencies to extend knowledge and to cultivate a lively interest in subjects of all kinds. The fact that such activities fulfilled a recreational need as well as an educational one may account for their popularity. They served to stimulate the mind and to inform, but the more relaxed, friendly, informal ambience, very different from the disciplined social environment of the classroom, was undoubtedly conducive to the formation of social linkages and confidence bridges between superordinates and subordinates.

The most important of these educative, recreational agencies were the Improvement Societies. That these societies were frequently associated with the town's religious institutions, with the clergy and the lay-leaders, may have expedited the process of socialization. In the latter half of the nineteenth century nearly every church and chapel in Burnley appears to have had a Young Men's Mutual Improvement Society and as often a counterpart for young women.(36) These clubs often came into being as spin-offs from Sunday school classes for adolescents. The meetings, usually held weekly, took the form of debates or lectures followed by informal discussion. The range of subjects covered is impressively wide and argues both a thirst for knowledge and an eager enjoyment of discussion and debate. While some societies applied themselves to the study of a single theme for a whole session, others investigated a different subject at each meeting. Prayers may have been said, but the topics covered appear to have been entirely secular.

One of the earliest of the Burnley societies was that formed in 1864 at Wesley Chapel in Hargreaves Street.(37) Its meetings were held on Friday evenings and amongst the local men of distinction who lectured there was Dr Brumwell who spoke on 'Digestion' and 'John Wesley, the Physician'. The interests of the Brunswick Society and of the Sion Society tended to be more politically orientated; various aspects of 'Nationalization' were investigated at some length by the former while the latter debated the comparative merits of 'Monarchy' and 'Republicanism'. The society attached to St Peter's appears to have had a preference for English literature for it studied the life and work of great literary figures - Shakespeare, Milton, Swift and so on. The societies at Westgate (dating from 1867), Mount Pleasant (from 1869), St Peter's (from 1879) and St Paul's (from 1880) chose to entitle themselves Young Men's Christian Societies but their programmes of events were very similar to those of the Improvement Societies. The Westgate Society, for example, devoted itself for a time to the study of art and encouraged an interest in self expression by mounting exhibitions of paintings.

Of individual men of mark in Burnley who took recreation-orientated education to the people, the Reverend R. Littlehales,(38) pastor of the Baptist chapel in Yorkshire Street for some twelve years (1875-87), is particularly noteworthy. His lectures on Sunday afternoons at the Mechanics' or at the Theatre Royal, and his talks on Monday evenings in Altham's Coffee Rooms appear to have generated great interest, perhaps because the speaker was reputedly an accomplished orator who spoke out fearlessly and with conviction about what he regarded as the social evils of the day: vice, gambling, intemperance, dog-coursing, pigeon-flying and the theatre.

There were many more dimensions to the recreational life of Burnley's religious centres. Churches and chapels in northern industrial towns were important focal points of social life and respectable recreation. News columns and advertisements in the local press provide a mine of information about the leisure activities made available; diversity, ranging from active participation to passive spectator involvement, arguably ensured attractions to suit most recreational preferences. Centres of worship organized special events: bazaars, concerts, picnics, tea parties, lantern lectures, sales of work, sewing circles, choirs, dramatic societies, bands and so on. By the 1880s many of Burnley's chapels and churches appear to have had football and cricket teams which held regular practices during the playing season and which competed in local league matches against other teams in the district.

Relaxation, entertainment and a sense of community were provided through the more relaxed medium of lantern lectures, picnics, concerts, trips to the seaside and celebratory tea parties to mark special occasions. Fund-raising activities, such as those involved in sales of work and sewing circles, gave shared expression to a sense of Christian duty and moral responsibility as well as fulfilling the more obvious leisure purpose. Dramatic societies, choral societies and brass bands provided recreational outlets for those talented in the performing arts.

Employing enterprises were also centres of recreation sponsored 'from above'. At most of the larger firms employers appear to have made attempts to promote goodwill, community spirit and a family atmosphere by providing 'tea treats' for their workers at Christmas and on other occasions when there was cause for celebration. In Burnley, for example, Abram Altham(39) 'treated' his employees on his election to the Town Council; William Mitchell(40) gave a 'tea-treat' on his election as Burnley's MP. Celebrations were usually held in a workroom or storeroom at the mill or, where numbers were smaller, in the local chapel schoolroom, particularly if the employer was involved in lay-leadership duties. On such occasions food and drink, invariably excluding intoxicants, were supplied at the firm's expense, and employers, along with their families and works overlookers mingled informally with factory hands; tea was followed occasionally by dancing but more usually by a concert for the entertainment of the assembled throng. At these gatherings volunteer performers, led most conspicuously by 'accomplished' members of the employer's family, led the entertainment with songs, recitations and musical pieces performed on the pianoforte.

Such celebrations tended to be strongly imbued with the ideals of chapel-bred temperance, a virtue which featured overtly as a proxy for respectability in the moral context of the era. Temperance, widely regarded in nineteenth-century middle-class opinion as requisite to the self-respect of the masses, vital to labour efficiency and indispensable to municipal law and order, was more explicitly fostered in Nonconformist spheres, but Tory Anglican opinion ran along roughly similar lines about the need to divert the recreational preferences of the lower orders away from the excesses of intoxication. In efforts to counter the leisure-time attraction of the pubs, inns and taverns employers sometimes built or subscribed to the maintenance of coffee rooms and tea rooms.

In Burnley Abram Altham(42) 'without any intention of profit' built a coffee room where the local Baptist minister gave regular lectures, reportedly well attended, on the cause of temperance. In countervailing efforts to neutralize the magnetism of the inns and taverns in Warrington the Quaker Crosfield family(43) offered financial and administrative assistance in the provision of tea and coffee rooms, a circulating library and a horticultural society. The family was unstinting in financial aid and organizational zeal to foster the growth of 'rational', uplifting and harmlessly enjoyable leisure activities. Leisure, recreation, relaxation and pleasure were to be condoned but it was essential that activities were directed into desirable channels. In the summer of 1864 John Crosfield presided over the organization of the Bank Quay flower show held under the auspices of the recently formed horticultural society of which he was a patron. His address to the crowd on that occasion discloses a great deal not only about his personal philosophy but about middle-class attitudes in general towards the recreation of subordinates:

> . . . there is much good to be got from the cultivation of flowers; the pursuit has a moral tendency, and is a great inducement to a man to spend his time at home with his family, instead of at the public house, where many temptations beset him.(44)

In 1875 John Crosfield became a shareholder in a limited company to provide temperance coffee and cocoa rooms throughout Warrington, together with reading rooms and club rooms to enable workmen to spend their leisure hours in a rational and sober manner.

Of the recreational opportunities provided 'from above' by employers works trips, or more specifically company-sponsored railway excursions, are perhaps the best known. These were common in Burnley in an era when an expanding railway network linked the major industrial towns of the North West with the expanding seaside resorts of the Lancashire coast (such as Blackpool, Southport, New Brighton and Morecambe) and to the more accessible Welsh resorts. At the Crosfield soap and chemical producing firm in Warrington the works outing had become firmly established as an annual event by the beginning of the 1870s. Roughly two hundred and fifty of Crosfield's employees went to Llangollen in 1861; in 1886 as many as one thousand went to Blackpool.(45)

The individual and collective reputations of social leaders were enhanced by their philanthropic activities. Philanthropic efforts encompassed not only health, education and religion but included leisure amenities also. The provision of parks, gardens and recreation fields was favoured and actively promoted; open spaces such as these were viewed as worthwhile social amenities which improved public health through opportunities for exercise and fresh air, and which countered the attraction of more pernicious recreational alternatives. In Warrington(46) a gift of £9,500 from George Crosfield in 1872 enabled the Town Council to purchase Bank Hall and its surrounding grounds for conversion into a Town Hall, public park and gardens. In Burnley land to provide parks and gardens, a favoured form of philanthropy, was sometimes given during the lifetime of the benefactor, as in the case of Queen's Park, an extensive area of some twenty-eight acres, Thornber Gardens adjacent to the hospital, and Towneley Park, sold to the Corporation for a sum well below its current market price by Lady O'Hagan. In other cases parks were bought with money bequeathed to the town for the purpose as in the case of Scott Park and Thompson Park.(47)

Access to elective and selective office conferring decision-making authority in the conduct of local affairs was dependent upon the individual's local reputation as a capable, responsible and respectable townsman; it depended also upon his ability to legitimate his claim to leadership by persuading others that his values and ideals, whether moral, religious or political, were conducive to the wellbeing of the community in general. This does not necessarily mean or prove that subordinates were successfully socialized in dominant ideology and that the general response was one of deference. It does suggest that there were sites of consensus. It is true that in nineteenth-century Burnley the structure of social relationships and interaction was such that large numbers were exposed to influences from above in the spheres of education, religion, work and recreation and that these influences had the potential to foster vertically structured allegiance with a predominantly middle-class group of leaders. Mechanisms to socialize attitudes and aspirations, reactions and responses were certainly in existence, but this does not prove beyond all doubt that the mechanisms were effective. As we have seen, the structure of authority and influence which obtained in the workplace was replicated beyond it. The multi-functional role of employer-dominated religious institutions, which served as the focus not only of Christian worship but also of education, recreation and philanthropy, meant that leaders here had a strategic advantage in whatever efforts were undertaken to legitimate their leadership, but this is not conclusive proof that acceptance of the leadership was secured through a process of socialization in dominant ideology. Deference was not necessarily the end product. Influence of this kind needs to be considered not only from the viewpoint of the would-be socializers, if such they can be termed, but also from the viewpoint of those who were to be socialized.

References

1. Bennett, W., *History of Burnley*, Burnley Corporation, 1951, iv, ch. 4.

2. Mouffe, C., ed., *Gramsci and Marxist Theory*, Routledge and Kegan Paul, 1979; Gramsci, A., *Selections from the Prison Notebooks*, New Left Books, reprinted 1971.

3. Abercrombie, N. , *et al.*, *Dictionary of Sociology*, Penguin, 1984, p. 201; Danziger, K., *Socialization*, Penguin, 1971.

4. The claim that subordinates were successfully socialized by their social superiors is questioned in Thompson, F.M.L., 'Social Control in Victorian Britain', *Economic History Review*, 2nd Series, XXXIV, 1981, pp. 189-208. The dominant ideology thesis is reviewed and critically assessed in Abercrombie, N. and Turner, B.S., *The Dominant Ideology Thesis*, Allen and Unwin, 1980.

5. Danziger, K., *op. cit.*; Parsons, T. *et al.*, *Family, Socialization and Interaction Processes*, Free Press, New York, 1955; see also Kuper, A. and J. eds, *The Social Sciences Encyclopedia*, Routledge and Kegan Paul, 1985, pp. 775-6.

6. Abercrombie, N. *et al.*, *Dictionary . . .*, pp. 144-5.

7. *Ibid.*, pp. 76-8; Durkheim, E., *The Elementary Forms of Religious Life*, Allen and Unwin, 1912 edition reprinted 1954.

8. Abercrombie, N. *et al.*, *Dictionary . . .*, p. 178.

9. *Ibid.*, p. 91; Gramsci, A., *op. cit.*

10. Abercrombie, N. *et al.*, *Dictionary . . .*, p. 195.

11. For differing interpretations of the nature and extent of religion as a socializing agency see Hart, J., 'Religion and Social Control in the Mid-Nineteenth Century' in Donajgrodksi, A.P., ed., *Social Control in Nineteenth-Century Britain*, Croom Helm, 1977; Perkin, H.J., *Origins of Modern English Society, 1780-1880*, Routledge and Kegan Paul, 1969, chs 8 and 9; Thompson, E.P., *The Making of the English Working Class*, Gollancz, 1963, ch. 11; Hobsbawm, E.J., *Labouring Men*, Weidenfeld and Nicolson, 1964, ch. 3; Thomis, M.I., *The Town Labourer and the Industrial Revolution*, Batsford, 1974, ch. 9;

Halévy, E., *The Birth of Methodism in England*, translated and edited by Semmel, B., Aldine, Chicago, 1971; Halévy, E., *A History of the English People*, Penguin, 1937; McLeod, H., *Religion and the Working Class in Nineteenth-Century Britain*, Macmillan, 1984.

12. Parkin, F., *Class Inequality and Political Order*, MacGibbon and Kee, 1971, ch. 2, especially pp. 70-6.

13. Bennett, W., *op. cit.*, ch. 9.

14. *Ibid.*, pp. 157-60.

15. *Burnley Notabilities: Press Cuttings, 1971, loc. cit.*

16. *Men of Burnley: Press Cuttings, 1963-5, loc. cit.*

17. *Men of Burnley: Press Cuttings, 1961-3, loc. cit.*

18. *Ibid.*; obituary of W.C. Hargreaves, *Burnley Gazette*, 22 Dec. 1900.

19. *Burnley Notabilities: Press Cuttings, 1971, loc. cit.*; obituary of Robert Handsley, *Burnley Gazette*, 21 Oct. 1903.

20. *Men of Burnley: Press Cuttings 1963-5, loc. cit.*

21. Appendix, Table X.

22. Bennett, W., *op. cit.*, ch. 9.

23. *Ibid.*, pp. 151-2.

24. *Ibid.*

25. *Ibid.*

26. *Ibid.*, chs 9 and 10; Young, M.E., 'The Burnley School Board, 1871-1891', M.Ed. dissertation, Manchester University, 1973.

27. Bennett, W., *op. cit.*, chs 9 and 10.

28. Musson, A.E., *Enterprise in Soap and Chemicals: Crosfield's of Warrington, 1815-1965*, Manchester University Press, 1965, ch. 10.

29. Bennett, W., *op. cit.*, p. 170, chs 10 and 14.

30. Lawson, J. and Silver, H., *A Social History of Education in England*, Methuen, 1973, chs 8 and 9.

31. Bennett, W., *op. cit.*, ch. 10; Young, M.E., *op. cit.*

32. Perkin, H.J., *op. cit.*, p. 70.

33. Quoted in Bennett, W., *op. cit.*, p. 181.

34. *Ibid.*, pp. 180-5.

35. *Ibid.*, p. 153.

36. *Ibid.*

37. *Ibid.*, ch. 10.

38. *Ibid.*, pp. 150, 165.

39. Abram Altham's obituary, *Burnley Gazette*, 1 Aug. 1885; see also *Burnley Notabilities: Press Cuttings, 1971, loc. cit.*

40. *Men of Burnley: Press Cuttings, 1961-3, loc. cit.*

41. Bennett, W., *op. cit.*, pp. 154-6.

42. Abram Altham's obituary, *Burnley Guardian*, 1 Aug. 1885.

43. Musson, A.E., *op. cit.*, ch. 10.

44. Quoted *ibid.*

45. *Ibid.*, ch. 10.

46. *Ibid.*

47. Many details of leaders' personal philanthropy in *Men of Burnley: Press Cuttings, 1961-3; Men of Burnley: Press Cuttings, 1963-5; Burnley Notabilities: Press Cuttings, 1971, loc. cit.*

PART TWO

REACTION:
RESISTANCE AND ACQUIESCENCE

5

The Political Response

Introduction

Despite the successive waves of discontent in the relationship between masters and men in the economic sphere, in which more militant and aggressive unionism suffered a whole series of bitter and often unsuccessful confrontations with the employers, recurrently hostile industrial relations did not lead to a wholesale rejection of the masters from the positions of leadership they occupied outside the workplace. They continued in their roles as leaders in the Town Council, the School Board, the Board of Guardians and so on, though employers tended to come forward for election in smaller numbers as the period progressed. When, from 1883 onwards, resurgent Toryism in Burnley offered other middle-class leaders with an alternative policy for municipal government there was no mass stampede on the part of the electorate from its long Liberal allegiance. When, from the early 1890s, Socialism offered not only an alternative political ideology but also representatives from a different social class, the electorate was even more reluctant to transfer its support. The absence of a more decisive swing to either Toryism (which promised a better deal to less affluent ratepayers) or to Socialism (which offered a working-class political solution in a town with a disproportionately large wage-worker population) is puzzling, given the backdrop of industrial unrest and discontent in the period. The persisting majority preference in the election of town councillors was for Liberal representatives. In this chapter we look more closely at subordinates' responses to the opportunities available to them in three main spheres: industrial relations, Parliamentary elections and local elections to the Town Council.

143

Reactions: industrial relations, trade unions and politics

Political mass movements amongst the subordinate class disappeared in the North West after 1848 with the demise of Chartism. No subsequent movement was able to integrate and mobilize the economic and political grievances of wage-workers on a comparable scale during the later Victorian era. Certainly there were confrontational episodes in the sphere of industrial relations, often imbued with anger, sometimes geographically extensive in scope and hard-fought by the trade unions. Yet such conflict was not translated into political protest. As Walton has shown, it 'consistently lacked an overt or sustained political dimension, and the Lancashire working class became firmly assimilated into the orthodox two-party system which crystallized nationally in mid-Victorian times.'(1) Political allegiances to the Liberal and Tory parties became so deeply entrenched that the embryonic Socialist parties which came into being in the late nineteenth century found it difficult to make headway.

This state of affairs is nowhere better illustrated than in Burnley. After 1848 Burnley Chartism maintained a sporadic, bush-fire presence which burned itself out after a few years. Industrial conflict persisted, however; it was sometimes violent, widespread and sustained, but no longer did it link up overtly with politics.(2) In 1858 Engels noted with regret the appearance of what he termed a 'bourgeois proletariat' in pursuit of reform and material improvement within the prevailing socio-political structure. This new stability in the stratification order was already apparent during the years of the 'cotton famine'.

The 'cotton famine' of the early 1860s brought mass unemployment and regionwide deprivation to industrial Lancashire in general. Towards the end of 1862 49 per cent of *all* operatives were without work in the twenty-eight Poor Law Unions of the cotton districts, 35 per cent were working less than full time, and only 16 per cent were working full time. On average unemployment remained at over 30 per cent throughout 1863 and 1864, with much higher concentrations in some blackspots.(3) In Burnley the 'cotton famine' ruined several manufacturers including the owners of Parsonage Mill, Rake Mill, Newtown, Marles, Ashfield in Trafalgar Street, Lane Bridge and Spruce Mill.(4) This was economic crisis on a grand regional scale, yet in general it was met with resignation and fortitude on the part of wage-workers rather than with anger and violent protest. Moreover, there was no regionwide resurgence of Chartism, despite the fact that the Chartist movement had had a flourishing presence in the North West little more than a decade earlier. This is not to suggest that subordinates' response to the vicissitudes of the early 1860s was one of pervasive uninterrupted passivity, but to underline the point that 'resistance to authority on specific issues never threatened to broaden out into a general political critique.'(5) Certainly there were sporadic disturbances and even riots - at Ashton and Stalybridge, for example. In the Burnley district alarmed magistrates discussed the possibility of a full-scale uprising, for there were passionately angry outbursts amongst the unemployed - but protest was about the terms and conditions attached to the receipt of poor relief, about the level of relief payments, about the allegedly stringent application of labour and school attendance tests, and about discrimination in the distribution of relief to the disadvantage of trade unionists. The feared uprising did not materialize. Subsequently, Burnley's leaders commended the strong spirit of independence, pride and resourcefulness of unemployed operatives who had weathered the storm with fortitude and who had displayed a marked reluctance to seek charity or relief from the Poor Law Guardians before personal savings were exhausted. Accommodation to mischance, however, as Walton convincingly argues, should not be confused with passivity; Lancashire workers in Burnley and elsewhere were 'not as supine in adversity as their social superiors subsequently preferred to believe, although their resistance seldom took overtly political form . . . .'(6)

Thrift, prudent forethought and practical frugality may supply partial explanation for the perceived quiescence of distressed workers. Personal saving through banks, building societies, friendly societies and the co-operative society undoubtedly served to ameliorate the experience of hardship; but the institutions of working-class thrift did not so much prevent destitution as delay it, although the 'habits of mind which encouraged the grim, dogged accumulation of ultimately substantial savings from inadequate wages may well have been conducive to the silent endurance of a deeper adversity.'(7) More importantly, however, the 'cotton famine' generated less violent class hostility and less serious disruption of law and order than earlier and later trade depressions because the fundamental causes were perceived to be external, remote and beyond the control of factory masters. Indeed, employers were the more likely to be respected for their efforts to keep their mills open than to be reviled for the introduction of wage cuts and short-time working.(8)

That the economic crisis of the 'cotton famine' years was acknowledged to be the result of exceptional circumstances in which Lancashire cotton masters played no causal part goes some way in explaining the absence of major political upheaval in the 1860s. Yet political quiescence also characterized the three decades which followed when circumstances were very different. Many urban wage-workers received the right to vote both in municipal and Parliamentary elections with the extension of the franchise later in the 1860s, and the secret ballot, introduced in 1872, all but eliminated the risk of reprisals for the worker whose political preference differed from that of his employer. The practical opportunity plus the ways and the means to effect radical political change were there; moreover, during the last three decades of the nineteenth century there was economic discontent, in part at least directly attributable to the activities of employers, to provide a potential cause for rejection of their political leadership. There were recurrent waves of industrial unrest in both cotton and coal during these years and the causes of wage cuts and lay-offs were not perceived to be entirely beyond the individual and collective control of the employers. Anger and hostility in industrial relations erupted into strikes and on occasions into running riots in the streets, yet even here energies and grievances were not diverted into radical politics as a means to economic redress or to social reform.(9) Certainly in the industrial towns of the North West there are a few exceptions to this generalization, as Walton shows, but the characteristic response was acquiescence in the two-party political *status quo*. Burnley is typical in this respect, though less typical in its majority preference of Liberalism.(10) In nearby Blackburn and many other towns in the region Tory predominance persisted.

The organization of workers into trade unions and employers into masters' associations is testimony to the claim that workplace relationships were conceptualized in oppositional terms. There were recurrent confrontations, mutual recriminations, and strikes countered by lockouts during trade recessions when the main causal factors were not perceived to be entirely exogenous. In Burnley(11) there was a selective strike at targeted mills (sustained at one factory from February 1872 to October 1873) to force employers to adopt a standard 'List'. As we have seen, production in the cotton trade was brought to a standstill by the disturbances of 1878; workplace conflict, spilling out into the streets, led twice to the reading of the Riot Act. Strikes recurred in 1884 when, despite the recovery of trade, Burnley cotton masters refused to restore wages after cuts imposed the previous year. During the first decade of the twentieth century there were strikes at some of Burnley's mills over the redeployment of labour and the introduction of new labour-saving technology such as the automatic shuttle which threatened jobs. The 1908 strike, which occurred during a six-months-long recession, brought out 20,000 operatives. Many of the strikers, urged on by 'extremists' dissatisfied with the tentative policy of the union committee, marched on the workhouse, tried to rush the Town Hall when the Council was in session, and attacked the Weavers' Institute to demand higher unemployment benefits than those currently permitted under union regulations. Another major strike occurred in 1911; industrial action, prompted by the employment of non-unionized labour in the mills, continued for three weeks until the dispute was settled through the intercession of a specially appointed Conciliation Board.

In Burnley the recurrent strife in cotton was paralleled in coal, and in the latter case, again, there were no 'exceptional circumstances' such as those which caused the textile recession of the 'cotton famine' years. There was a ten-months strike by one hundred colliers at the Cliviger pit in 1860 over the demand for a pay increase of one shilling on every twenty-five loads of coal. A strike in 1867, again by the Cliviger miners, concerned demands for wage increases in consideration of a 10 per cent increase in coal prices. Another strike occurred at the Bank Hall pits in 1872 when coal prices began to rise again after its price, and therefore also wage rates, had fallen by 25 per cent between 1869 and 1872 - the trigger was the dismissal by the mine-owners of members of the deputation of workers' representatives requesting a pay rise. There followed a wider strike affecting most of the mines in the Burnley district and involving roughly 1,200 men and boys in July 1873 when the coal-owners announced their intention of employing only non-union men in the future. The unsuccessful outcome of the strike and employers' offensives to suppress unionism all but stifled the Miners' Association out of existence in Burnley for several years, and it was not until 1889 that the next major strike occurred. Again, the focus of disagreement was the level of pay, along with other factors affecting remuneration and working conditions: the appointment of checkweighmen, the abolition of royalties, an eight-hour day, a five-day week and recognition of the union. At the Beehole colliery miners also demanded wider roads to facilitate higher productivity and therefore also higher pay. A strike at the Clifton mines in 1892, supported by sympathizers from other pits in the area, was once again confined to work-related issues. Thereafter, industrial relations in the coal industry remained in a state of turbulence, with resistance to wage reductions in 1894, a fifteen-week strike over pay in 1898, a six-week stoppage at the Cheapside pit in 1900, a seventeen-week walkout in 1910, and a four-week strike in 1912. As a generalization, on the occasion of industrial relations conflict the demands of Burnley wage-workers never went beyond the narrowly economic.

Oppositional workplace relationships of this kind were not unique to Burnley, of course. Examples proliferate throughout industrial Lancashire. The Preston cotton strike and lockout of 1853-4, which lasted nearly a year, was both protracted and imbued with anger, but it was organized by a 'moderate and respectable leadership which commanded the grudging admiration of even the most hostile middle-class observers.'(12) In Blackburn confrontational violence surfaced in 1878 on the wave of weavers' strikes which washed across textile Lancashire that year; the spokesman for the employers had his house sacked and looted, and 'even Harry Hornby was not immune to the physical fury of the rioters.'(13)

The later nineteenth century is characterized by endemic industrial relations turbulence which persisted even when employers took steps to defuse it. The salient point, however, is that workers, whether unionized or not, were not turning to radical politics in significant numbers to promote their interests. Workers' economic aspirations for improvement in employment conditions were to be pursued through the trade unions using tried and tested methods with resort to strike action if necessary.

Political objectives were perceived to be achievable within the prevailing two-party socio-political structure. For the time being at least, many unions preferred to distance themselves from the embryonic Socialist parties. Until the end of the nineteenth century the class conflict which occurred focused on the workplace and it was expressed in economic rather than political terms. As Clarke observes, the cotton unions as such 'had sought to avoid involvement in party politics.' This principle was exemplified in 1885 by the events in Blackburn when the 'radical inclinations of the original weavers' leadership spurred on the creation of a powerful and Tory-orientated rival organization.'(14) In these years the cotton unions' primary political objectives 'involved lobbying for specific reforms on issues relating to such topics as hours and working conditions, and this form of pressure-group activity had little to do with wider party divisions.'(15) Even in the case of the miners, their more sustained political involvement regionally was with pressure-group tactics for protective legislation. In general, as Joyce convincingly argues, the Trades' Councils which emerged in most sizeable industrial towns in the mid-

Victorian period tended to avoid party-political issues and 'individual unions almost always declared that they were above politics.'(16) In Walton's words:

> Lancashire's trade unions were steadily gaining in strength and industrial muscle during the second half of the nineteenth century; but until the turn of the century and afterwards they were unwilling to convert their influence into effective independent political clout.(17)

The attitude of the leadership of the Burnley branch of the weavers' union provides an exemplary case. David Holmes, a founding member of the Burnley branch and its president for thirty-five years, was a Gladstonian Liberal, but he would never allow the committee nor mass meetings of weavers to start discussions of political theories. He expressed what undoubtedly was the majority view when he asserted that the true function of the union was to 'improve conditions in the mills and to maintain the prosperity of the textile trade.'(18) Holmes consistently refused to permit the theories of the established parties to influence the union's industrial policy and in this he had the backing of the union's secretary, John Strickland, and of the majority of his committee. The union was equally aloof in its attitude towards Socialism. The founders of the Burnley branch of the Social Democratic Federation were anxious to win over the influential weavers' union, but their overtures were given a cool reception. The first open quarrel occurred in 1894 when objections were raised by some Socialist operatives over the right of the committee to elect representatives to the Trades Union Congress. The internal dispute threatened to disrupt the whole society two years later during a meeting held in the SDF rooms in St James's Hall to discuss the formation of a rival union: the New Textile Operatives' Society (Weavers' Dept).(19) Though the rival centre was established it was short-lived and the breakaway operatives subsequently returned to the Burnley branch of the weavers' union. For some years thereafter peace was maintained, with only occasional outbursts from Socialist members.(20)

Early working-class representatives, David Holmes of the weavers' union and John Leeming of the miners' union, for example, were elected into local government office as Liberals,(21) but the Burnley Trades' Council, formed of representatives, including Holmes and Leeming, of many local trade unions, would not at first officially support any political party on the premise that the Council's function was primarily an economic one and that its funds and its energies should be devoted to gains for its members in the industrial sphere.(22) As an organized group it eschewed party politics, urging that individuals were free to vote for whichever candidate was judged to be most sympathetic to the interests of the working man.

Reaction: the Ratepayers' Association

The attitude of the Burnley Trades' Council was echoed in 1892 by a newly formed and surprisingly short-lived Ratepayers' Association. John Leeming (Trades' Council and Miners' Association), M. Battle (president of the Burnley Trades' Council), William Rawson (president of the Powerloom Weavers' Association) and other trade union and Trades' Council personnel figured in its leadership and stamped it with a specifically working-class identity.(23) Several meetings were held in May, June, July and August of that year, when working-class dissatisfaction was being strongly expressed with the 'ways and means of the Corporation in carrying out the administration of the Town's affairs.'(24) Several issues were raised in discussions imbued with consciousness of class. There was resentment about the Corporation's refusal to raise the wages of refuse collectors, though it was prepared to grant salary increases to high-ranking officials employed at the Town Hall and in the Police Force, and it saw fit to pay 'very handsomely a Town Clerk who was not even a Burnley man.'(25) Moreover, a new Clerk of Works had been appointed 'to walk about with his coat on all day at a salary of £3 per week of the ratepayers' money.'(26) There was indignation over the cost involved in the 'furnishing of a lavish reception room at the Town Hall.' There were 'uncomplimentary comments' about the ineptitude of the Town Council in its handling of the water works scheme, 'the estimated cost of which had been £50,000 but which had in fact cost the ratepayers £160,000, while at the same time its capacity was 20 million gallons less than anticipated.'(27) In the case of the Duckpits sewage works, £42,000 had already been spent on experimental schemes and the system was still inefficient. Furthermore, Alderman Keighley had abused his position by indulging in 'land grabbing' and a great deal of 'Council jobbing' had gone on in connection with the Gannow Bridge project.(28) Things were no better, it was alleged, in the case of the Guardians who had paid no less than £1,400 in architect's fees alone for a 'new palatial pauper infirmary', for which the 'most costly building materials' were to be used and which promised to be not only 'unnecessarily ornate' but 'unnecessarily and expensively modern'

in the use of 'hot-air heating'.(29) It was unanimously agreed at
the meeting that it was high time working men took things into
their own hands and had on the Town Council and the various
Boards, 'men to represent them, of their own interests.'(30)

From the outset the leadership of the Association urged the
need for protests of a 'non-political character' about the policies
of Burnley's Town Council. Ratepayers were exhorted to use
their voting power(31) to elect on to Town Council working men
or others, regardless of class or party, known to be sympathetic to
working-men's interests. However, after a promising start, the
Association appears to have lost its momentum by the end of the
year, and to have had no further impact as an organized force
upon the town's affairs.

In general the employer-dominated Liberal majority in the
Town Council seems to have been accepted as a relatively effective
set of leaders, despite sporadic outbursts of adverse criticism
from the Ratepayers' Association. There was extensive provision
of social amenities: gas, water, a planned sewerage scheme, street
paving and lighting, cemetery and market control, a fire brigade,
a police force and, more belatedly, electricity, transport and
sponsored recreation grounds. Certainly there were some
technological inefficiencies and some expensive mistakes, yet the
town was generally well-served in all the spheres vitally affecting
urban environmental conditions.(32) Moreover, high-cost projects,
which municipal enterprise such as this necessarily required, did
not apparently hurt the local ratepayers nearly so badly as critics
within and without the Town Council claimed. The Ratepayers'
Association was remarkably inactive throughout the period except
for the late 1870s and a brief revival in 1892, and evidence
suggests that the Tory 'Economy Party' failed to muster mass
support because the rates were not intolerably high. An editorial
in the *Burnley Gazette* in 1877 entitled, 'The One Ratepayer',
countered Tory accusations of mis-spending with dismissive
derision.(33) Tory allegations that the Town Council was exceeding
its borrowing powers, was heading for bankruptcy, and was being
inordinately extravagant with ratepayers' money, had led to a
Local Government Board Inquiry held in the Council Chamber,
which was attended by only 'one ratepayer'. Editorial opinion in
the pro-Liberal *Burnley Gazette* is suffused with exasperation:

> What about the Ratepayers' Association? Surely it bodes ill for that
> embryonic organization that only 'one ratepayer' could be found to
> take so much interest in our municipal economy as would carry
> him to the Town Hall on the occasion of an inquiry so important as

the one held last week by Lieutenant Colonel Cox. If the ratepayers are too thoughtless and indifferent to interest themselves in 'Municipal Affairs', except at election time, is it consistent that they should be such very savage critics of the peccadilloes of their representatives? . . . Perhaps it is the case that the Town Council serves the community as a whole not worse, but a little better, than they deserve . . . . They are indifferent to occasions to protest and show their feelings . . . . They know that they are well-served and are content to let well alone - except for anonymous Conservative scribblers to the press.(34)

Tory accusations of high rates and mis-spending recurred regularly at election time but, though rates had undoubtedly risen, Burnley was still, according to the Liberal press in 1884,(35) a low-rate borough compared with similar local towns. While the current rate was:

	6s. 4d.	per head in Burnley
it was	2s. 0d.	per head in Blackburn
	13s. 6d.	per head in Bolton
and	15s. 10d.	per head in Rochdale.

Similarly the current price of gas in 1884 was:

	2s. 6d.	per 1000 cubic foot in Burnley
compared with	3s. 3d.	to 3s. 6d. in Blackburn
	2s. 8d.	in Bolton
and	3s. 0d.	to 4s. 0d. in Rochdale.

Water also was cheaper in Burnley, it was claimed, and while the cost of the Town Hall seemed high, critics were reminded that the building served a fourfold purpose since it also incorporated the public baths, the police station and the Borough Police Court.(36)

By 1887, though Burnley rates had risen to:

	7s. 9d.	per head of the town's population
they were	10s. 6d.	per head in Accrington
and	13s. 6d.	per head in Blackburn.

While Burnley's gas by that year had fallen to:

                              2s. 3d.   per 1000 cubic foot
          the price was   3s. 1d.   in Blackburn
                   and   2s. 11d. in Accrington.(37)

Two factors appear to have been involved in the Liberal faction's ability to maintain relatively low rates and charges while providing and maintaining what, in the context of the era, were relatively efficient urban amenities. Arguably, extensive dissatisfaction with the services provided by the Liberal leaders would have reflected more positively in the transfer of electoral support to the Tory 'Economy' Party in municipal elections, or in an earlier and readier preference for Socialist representatives. Firstly, as businessmen involved in large family firms and business partnerships, many councillors were men of experience in the organization of credit and the handling of major projects involving risk and large amounts of loan capital. Though there were difficulties and some mistakes were made, the Council steered well clear of bankruptcy, negotiated large loans successfully and handled the repayment of debts without undue pressure upon the ratepayers.

Secondly, in addition to the advantages of financial and business acumen, the Town Council had alternative sources of revenue to supplement the rates. The sale of municipal gas and its by-product, coke, brought increasing profits from the beginning of the 1880s. The selling price of each was relatively low since large-scale production coupled with new technology brought economies of scale and falling unit costs.(38) Water was also a valuable source of revenue and, after an initial period of difficulty, municipal markets and the abattoir brought in more modest but consistent returns.(39) Additionally, County Borough status,(40) achieved in 1889, enabled the Burnley Council to issue, and to receive revenues from, 'all manner of licences' and gave the Council access to government grants for the maintenance of highways and bridges. Majority electoral preference suggests that, generally, the employers in their roles as Liberal Town Councillors provided satisfactorily efficient, cost-effective market products.

Reactions: Parliamentary politics

When the new parties of the Left emerged in the late-Victorian era they were to find the established bipartisan political structure very difficult to penetrate,(41) despite the electoral reforms of the late 1860s which extended voting rights in both Parliamentary and municipal spheres. In textile Lancashire the 1867 Reform

Act transformed the pattern of Parliamentary elections. The Act was a major, far-reaching piece of legislation in that it increased Lancashire's twenty-eight Parliamentary seats to a total of thirty-six, and it brought household suffrage to the boroughs, thereby increasing the electorate in the cotton town constituencies fivefold or sixfold. It thus, as Walton observes, 'gave working-class voters a clear predominance in the manufacturing towns . . . .'(42) In the 1865 general election Lancashire's Parliamentary seats had been evenly divided between the Liberals and the Conservatives; in 1868, under the reformed system, the Conservatives gained twenty-four seats and the Liberals twelve. In the cotton constituencies overall a twelve to six Liberal lead in 1865 was reversed in 1868 when the Conservatives won thirteen of the twenty seats. The Conservatives' predominance in Lancashire proved to be no transitory phenomenon. They held most of their gains in 1874 and, though some ground was lost in 1880, it was recovered in 1885 after the further extension of the franchise the previous year. Thereafter, the Conservatives maintained their regional majority until the Liberal landslide of 1906.(43)

Conservatism had widespread support amongst wage-workers in the industrial towns. Burnley was untypical in this respect; here it was Liberalism which predominated. In 1850 Burnley formed part of the Northern Division of Lancashire which returned two members of Parliament, but the local community regarded this as highly unsatisfactory for an increasingly populous industrial town. Burnley therefore pressed to be given the status of a Parliamentary borough returning its own member.

Political meetings to discuss the issue were already being held in the town in 1852; in April of that year a petition, seventy-seven feet in length and signed by 2,744 ratepayers, was sent to Parliament. Russell's Reform Bill of 1854 included Burnley in the list of proposed new boroughs but the Bill was defeated. Further meetings were held in Burnley in 1854 when the Conservative leader, Disraeli, took up the cause of Parliamentary reform, but expectations again remained unfulfilled. The issue was revived once more in 1865, and in February 1866 a Burnley Reform Association was formed by leading Liberals: William Thomas (chairman), S. Kay (secretary), J. Kay, Richard Shaw (later MP), T.T. Wilkinson, Lord Massey, John Barnes, R.C. Sutcliffe, Dr Coultate, Captain Creeke and Andrew Ogle. One of the Association's first moves was to despatch another petition to Lord Russell pressing for Parliamentary reform. This second petition was 'eighteen yards long, nearly six pounds in weight and signed by 4,507 ratepayers.'(44) Russell's reform proposal was rejected by the Commons but in 1867 Disraeli was able to secure the passage of the Parliamentary Reform Act under which Burnley became a Parliamentary borough returning its own member of Parliament.

Early in 1868 there was enthusiastic activity in Burnley by both the Liberals and Conservatives in preparation for the coming general election. Both parties mounted campaigns to win the votes of newly enfranchised wage-workers, forming political clubs to this end. From the outset there was mutual animosity rooted in religious sectarianism. A town meeting summoned by the Liberal Nonconformist mayor sent a petition to Mr Gladstone pressing for the disestablishment of the Irish Protestant Church which, it was hoped, would inhibit the spread of Fenianism. In retaliation the Tories formed the Constitutional Club a week later explicitly to defend the Constitution and the Church of England. Both parties formed committees and sponsored rival candidates for Parliamentary election. The Liberal Committee, peopled in the main by leading Nonconformist employers, included all the founder members of the Reform Association along with J.H. Scott, Dr Dean, Dr Brumwell, T. Nowell, Mark Kippax and the agent, Joshua Rawlinson. They nominated as their candidate a local man from 'a very old Burnley family' - Richard Shaw, solicitor of Holme Lodge. In general he could expect support from workers in the textile trades and from Nonconformists.

The rival Tory Committee consisted of J.E. Hargreaves, George Slater, John Folds, John Heelis, John Butterworth, William Milner Grant (proprietor of a private school), John Greenwood, Thomas Dugdale, James Fishwick, Dr Smirthwaite, Dr Bulter (headmaster of the Grammar School), Canon Townley-Parker and Robert Handsley (agent to the Thursbys). The Tories nominated General Scarlett of Bank Hall as their candidate. He could rely upon the support of the Anglican Church and the mining community. The General was a director of the Hargreaves colliery, related via the Hargreaves family to the landed mine-owning Thursbys. The Reverend William Thursby had married the elder daughter of Colonel Hargreaves; the Colonel's younger daughter was married to General Scarlett. Both the Thursby and Hargreaves families had local mine-owning interests.

The enthusiasm which characterized Burnley's run-up to the Parliamentary election of 1868 was punctuated by recriminations, accusations and counter-accusations. When the electoral lists were reviewed in September of that year, as many as three hundred names, allegedly inserted while the books had been deposited at Dugdales in Lowerhouse, were struck off. Bitter attacks ensued, and as nomination day approached there were several breaches of the peace; posters were torn down or defaced, windows were smashed, Pentridge Mill (owned by Mr Lomas, the mayor) was attacked, and there was fighting in the streets by rival gangs. There were angry accusations against the General - of keeping up the price of coal, of obstructing the establishment of a town cemetery opposite Bank Hall, and of being the son of a judge who had passed sentence upon several Chartists.(45)

Denunciations of this kind were countered with partisan fervour, with arrays of banners, rallies and street canvassing. On the occasion of the election of Burnley's first member of Parliament, the Liberal candidate, Mr Shaw, was declared to have been elected by a show of hands. The Tories protested and there followed a second show of hands which again, according to the mayor, gave victory to Mr Shaw. The Tories challenged the result once again and demanded a poll. This too, held the following day, favoured Mr Shaw by 2,620 votes to General Scarlett's 2,238.

This set the electoral pattern in Burnley for the rest of the century, even after the 1872 Act, introducing the secret ballot, had reduced the risk of bribery, intimidation and corruption. The Liberals were successful again in the Parliamentary election of 1874. The Liberal Association put forward Mr Shaw (the retiring member) as their candidate. The fact that the Conservative candidate, Mr W.A. Lindsay from South Kensington, was up against a well-known local man probably did little to further Toryism in Burnley. The Liberals maintained their success in Parliamentary elections(46) until 1900 when the Conservative candidate, Mr W. Mitchell, was elected. (On Mr Shaw's death in 1876 he was succeeded by Mr Peter Rylands, an ironmaster of Warrington.)

The 1886 election was an interesting two-man contest in which a Liberal candidate was opposed by a Liberal-Unionist. In the election of 1885 Mr Rylands had been returned to Westminster. He numbered amongst those members of the House of Commons who opposed Gladstone's Home Rule Bill which proposed to create an Irish Parliament to be largely independent of Westminster. The Irish Policy led to the defeat and resignation of the Gladstonian Government. In Burnley the Liberal Association met to decide upon a candidate for the election to be held on July 10th 1886. Mr Rylands's opposition to the Home Rule Bill had lost him much support and at the meeting only thirty-three of the 244 people present voted for his candidature; the majority were in favour of nominating James Greenwood of Cumberland Place. In the event, the minority adopted Mr Rylands as Liberal-Unionist candidate; the majority nominated Mr Greenwood as a Liberal. Mr Rylands won the seat because he was able to muster the local Conservative vote - the Conservatives had not fielded a candidate of their own - but he won by a narrow majority of only forty-three votes.

Rylands's death in 1887 led to a by-election in Burnley. Again, the Liberal candidate, Mr John Slagg, a Manchester merchant and chairman of the National Reform Union, won against the Conservatives' nominee, Mr J.O.S. Thursby, son of Colonel Thursby and grandson of the Reverend William Thursby. When Mr Slagg retired through ill-health in 1889, the new Liberal candidate, Mr Jabez Spencer Balfour was returned unopposed; Mr Balfour was returned again in 1892 when he defeated the Conservative contestant, Mr Edwin Lawrence. Liberalism prevailed in 1893 and 1895, represented on both occasions by the Hon. Philip Stanhope. Thereafter, Conservative and Liberal successes alternated up to the First World War, beginning with the election of the Conservative candidate, Mr W. Mitchell, a local man, in 1900.

Interest in Parliamentary elections was reflected in and promoted by a proliferation of political clubs(47) with increasing memberships. The Reform Association spawned other Liberal clubs in Burnley: Gannow established in 1870, Burnley Lane in 1871, and Fulledge, Elmwood Street and Accrington Road all in 1877. All had strong links with Nonconformism. To promote Toryism amongst workpeople in general, members of the original Burnley Constitutional Club actively involved themselves in the establishment of the Burnley Working Men's Constitutional Club. The association with Anglicanism is unsurprising. The Club was inaugurated at the Church Institute by a tea-party attended by thirteen thousand people; it subsequently held a demonstration at which ten thousand gathered before marching in procession to Bank Hall to present General Scarlett with two vases (valued at £300) and to declare their loyalty to the Conservative cause. Eighteen months later, in acknowledgement of this support, the General gave £1,000 to establish a Conservative Sick and Burial Club. Other Conservative clubs included Lane Head established in 1875, Oxford Road in 1877, Wood Top also in 1877, St Andrew's in 1889 and Burnley Wood in 1891. In 1877 the Primrose League, led in Burnley by prominent Churchmen, Canon Townley-Parker and Mr J.O.S. Thursby, established four 'Habitations': St Peter's, Bankhouse, Trinity and Gannow.(48)

Socialism appeared belatedly on the political scene. Its leaders had a clear understanding of the need for local consciousness-raising initiatives and they recognized that the trade unions were potentially the most effective agencies through which to rally wage-workers' support. Mr Henry Broadhurst, an Under Secretary of State for Home Affairs, visited Burnley in 1882 and in a public speech urged the establishment of a Council representing all local trade unions. This advice led in December 1882 to the formation of the Burnley and District United Trades' Council, but the formation of the Trades' Council, led as it was by older unionists with pre-established loyalties and allegiances, did not lead, in the short term at least, to mass espousal of Socialism. Among the Council's early leaders were David Holmes, John Strutt, John Strickland, J. Battle, T. Etherington, J. Leeming and S. Woods. In 1882 only eighteen trade unions sent representatives to the Council; it was not until 1894 that the number had risen to thirty-seven.

The Trades' Council held regular meetings at the Working Men's Club in Keighley Green, but its deliberations appear to have concentrated upon practical ways and means of furthering the interests of working men within the rules governing the prevailing two-party political structure. Certainly current issues in national policy were discussed but debate upon political theories as such was not welcomed. The focus was upon immediate practicalities relating to conditions of employment and to urban services and amenities affecting the local community beyond the workplace. The Council discussed the best means of protecting workers' interests and fought successfully for an increase in the number of fixed holidays. In local matters it urged the establishment of a Burnley Free Library, the abolition of the smoke nuisance, and the more effective application of the Food and Drugs Act. In the sphere of national issues it supported the payment of members of Parliament and limitation of the number of destitute immigrants allowed into Britain.(49)

Discussion of political theories was actively discouraged. David Holmes, president of the Weavers' Union, repeatedly insisted that his union was a labour organization whose proper function was to safeguard and improve members' employment conditions; neither individual unions nor the Trades' Council were political clubs for the propagation of new doctrines of state control of industry. Certainly some of the union officers were politically active in Burnley, but the entrenched majority link was with Liberalism. David Holmes represented Daneshouse on the Borough Council for nine years as a Liberal-Radical; Mr Strickland (secretary of the weavers' union from 1880 to 1891) was a founder-member of the Burnley Reform Club. It is true that Mr S. Wood of the miners' union was secretary to a radical society which discussed and promoted Socialism, but the majority of union leaders within the Trades' Council believed that the betterment of social conditions was achievable through the kind of legislation that the established political parties had already shown themselves willing to enact at central government level. More was to be gained by this means. It is unsurprising, given pre-constructed well-entrenched patterns of personal and party loyalties and the achievements already forthcoming through tried and tested means, that there was no immediate mass defection to the new Socialist parties.

There were, of course, *some* Socialists amongst Burnley's trade unionists, and several Socialist leaders who visited the town campaigned to increase their support, but wage-workers' persistent rejection of the new doctrines suggests that, in their own eyes, they were as capable of rationally appraising a novel political alternative as they had been of assessing the relative merits of Liberalism and Conservatism. Early Socialism was associated with extremism. There was as yet insufficient knowledge of, and familiarity with, its exponents as people, whereas the leaders of the established parties had local reputations built over many years and had shown themselves willing to preside over a gradualist process of reform which was already underway.

When a branch of the Social Democratic Federation was founded in Burnley around 1890 to propagate the theories of Karl Marx, friction between the Socialists and the trade union leaders was inevitable. The SDF took rooms in St James's Hall and arranged for prominent Socialist lecturers to visit the town. In 1891 Robert Blatchford (Nunquam of *The Clarion*) gave three lectures - on 'Discontent', 'Palliatives' and 'Revolution'. He was followed by H.W. Hobart of the London Working Men's Association and in 1892 by Keir Hardie who lectured in Brunswick on Socialist theories. There were regular open-air meetings and for some time three lectures were given each Saturday and Sunday in St James's Hall. Henry Hyndman himself, founder and leader of the SDF, came to Burnley to further the cause of Socialism. In Bennett's words:

> He was very wealthy, educated at Eton and Cambridge, rather proud and dominant and resented criticism; he always attended meetings in top hat and frock coat.(50)

Many operatives, unsurprisingly, found it difficult to identify with Hyndman on a personal level and to reconcile his espoused ideology with his background and lifestyle. Yet Hyndman's eloquence, energy and hatred of meanness won him some support amongst those Burnley operatives 'who could overlook his foibles.'(51) A Socialist Club was opened to increase support in the town - but Mr Hyndman came third each time he contested for Parliamentary election in Burnley: in 1895, 1906 and both elections in January and December of 1910. In 1895 Dan Irving came to Burnley to organize the SDF more effectively. He was the driving force behind the first Socialist demonstration in the town on May 1st of that year and, according to Bennett, arranged for a daughter of Karl Marx to lecture to local audiences. The previous year G.B. Shaw had spoken on social democracy.

In retaliation against the activities of the Socialists, a Non-Socialist Club was opened in 1894 in Union Street. A wordy warfare broke out that year when, at a gathering in Burnley, George Lansbury attacked the Labour Electoral Assembly, a national organization supported by the Radical-Liberals. By 1896 relations between the Radical-Liberal and Socialist members of the weavers' union had become so strained that the latter attempted to found a breakaway organization more explicitly political in its objectives - the New Textile Operatives' Union (Weaving Department) with its headquarters in St James's Hall. The union was short-lived, however, not least because, though there were many sympathizers, they saw their immediate priorities as best served by the long-established institutions.

Undoubtedly interest in Socialism was growing, albeit slowly, amongst Burnley's operatives, but support was split in 1897 with the founding of an alternative Socialist centre, the Burnley branch of the Independent Labour Party. From the outset the ILP vied with the Burnley branch of the Social Democratic Federation for membership - to the confusion of potential Socialist recruits. In the early years, at least, the relationship between the SDF and the ILP in Burnley was one of competition rather than collaboration; both sought to win support via the trade unions. The ILP, led nationally by Keir Hardie, had amongst its many objectives the immediate amelioration of the condition of the working classes by state action, and ultimately the complete reorganization of society on the basis of Socialist principles. The SDF, in contrast, stood for a rigid Marxism and could not work with the ILP whose principles implicitly required state legislation; nor would the SDF agree that workers should support the nominees of other political parties - the Liberals, Liberal Unionists and Conservatives - if they had no candidate of their own.

Both the ILP and SDF continued rival policies seeking to

politicize the trade unions. This proved to be a protracted uphill struggle, however; activists met with some resistance both from individual unions, particularly the weavers' union, and from the Burnley Trades' Council. It was not until 1903 that the Burnley Trades' Council took the decision to affiliate itself to a political group - not, however, to the SDF or the ILP, but to the Labour Representation Committee. Even then, the Burnley branch of the weavers' union held aloof for a further two years.

The Labour Representation Committee, founded in 1900 as a federation of trade unions and Socialist organizations, had as its objective the establishment of a Parliamentary Labour Party (the LRC became the Labour Party in 1906). By officially associating itself with the LRC the Burnley Trades' Council accepted the duty of working with the SDF and the ILP. Yet, as Bennett observes:

> . . . a lurking desire of the older Burnley trade unionists to maintain their original position was evident in the request that if Mr Hyndman was too ill to contest the next election, a Labour non-Socialist should be nominated; there was also the fear that many Labour-Radicals would not vote for a Marxist, though sponsored officially by the Labour Representation Committee.(52)

The first annual conference of the national SDF was held in Burnley in 1904 and the following year the Burnley branch of the Labour Representation Committee held its first meeting.(53) The local bond between trade unionists and the Socialists was apparently complete, yet the policy of co-ordinating the activities of all the parties of the Left did not produce the anticipated results. Socialism in Burnley continued to be bedevilled by divisions and conflict which produced political disunity amongst members of the Burnley branch of the weavers' union. In August 1908, during a trade recession which created widespread unemployment, twenty thousand operatives held a demonstration at which union officials were castigated for their refusal to increase the level of union relief benefit paid to unemployed members.

Conflict amongst the weavers affected the unity of the Burnley Trades' Council for, though the moderate majority deplored excesses, there was a strident minority who condoned and applauded the demonstrators' means, methods and objectives. Subsequently, several members of the SDF advocated secession both from the Trades' Council and the unions. These recalcitrants, dubbed the 'Impossiblists' by Dan Irving, who regarded working-class solidarity as an essential foundation upon which to build an effective political party to represent labour, attempted to set up yet another rival Socialist centre - the Burnley Branch of the Socialist Party of Great Britain.

The Branch was short-lived, but its existence did little for the already fragmented image of early Socialism; nor did the extremist rhetoric which accompanied the campaigning activities of some Socialist groups do much to attract the support of the moderate majority. In the Parliamentary election of 1906 the Liberal candidate, Mr Fred Maddison, was returned with a majority of 324 over the Conservative, Mr G.A. Arbuthnot, while Mr Hyndman was at the bottom of the poll with 4,932 votes out of a local electorate of some 16,000. Mr Hyndman was at the bottom of the poll again in the two Parliamentary elections held in January and December in 1910, the 4,948 votes he gained in January being reduced to 3,810 in December.(54)

Reactions: local politics

The dominance of Burnley's employer-led Liberal faction was contested in three main ways in the later nineteenth century. Firstly, it was challenged by members of other social strata who put themselves forward for contested election to the Town Council, the Board of Guardians, and the School Board, so that the ranks of the entrepreneurial middle-class leaders were gradually diluted by increasing numbers drawn from other sections of the middle class and, following on more slowly in their wake, by wage-workers or, more usually, their elected union officials. Secondly, it was challenged by resurgent Toryism, with an alternative political policy and, thirdly, it was challenged by the Socialist proponents of an alternative political ideology. In this section we consider the electorate's response to the political opportunities available to them.

The later years of the period witnessed the resurgence of the local Tory party led by a young, more vigorous group of political aspirants who scorned the apathy of the older generation and made a new, more decisive bid for leadership in the main agency of local government - the Town Council. A policy of 'economy' was calculated to appeal to rate-paying wage-workers, particularly those sections of the electorate most involved in recurrent industrial friction, and it was advocated by a new group of leaders whose interests were less clearly identified with the employer class. The Tory challenge was followed up, more slowly, by the challenge of an altogether new political element in the form of

Socialism. Yet the electorate continued to endorse Liberalism's hegemony in the Town Council, and the subordinate class continued to vote into office personnel drawn for the most part from superordinate social strata.

Challenge to the predominance of the entrepreneurial middle class occurred as a slow infiltration by members of other classes into positions of authority where leading employers had been so conspicuous during the 1870s and early 1880s.(55) A particularly sensitive area registering signs of change in the social composition of the leaders is the electorate's annual choice of representatives voted on to the Town Council. While the aldermen represent a strong element of continuity of personnel, since the office was held on a six-yearly basis, the annual municipal elections affecting one-third of the body of ordinary councillors allow changes in electoral preference to be more readily discernible. Table IV shows that it is only from 1893 onwards that the percentage of major employers returned annually to the Town Council follows a steady decline.(56) Only on rare occasions were more than three large employers elected at any one time after this date. There is a marked increase, however, in the participation of other sections of the middle class - of small businessmen from 1883, of shopkeepers and dealers from 1884, and of professionals from 1889.(57) Working-class participation, beginning in 1889 with the election of the president of the weavers' union, David Holmes, follows thereafter a slow and unsteady course, though press reports offering details of annual nominations indicate that from 1890 members of the working class in fact were bidding regularly, but often unsuccessfully, for election to the Town Council.(58) Along with David Holmes,(59) working-class successes, Fred Thomas,(60) John Leeming,(61) John Sparling(62) and John Tempest,(63) were all sponsored, albeit belatedly in the period, by individual unions or by the local Trades' Council.

Press accounts of nominations and election results show that it was not so much that representatives of the other classes were being elected in preference to the large employers, but that the large employers were not coming forward for election on the same scale as before.(64) Generally, it would seem to be the case that, though one or two major employers were rejected by the electorate (and these, significantly, rarely contested again), where they offered themselves as candidates, they were usually successful. Conversely, though later in the period working men contested quite vigorously, often supported by their unions, by the Trades' Council or by local Socialist groups, their election was comparatively rare before 1914.(65) Working-class candidates had earlier electoral successes on the School Board and on the Board of Guardians, but here, too, their proportional representation *vis-à-vis* other social classes was extremely small. David Holmes was elected to the School Board in 1883(66) and by 1892 had become the town's first 'working-class JP'.(67) John Leeming, miners' agent, had been elected to the School Board by 1892 and was joined there by John Sparling in 1898.(68) Significant also in the period was the appearance of women in elections. In the 1890s Lady O'Hagan was elected to the School Board and the Board of Guardians, and on the latter body she was joined subsequently by doctors' wives, Mrs Robb and Mrs Brown.(69)

The gradual decline of active interest in municipal affairs on the part of the large employers is difficult to explain and it seems likely that several factors were involved. A long period of intermittent but persistent industrial friction may ultimately have affected their willingness to submit themselves to any unpleasantness or harassment which might occur in the process of electioneering, so that new men were sometimes deterred from following in the footsteps of the older generation of leaders. Additionally, with the spread of limited liability and the joint stock form of company organization,(70) a number of employers left their business interests in the hands of professional managers and moved away from the area, losing direct contact with the town's affairs. In the case of the Masseys, for example, C.J. Massey moved to Scotland, and then to Clitheroe, and, though he maintained contact with many of his friends in the town, the long tradition of Massey participation in local politics was broken.(71) In the case of the Barnes family, though less is known, at least part of the family had settled in Southport by the end of the period. At this time, Miss Barnes, whose generosity was proverbial, was sending donations to various causes in Burnley from her home in this fashionable seaside resort.(72) Occasionally also, the older class of leaders had by the end of the period moved up from small town politics into higher circles. The Dugdales, for example, whose Lowerhouse mill colony had by 1889 been absorbed within the larger area of the town as a result of urban spread and the extension of the borough boundaries, had moved into the county magistracy, and at least one member of the family had developed business interests in the Lancashire and Yorkshire Railway Company.(73)

It would be erroneous, however, to overstate the decline of the traditional employer class. What requires explanation perhaps, is not so much why their numbers gradually declined, but rather why they lingered on as leaders for so long in Burnley while their demise was so clearly evident in other towns such as Darwen.(74) In 1903 Burnley Town Council contained no less than four members of the highly influential Thornber family who ran one of the town's largest textile businesses.(75) More significantly, the employers long retained their hold on municipal affairs as aldermen, an earlier employer clique giving way later in the period to a new clique of similar social composition as the veterans retired or died.(76) Whereas in earlier years, aldermen were representatives of family firms, in later years they were sometimes directors of limited companies, as in the case of Elijah Keighley, J.M. Grey and E. Whitehead.(77) In Burnley, in the short term at least, limited liability and the joint stock form did not necessarily preclude participation in local politics. In addition, friction in industrial relations, though it may in part account for the apparent reluctance of the entrepreneurial middle class to offer themselves for election on the same scale as before, was nevertheless not associated with the wholesale rejection of them as a class by the electorate.

The period was one of long Liberal predominance in the Town Council. There were several years when the Conservative bid for office met with scant success, followed by a six-year period of uncontested elections. The electorate was, therefore, left with reduced choice at election time, but the withdrawal of the Tories is in itself a reflection of the well-established and apparently immutable political preference of the vote-casting public. The abdication from the Town Council of the Tory faction in 1877, led by Robert Handsley, John Butterworth, George Haslam, Adam Dugdale and John Greenwood,(78) left the municipal stage almost entirely to the Liberals, collectively committed to what the Tory opposition represented as a 'big-spending' policy. Some of the more influential Tories - the Thursbys, the Scarletts and Colonel Starkie, who were all actively involved in county matters - were uninterested in direct participation in municipal government.

The long period of Tory apathy was brought to an end in 1883 when there began a new, more purposeful and dynamic Tory challenge led by a younger, more vigorous element exasperated with the apathetic inaction of the older generation of leaders, some of whom had gravitated to the ranks of the county magistracy.(79) The first political challenge to the Liberals, therefore, came from Liberalism's traditional middle-class rival. Resurgent Toryism offered to the borough electorate an alternative policy, clearly outlined in the *Burnley Express*.(80) Its policy in the municipal sphere was 'economy', and though based upon the policy line of the older local leaders, it was now propounded with a new, more forceful, collective determination in a bid to rally the support of working-class ratepayers and of the drink trade. Preliminary successes in 1882 and 1883(81) were followed by strenuous propagandist campaigns in 1884 when the pro-Tory *Burnley Express* published a special election issue. In 1883 the Tories had contested six out of the eight wards.(82) An editorial in the *Burnley Express* of that year stated:

> It is many years since the municipal elections in Burnley were fought as they were on Thursday. Hitherto, the Conservative party has been content to allow the Liberals undisputed possession of all seats in the Council and both parties have grown so accustomed to that state of things that the Liberal monopoly had come to be regarded as a natural consequence . . .. The very announcement of a determination to contest their [Liberal] claim to such a right has been looked on as little less than an insult . . .. Previous Conservative neglect of their duty to the constituency [was] due to disheartedness in successive disasters or to lethargy in the belief that Burnley is overwhelmingly Radical . . .. This deplorable state of things has been allowed to prevail for an almost incredible length of time, but recently it was decided to make an attempt to rectify the situation.(83)

In 1884, the Conservatives contested all eight wards for the first time since 1868. Liberal astonishment at the temerity of these young Tory upstarts was expressed in a heavily sarcastic editorial in the pro-Liberal *Burnley Gazette*:

> These new young Tories are going in for a majority and for winning back all the wards! They are fighting the Liberals all along the line - in every ward! They aim to fill the whole Council with Tories!(84)

The mid-1880s, therefore, saw the beginning of a new, sustained determination on the part of the Tory faction to challenge Liberal predominance. 1884 marks the start of the long Conservative fightback to extend their support base amongst the voting public and to gain a voice in municipal affairs.(85)

In the local context the Tories were the 'economy' party. They now began a series of publicity campaigns to arouse indignation about the 'mismanagement of ratepayers' money' and what they claimed to be exorbitant rates necessitated by the 'high-spending' policy which the Liberals had embarked upon. An extravagantly expensive and largely unnecessary Town Hall, the 'newest corporation undertaking . . . in the Municipal Building Craze,'(86) was likely, it was claimed, to add to the town's debts. In recent years, rates had 'already risen from 1s.0d. to 3s.10d. in the pound, and were likely to soar higher.'(87) An attack was made upon the new rates for public houses. Examples from a lengthy list quoted in the *Burnley Express* included:

> the Cross Keys whose rates had risen from £93 10s. 0d. to £187 0s. 0d.; the St Leger whose rates had risen from £46 0s. 0d. to £113 0s. 0d.; the Clock Face whose rates had risen from £50 0s. 0d. to £119 0s. 0d.; and the Boot Inn whose rates had risen from £59 10s. 0d. to £103 0s. 0d.(88)

At the same time much was made of the 'injustice' of the current rating system which favoured employer-owned mills, workshops, sheds and other work premises compared with the cottages, dwelling-houses, licensed public houses and shops. The less affluent were required to pay a disproportionately large share of the town's total rates bill.(89) Thomas Hargreaves, a leading figure in the Tory resurgence, drew attention to the philanthropy of the Tory Thursbys, 'unmatched in the area and apparently going unheeded and unrewarded by townsmen who had benefited for years from the family's munificence.'(90) The Tory press mounted both political and personal attacks upon the Liberal Council, and it is evident that the hitherto somnolent Tory party was now fully awake to its public duties.

This new assertiveness was not rewarded with sweeping successes at the polls, however.(91) For nearly a decade, the Tories had to be content with relatively modest gains, mainly in the 'church wards' of St Peter's, Trinity and St James's - a reflection of the link between Anglicanism and Toryism. From 1890, the number of Tories returned in annual municipal elections increased somewhat, though their numbers rarely exceeded those of the Liberals.(92) What is significant here is that, though there was no wholesale defection to the Tories, the party did not capitulate. 1884 marks the beginning of a long, steady and sustained Tory fight back in which annual elections were consistently contested in most wards.(93) That the electorate had the opportunity and the means to eject the Liberals but refrained from doing so suggests that most people were content with the political *status quo*. In addition to ongoing complaints about Liberal extravagance there were, later in the period, accusations of discrimination; in Tory wards, Councillor Slater alleged, it was difficult to get anything done for the resident ratepayers, and the drink trade was 'persecuted' because 'the Town Council was in the grips of the Temperance Party.'(94)

There was no immediate landslide to the Tory ranks, but by

the end of the period Tory persistence had had some effect. In 1900, as we have seen, the town elected its first Tory MP(95) - a local cotton manufacturer, William Mitchell, who had interests in several of the town's largest mills. From 1900 till the outbreak of World War I, in fact, Burnley had an alternating succession of Conservative and Liberal MPs,(96) which suggests that within the constituency Conservative and Liberal support was now more or less evenly balanced. Conservative gains in the Town Council brought a Conservative mayor, Albert Carrington, in 1904 and by 1905, there were two Conservative aldermen out of the twelve who led the Council.(97)

The extent to which the changing proportion of Tory personnel in the Town Council was reflected in an increasingly modified Liberal policy in municipal affairs is difficult to assess. In the 1890s, according to press comments, the Tories used their powers less effectively than they might. As it was observed in the *Burnley Gazette* in 1892:

> The cry of 'economy' has always been the electioneering cant of the Tory party at the Municipal Elections but . . . that there is no sincerity in it is evident from the fact that they never bring it to its test by any specific charges and never show in any single instance where the Tories have opposed any unnecessary expenditure which has been carried against Tory votes by a Liberal majority . . .. They simply raise the cry at election time and then their masterly inactivity in the Town Council shows how hollow and insincere is their zeal in local elections.(98)

Perhaps the best measure of ongoing Liberal influence in the borough is the change which had occurred in the policy of the School Board by 1890. Throughout the 1870s and 1880s more or less equal numbers of Tory Anglicans and Liberal Nonconformists had collaborated in a mutually agreed policy of keeping elementary education under denominational control(99) and, while several new schools had been built, none of these had been built by the Board as such.(100) By 1890, however, the ideas of the Church and Nonconformist elements on the School Board were clearly divergent. While the Church Party continued to advocate a policy of denominational control, the Nonconformists began to urge a policy of taking over voluntary schools, if this was the wish of the managers, and of providing state-controlled Board Schools. The two rival factions were now clearly identified in the press as the 'Voluntarists' and the 'Progressives'.(101) The Socialist, Dan Irving, now a member of the School Board, joined forces with the Progressives and, though he played a significant role in the pressure group for non-denominational schools, it is clear that it was the Liberal Nonconformists who provided the group's numerical voting strength on the Board against the Anglican Tories.

The first member to come out clearly as an advocate of Board Schools was John Baron, a Liberal Methodist, who in 1883 had refused to serve a further three-year term on the Board in protest at the failure to build two Board schools as recommended by the Education Department. The Board, he alleged, was a 'mere attendance committee.'(102) In the years which followed, a Liberal non-sectarian member of the Board, weavers' union president, David Holmes, consistently argued the merits of state education(103) and by the end of the 1880s the two factions were opposed. Though the voluntary schools continued to be the main providers of elementary education, the Progressive policy was clearly behind the building of the first two Board schools in the early 1890s.(104) Thereafter, there was an increasing tendency for the Board to take over the elementary schools of the less affluent Nonconformist sects.(105) Until the 1890s, the Board had consistently refused requests to do so.(106)

It would seem, therefore, that, whereas Tory representation did not appear decisively to redirect or modify Liberal policy in the Town Council, the change in Liberal Nonconformist attitudes on the question of education was of major significance in modifying the School Board's policy from the early 1890s.

Late in the period the embryonic Socialist parties offered the electorate a third option in elections for the Town Council. Socialist ideologies took root more readily amongst the younger, more militant trade unionists opposed to the conciliatory pro-Liberal political stance of the older generation of union leaders. The first working-class Socialists began to infiltrate the various elected bodies of the town in the 1890s. Significantly, the first Socialist on the Town Council, John Tempest,(107) was attacked most strongly in the Council Chamber by weavers' agent, David Holmes,(108) who, as a working-class representative of the older generation, conformed to the local traditional pattern of allegiance to the Liberals.

The Socialist cause in Burnley, as we have seen, was given considerable impetus by the visits of national leaders. In 1891 for example, Robert Blatchford, or 'Nunquam' of *The Clarion*, and H.W. Hobart of the London Working Men's Association, addressed rallies in Burnley.(109) The following year, Keir Hardie lectured in Burnley on Socialist theories and open-air meetings(110) were held regularly on Saturdays and Sundays when local and national activists worked systematically to increase support. The charismatic Henry Hyndman, founder and leader of the SDF, was in the town in 1894(111) when a number of Socialist clubs were formed. The following year, Dan Irving, national secretary of the SDF, came to Burnley, took up residence in the town as Socialist leader and organizer and rapidly developed an active interest in local politics.(112) In the 1890s also, propagandist lectures were delivered in Burnley by Ben Tillett of the London Dockers' Union and in later years by Margaret Bondfield, George Lansbury, H.R. Taylor of the London Trades' Council, Philip Snowdon and Ramsey MacDonald himself.(113)

Sustained local organizational identity was at first difficult to attain, however. Socialism was for some years fragmented; separate factions competed for support and on occasions even contested against each other in local elections.(114) Socialist banners under which working men fought in municipal elections included the SDF, the ILP, the Labour Electoral Association, the Trades' Council, the Labour Representation Committee, the Co-operative Society, and the Socialist Party of Great Britain which represented a revolutionary kind of Socialism(115) - to the confusion of the electorate and the exasperation of the seasoned leadership of the established, 'respectable' middle-class parties. Moreover, the association of Socialism with the more extremist and volatile element amongst the unions was calculated to excite suspicion rather than confidence amongst rational moderate-minded wage-workers.(116)

Dan Irving, who arrived in 1895, provided the town with a resident, experienced campaigner, and around him there emerged a nucleus of Socialist leaders consisting mainly of trade union officers: John Battle, John Tempest, John Sparling and Thomas Etherington.(117) These activists worked more systematically to spread Socialist theories amongst their fellow unionists and to extend Socialist influence in the town by contesting elections to the School Board, the Board of Guardians and the Town Council. Rallies, meetings and lectures were regularly but briefly reported in the press, and nomination lists indicate that from 1890 Socialists were regularly bidding for election to the Town Council.(118)

Successes were elusive, however. The first Socialists on the Council, John Tempest of the weavers' association and John Sparling of the miners' union, were elected in 1892(119) but neither was re-elected in 1895.(120) In 1902 Dan Irving and D. Jones, a grocer, were elected as Socialists(121) and the following year they were joined by Fred Thomas(122) of the Trades' Council, but generally successes were few and far between.(123) It is evident from Table IV, that though the Socialist challenge was both vigorous and persistent and, by the end of the 1890s, more efficiently organized, the electorate was not readily won over by its ideology. On the School Board and the Board of Guardians, also, successes were equally sparse. Dan Irving, for example, had secured his election to the Board of Guardians by 1901,(124) and to the School Board by 1898(125) along with John Sparling, but it is apparent that Socialists present on such a small scale in the various elected bodies, stood little chance of modifying existing local policies or of imposing their own policies on other members of the boards.

The Socialist challenge in local affairs was paralleled by the Socialist bid for Parliamentary representation in general elections beginning in 1895 with Henry Hyndman.(126) By 1906 and 1910 Hyndman had secured a larger body of political support in the town,(127) but the Socialists did not capture Parliamentary representation in the town until 1918 when Dan Irving became Burnley's first Socialist MP(128) after residing in the town for more than two decades.

It is evident, therefore, that though the dominant Liberal faction was challenged in the period, firstly, by resurgent Toryism in the mid-1880s and, secondly, in the late 1880s and 1890s by Socialism, Liberalism proved to be remarkably resilient to the end of the century. The Liberals were not ejected *en masse* from their positions on the Town Council, School Board, Board of Guardians and so on, though their ranks were gradually diluted by increasing numbers of Tories and the first few Socialists to secure the confidence of the electorate. Throughout the period Liberal policy and Liberal influence were clearly reflected in the political composition of the aldermen.(129) The subsequent pattern of general election results from 1900 to 1914(130) signified, erroneously, that the Tories rather than the Socialists were to be the more formidable opponent in the future.

Part of the explanation for subordinates' acquiescence in the prevailing socio-political order is to be found in the circumstances outlined in this chapter.

In the sphere of Parliamentary representation, arguments premised upon local preference for local candidates are plausible but unsustainable. It is true that two successful contestants, Richard Shaw and William Mitchell, were both Burnley men - but so were J.O.S. Thursby and John Greenwood, both of whom were unsuccessful. That Shaw and Mitchell were Liberals while Thursby and Greenwood were Tories suggests a strong working-class preference for the Liberal party, possibly because of that party's willingness to introduce reforms which benefited the less privileged. But in other industrial towns in the region it was the Tories who won majority support; they too had a proven record of concern with the social welfare of the disadvantaged. The Socialist newcomers had not yet had the chance to prove their worth, and were still at the stage of persuading people to allow them the opportunity to do so.

Burnley people's preference in Parliamentary elections reflected their choice in elections to the Town Council; there too, as we have seen, Liberalism was the majority choice. Many Liberal councillors were leading figures in the party's political clubs, they were involved in the selection and nomination processes, and they were active in canvassing support for their chosen candidate in general elections. It may be the case, therefore, that those whom the electorate trusted with the task of decision-making at the local level of government were accepted as capable of sound judgment in the choice of Parliamentary candidates; if the Liberals performed efficiently in local government, they were likely to perform satisfactorily in central government.

This seems sensible enough - but it returns us to the task of explaining the majority preference at the local level. Many of the men voted on to the Town Council were employers. Though there was much cooperation, goodwill and community spirit, workplace relationships were nonetheless conceptualized in oppositional terms; yet recurrent, often embittered industrial conflict imbued with class consciousness was not at this stage projected into the political sphere. Dissatisfaction with some of the decisions of the Town Council was expressed, not via the unions as such, but by union men who formed a pressure group, the Ratepayers' Association, designed for the purpose of expressing a specific set of grievances which were not employment-related. The issues were thus compartmentalized. Significantly, the electorate continued to vote Liberal employers into local government. Part of the answer undoubtedly lies in the fact that the leaders were men who were well-known either personally or reputationally for the services they performed in dimensions of community life other than the workplace, not least the voluntary social services they undertook through the agency of the religious institutions. The churches and chapels had effective channels of communication with townspeople through the medium of education, recreation, philanthropy and social welfare including pastoral care. In Burnley these links were more extensive in the case of the Nonconformist chapels than those of the Anglican churches. In the case of the chapels, relationships were less formal.

The social distance between the leaders and the led was narrower. The leaders themselves were less remote and the extent of social interaction with the disprivileged was greater.

Certainly there were occasions of protest both within and without the workplace. More significant, however, was the general level of acquiescence in the socio-political structure, an acquiescence which underlies the prolonged predominance of the Liberal employers in positions of decision-making authority in Burnley. The argument outlined above may go some way in explaining the phenomenon, but we need to consider other possibilities before our conclusions are reached. Can the general response be represented as deferential? Did the religious, educational and recreational services provided 'from above' have the effect of socializing subordinates in attitudes, aspirations and expectations deemed desirable by the providers? Did subordinates surrender to the ideology of submission?

References

1. Walton, J.K., *Lancashire: A Social History, 1558-1939*, Manchester University Press, 1987, ch. 12.

2. *Ibid.*, p. 241.

3. *Ibid.*, pp. 241-2.

4. Bennett, W., *The History of Burnley*, Burnley Corporation, 1951, iv, p. 98.

5. Walton, J.K., *op. cit.*, p. 241.

6. *Ibid.*, p. 242.

7. *Ibid.*, p. 243.

8. Augar, P., 'The Cotton Famine, 1861-65', D.Phil. thesis, University of Oxford, 1979; Oddy, D.J., 'Urban Famine in Nineteenth Century Britain', *Economic History Review*, 2nd Series, 1983, p. 36.

9. Russell, A., 'Élites at the Local Level of Society: Social Leadership in Burnley, 1870-1900', M.A. dissertation, University of Lancaster, 1976; Trodd, G., 'Political Change and the Working Class in Blackburn and Burnley, 1880-1914', Ph.D. thesis, University of Lancaster, 1978.

10. Joyce, P., 'The Factory Politics of Lancashire in the Later Nineteenth Century', *Historical Journal*, XVIII, 1975, pp. 525-53; see also Joyce, P., *Work, Society and Politics: The Culture of*

the Factory in Later Victorian England, Harvester, 1980; Trodd, G., *op. cit.*

11. Many details of industrial relations confrontations are to be found in Bennett, W., *op. cit.*, ch. 6, and in Trodd, G., *op. cit.* For information on cotton and coal and the initiatives of Socialist activists in pursuit of working-class support via the unions see the excellent coverage in Howell, D., *British Workers and the Independent Labour Party, 1888-1906*, Manchester University Press, 1983, especially ch. 1.

12. Walton, J.K., *op. cit.*, p. 252; Dutton, H.I. and King, J.E., *Ten Per Cent and No Surrender: The Preston Strike 1853-4*, Cambridge University Press, 1981, pp. 54-5.

13. Walton, J.K., *op. cit.*, pp. 252-3; King, J.E., ' "We Could Eat the Police:" Popular Violence in the North Lancashire Cotton Strike of 1878', *Victorian Studies*, XXVIII, No. 3, 1985, pp. 439-71.

14. Walton, J.K., *op. cit.*, p. 264; Joyce, P., *Work, Society and Politics* . . ., p. 311; . Clarke, P.F., *Lancashire and the New Liberalism*, Cambridge University Press, 1971, pp. 84-5.

15. Turner, H.A., *Trade Union Growth, Structure and Policy*, Allen & Unwin, 1962, p. 127; Clarke, P.F., *op. cit.*, pp. 84-8; Watson, M.I., 'The Cotton Trade Unions and Labour Representation in the Late Nineteenth Century', *Northern History*, XX, 1984, pp. 207-16.

16. Joyce, P., *Work, Society and Politics* . . .

17. Walton, J.K., *op. cit.*, p. 265.

18. Bennett, W., *op. cit.*, p. 128.

19. *Ibid.*, pp. 128-9.

20. *Ibid.*

21. *Burnley Gazette*, 12 Oct. 1889.

22. Bennett, W., *op. cit.*, p. 143.

23. *Ibid.*, p. 75; *Burnley Gazette*, 28 May 1892, 1 June 1892, 4 June 1892 and 6 Aug. 1892.

24. *Burnley Gazette*, 28 May 1892 and 1 June 1892.

25. *Ibid.*

26. *Ibid.*, 28 May 1892.

27. *Ibid.*

28. *Ibid.*

29. *Ibid.*

30. *Ibid.*

31. *Ibid.*, 1 June 1892.

32. Bennett, W., *op. cit.*, pp. 79-94.

33. Editorial in *Burnley Gazette*, 6 April 1877.

34. *Ibid.*

35. *Burnley Gazette*, 1 Nov. 1884.

36. *Ibid.*

37. Figures for 1887 in Bennett, W., *op. cit.*, p. 97.

38. *Ibid.*, pp. 81-3.

39. *Ibid.*; see also Finance Committee Reports in *Minutes* of meetings of Burnley Town Council.

40. Bennett, W., *op. cit.*, p. 73.

41. Walton, J.K., *op. cit.*, p. 259.

42. *Ibid.*, p. 258.

43. Developments lucidly summarized *ibid.*, pp. 258-62.

44. Bennett, W., *op. cit.*, p. 137.

45. Many factual details of elections in nineteenth-century Burnley, *ibid.*, ch. 8; see also Trodd, G., *op. cit.*

46. Appendix, Table VI.

47. Bennett, W., *op. cit.*, ch. 8; Trodd, G., *op. cit.*

48. Bennett, W., *op. cit.*, ch. 8; Russell, A., *op. cit.*

49. Trodd, G., *op. cit.*; Bennett, W., *op. cit.*, ch. 8.

50. Bennett, W., *op. cit.*, p. 144.

51. *Ibid.*

52. *Ibid.*, p. 145.

53. *Ibid.*, p. 143.

54. Appendix, Table VI.

55. Appendix, Table I.

56. Appendix, Table IV.

57. *Ibid.*

58. *Ibid.*

59. Bennett, W., *op. cit.*, p. 128.

60. Fred Thomas elected in 1903: see election results in *Burnley Gazette*, 3 Nov. 1903.

61. John Leeming also elected in 1903: see *Burnley Gazette*, 3 Nov. 1903.

62. John Sparling elected in 1893: see election results in *Burnley Gazette*, 5 Nov. 1893.

63. John Tempest also elected in 1893: see election results *ibid.*

64. Annual publication in October press issues of nomination lists shows a declining interest on the part of major employers; see trend in Appendix, Table IV.C.

65. Appendix, Table IV.B.

66. Young, M.E., 'Burnley School Board, 1871-1891', M.Ed. dissertation, University of Manchester, 1973.

67. Bennett, W., *op. cit.*, p. 128; *Men of Burnley: Press Cuttings, 1863-5, loc. cit.*

68. Appendix, Table IX.

69. Burnley Board of Guardians, *Minutes* of meetings in late-nineteenth century, *loc. cit.*

70. Bennett, W., *op. cit.*, p. 98.

71. *Men of Burnley: Press Cuttings, 1961-3, loc. cit.*

72. The Barnes family does not appear in *Worrall's Directory* of 1896.

73. Hall, H., *Lowerhouse and the Dugdales: A Study of a Lancashire Mill Community*, Burnley and District Historical Society, undated, p. 16.

74. Doyle, M.B., 'Social Control in Over Darwen, 1839-78', M.A. dissertation, University of Lancaster, 1972.

75. *Minutes* of Burnley Town Council, 1903.

76. Appendix, Table V.

77. *Ibid.*

78. *Burnley Express*, 25 Oct. 1877.

79. Regular accounts in *Burnley Express* and *Burnley Gazette* of Magistrates' Court proceedings.

80. *Burnley Express: Special Election Issue*, 30 Oct. 1884.

81. Appendix, Table IV.B.

82. *Ibid.*

83. *Burnley Express*, 3 Nov. 1884.

84. *Burnley Gazette*, 26 Oct. 1884.

85. Cornford, J., 'The Transformation of Conservatism in the Late Nineteenth Century', *Victorian Studies*, VII, No. 1, 1963, pp. 35-66, identifies the mid-1880s as a period when the Tories were bidding more decisively in urban constituencies generally for election to local and central institutions of government.

86. *Burnley Express: Special Election Issue*, 30 Oct. 1884.

87. *Ibid.*

88. *Ibid.*

89. *Ibid.*

90. *Ibid.*

91. Appendix, Table IV.B.

92. *Ibid.*

93. *Ibid.*

94. *Burnley Gazette*, 6 Aug. 1892.

95. Appendix, Table VI.

96. *Ibid.*

97. Appendix, Table V.

98. *Burnley Gazette*, 29 Oct. 1892.

99. Young, M.E., *op. cit.*

100. Bennett, W., *op. cit.*, pp. 169-70.

101. *Burnley Gazette*, 5 Jan. 1895; Appendix, Table IX.

102. Young, M.E., *op. cit.*

103. *Ibid.*

104. Bennett, W., *op. cit.*, p. 176.

105. *Ibid.*

106. Young, M.E., *op. cit.* In the 1880s the School Board had refused John Baron's offer of the Methodist Iron School.

107. Bennett, W., *op. cit.*, ch. 8; *Burnley Gazette*, 3 Nov. 1893.

108. Bennett, W., *op. cit.*, p. 144.

109. *Ibid.*, p. 143.

110. *Ibid.*

111. *Ibid.*, p. 144.

112. *Ibid.*, p. 147.

113. *Ibid.*, pp. 143-6.

114. Reports of elections in *Burnley Gazette*, 4 Nov. 1908, 3 Nov. 1909 and 5 Nov. 1911.

115. Appendix, Table IV.B.

116. *Burnley Gazette*, 21 Oct. 1903. A Socialist supporter appeared before the Borough Magistrates after a physical assault on the person of Councillor Macfarlane whom the assailant accused of 'continually insulting Dan Irving in the Council Chamber'.

117. Names recur in lists of nominations in October issues of *Burnley Gazette* and *Burnley Express* in the 1890s.

118. Appendix, Table IV.B.

119. *Burnley Gazette*, 2 Nov. 1892.

120. *Ibid.*, 3 Nov. 1895.

121. *Burnley Express*, 5 Nov. 1902.

122. *Ibid.*, 4 Nov. 1903.

123. Appendix, Table IV.B.

124. Bennett, W., *op. cit.*, p. 147.

125. *Ibid.*

126. *Ibid.*, p. 253; Appendix, Table VI.

127. *Ibid.*

128. *Ibid.*

129. Appendix, Table V.
130. Appendix, Table VI.

6

The Lower Class Response
Radical or Deferential?

Introduction

Members of the entrepreneurial middle class appeared in disproportionately large numbers in the social structure of power and influence in urban industrial communities during the 1870s and 1880s. Their ability to maintain social control may have been facilitated by mechanisms enabling the leaders to socialize subordinates into a particular set of attitudes, aspirations and values. In this chapter we consider the lower-class response, in particular we consider whether it can be convincingly construed as 'radical' or whether it is more appropriately described as 'deferential'. The task is not straightforward since reactions varied according to changes in prevailing economic circumstances in the particular industry.

Terms, definitions, concepts and the historical evidence

It is necessary at the outset to define terms. The events and circumstances outlined in the foregoing chapters raise the problem of selecting an appropriate label to attach to the general response of the less privileged to the leaders' authority, given the somewhat contradictory strands in the evidence. Although the relationship between borough leaders and their local communities contained an element of friction, erupting into sporadic often barely controlled violence, it would be a distortion of the evidence to represent the overall perspective as one of 'continuous challenge' and a 'fluctuating but ever-present class warfare.'(1) A radical normative system, implicit in the terminology adopted by Dutton and King and inferred in the confrontational emphasis placed upon the events and circumstances they describe, would embody its own distinctive ideology and promote an alternative view of

180

society, involving principled rejection of, and organized opposition to, the prevailing structure of advantage and disadvantage. Lower-class reactions and responses in neither Burnley nor Preston nor other northern industrial towns covered in the present investigation suggest the emergence of a clearly identifiable radical value system drawing upon a set of precepts fundamentally opposed to those underlying the institutions of capitalism. According to Parkin, the social and generating milieu of the radical normative order is the mass political party based on the subordinate class.(2) In Burnley the borough electorate's apparently lukewarm interest in the policies of emergent Socialist groups and its ongoing preference for Liberal representation argue that, if radical values were espoused, they were not as yet widely disseminated. As we have seen, attempts were made by the Social Democratic Federation to win support. A local branch, founded in 1890, organized rallies and weekend lectures; visiting celebrity speakers included Keir Hardie, Robert Blatchford, Henry Hyndman and H.W. Hobart of the London Working Men's Association. However, despite the campaigning efforts of the early Socialist leaders and the availability of an alternative ideology, extensive electoral support for a Socialist political party in local and general elections was not a feature of Burnley politics until the twentieth century.

As far as can be ascertained, the relevance of an alternative mode of production based on workers' cooperatives does not seem to have generated extensive enthusiasm, and success for experimental cooperative enterprises proved elusive. Two worker-owned cooperative factories in Padiham, the Padiham Cooperative Cotton Society founded as early as 1848 by several hundred workers in the township peripheral to Burnley, and the Padiham Cotton League Company begun in 1862, both failed within a few years. A similar fate befell worker cooperatives within Burnley itself. The Burnley Cooperative Textile Society, formed in 1863, was scuppered by the 'cotton famine' and was eventually wound up in 1870. The Burnley Self-Help Manufacturing Society, founded in 1886 'to obtain for workers a greater interest in their labour,' failed in 1898 allegedly as a result of bad trade, jealousy between the different sections of workpeople and over-ambitious policy objectives. Two other worker cooperatives survived for an even shorter period. The Whittlefield Self-Help Company, formed late in 1887, took over 542 looms from J.H. Whitaker. The seven-year-old looms, valued at eight pounds each, were to be purchased over a period of four years by quarterly instalments. The Calder Vale Self-Help Company, formed in April 1888, acquired, again from J.H. Whitaker, 1,000 looms plus the Ashfield shed which housed them. Both of these enterprises failed in 1889 apparently because of falling prices during a trade depression. The Whittlefield Company lost £700 in the first six months of its existence and the Calder Vale Company lost £250 in four months. No more success attended the productive efforts of the Burnley Industrial Manufacturing Society with its 400 looms installed at Rake Head Mill. A scattering of other examples(3) could be cited but such would add little to the general observation that these experiments offered minimal challenge to the system prevailing locally. They appear to have been set up as economic expedients to preserve jobs under threat rather than as ideologically motivated impulses to confront and ultimately to supersede capitalist enterprise.

It was not only in Burnley that Socialism faced an uphill struggle. In Accrington the Independent Labour Party sponsored its first four Socialist candidates (including two miners, a stonemason and a shopkeeper) for election to municipal government as early as 1893(4) but not until the twentieth century, with the election of the first labour representative to the Town Council in 1905, did Socialist influence begin to make its mark under the political banner of the Social Democratic Federation. Ashton's Trades' Council fielded its first candidates in borough elections in 1892 when it contested all four of the town's wards, but not until 1911 was a Trades' Council candidate successful.(5) Even at this stage political attitudes tended to be ambivalent, however; the decision on affiliation to the Labour Representation Committee appears to have been delayed innumerable times between 1902 and 1911 and it is noteworthy that, despite anxieties expressed as early as 1888(6) about Ashton's backwardness compared with Bolton and Oldham in promoting worker representation in local elections, the Trades' Council had refused support for an ILP-sponsored candidate in the 1895 general election.(7)

If, as is argued here, generalizations implying the mass espousal of radical ideologies in these years are inappropriate, interpretations which, at the other extreme, appear to suggest the widespread presence of deference are equally questionable. The employers' influence, although extensive, was not total. Although for the most part the operatives' response to employers' political leadership was compliant, it cannot convincingly be construed as deferential.

In recent years the elastic manner in which the term 'deferential' has been applied to 'variegated and sometimes conflicting data' in the sphere of political investigation leads Kavanagh to suggest that 'it has outlived its usefulness as a term in academic currency.'(8) Newby and Bell, concerned with the investigation of broader social relationships rather than of narrowly political responses, urge the need for more precise usage(9) and, following Parkin, prefer to apply the term to 'individuals who endorse a moral order which legitimates their own political, material and social subordination.'(10)

Deferentials internalize the value system promoted by the dominant group, the dominant values in this context representing the perceptions and interests of the relatively privileged. Dominant values tend more obviously to represent the perceptions held by those in positions of authority; those groups who occupy the most powerful positions will also tend to have strategic access to the formal and informal means of legitimation. Deference results when the dominant class has been especially successful in imposing its own definition of social order on the less privileged.(11)

The deferential worker accepts as legitimate the dominant group's claim to leadership by virtue of the latter's inherently superior qualities and attributes, and endorses the group's view of his own subordinate position in the socio-economic structure as morally right. Inequality in the prevailing reward system with its pattern of privilege and deprivation, power and dependency, is viewed as both inevitable and just.(12) There are implications here for class relationships, for 'the more completely the subordinate class comes to endorse and internalize the dominant system, the less serious will be the conflicts over existing inequalities.'(13)

The dominant normative order is more likely to be internalized where there is extensive face-to-face experience of the economic, social and political judgments of dominant class members as, for example, in relatively isolated rural communities or small towns with well-established status systems based upon occupational community. 'Local status systems,' explains Lockwood, 'operate to give the individual a very definite sense of position in a hierarchy of prestige in which each "knows his place" and nothing in the prevailing circumstances causes him to question the appropriateness of his exchange of deference for paternalism.'(14) In a small community, with only limited contact with the outside world, a strong sense of localism develops and this fortifies the dominant group's attempt to impose a consistent and coherent set of ideas which buttress the legitimacy of its authority.(15) Newby, investigating deference amongst agricultural workers, draws attention to the effect of 'isolation' and 'totality' on the individual's perception of social reality; where the worker's subordination is a total one across all his many roles, he is all the more likely to internalize the dominant value system. The 'limited horizons' and restricted outside contacts of the village dweller serve to insulate him from influences offering alternative definitions of hierarchy and status.(16)

Although never completely cut off from external social influences in the nineteenth century, a sufficiently self-contained and total institutional framework was created in some villages so as to render the ideological hegemony of paternalist authority very extensive. However, caution warns against facile explanations which simplistically infer that the quiescent social and political behaviour frequently encountered in relatively isolated rural communities derives from deference. Quiescence may stem from genuine consensus. Alternatively, it may be the product of powerlessness rather than deference. A subordinate may have 'acknowledged this powerlessness and decided to make the best of his inferior situation, contriving to take it somewhat for granted while not necessarily endorsing it in terms of social justice' or feeling a genuine ideological commitment to the moral order of the superordinate stratum.(17)

The economic and social context of Burnley, of Joyce's Blackburn and of most sizeable industrial towns in the era fails to conform sufficiently closely to the type of environment most conducive to the propagation of deference; indeed, subordinate groups displayed certain deviant behaviour characteristics at times which the dominant group was hard-pressed to check. The multi-faceted authority of leading employers was widespread but, despite any socializing function performed by religious and educational agencies and the more explicitly coercive social control activities of police authorities concerned with the maintenance of law and order, there appear to be grounds to doubt that the internalization of dominant values occurred on a significantly wide scale.

Like Dutton and King's textile workers of Preston, Burnley workpeople engaged in the major industries in the locality do not seem to have comprehended the socio-economic framework in a unitary sense. Within the workplace they clearly viewed the relationship between employer and employee in dichotomous terms and convincing evidence of continuous, organic, harmonious unity is elusive. The existence of trade unions representing workers' economic interests, which are therefore potentially and often actually opposed to those of the employers, emphasizes social division and conceptualizes a conflict model of the reward structure which is clearly at odds with interpretations seeking to establish outright endorsement of the dominant code.

The Burnley branch of the East Lancashire Weavers' Association, for example, after a somewhat precarious existence earlier, was re-established in August 1870 and thence maintained permanent organizational identity to the end of the century, surviving even the violent clashes with established authority in 1878. The miners' union, with a membership numerically much depleted by a series of costly and mostly unsuccessful strikes, managed to survive despite the repressive strategies of the coalowners.(18)

The 1880s saw the spread of unionism in Accrington reflecting essentially oppositional attitudes amongst weavers, colliers, engineering workers and railwaymen. The town had a Trades' Council by 1893.(19) The *ad hoc* collection of money amongst other trades to assist striking weavers during the industrial unrest in the cotton industry in the late 1870s cautions against simplistic assumptions that loyalty-promoting benevolence sprang invariably 'from above'. The multiplication of examples would not be difficult. A more aggressive industrial relations posture was associated with the spread of general unionism in the later nineteenth century; but unions were in existence as a potential check upon employers' freedom of action in the North West long before this.

Unionism provided an alternative frame of reference in workers' perceptions of social relationships, reflecting and reinforcing horizontally-structured 'class' loyalties which, in the sphere of industrial relations at least, circumscribed employers' strategies to create a vertically-orientated framework of allegiance and dependence.

Rapid population increase and urban growth worked in the same general direction; urban development undoubtedly affected attitudes and perceptions by suggesting change and transformation, progress and advance, despite the rigours of the Great Depression. The urban communities of the northern industrial towns covered by the present study appear to have had none of the tight completeness of the factory-based, occupational neighbourhood groups with their communal identities which allegedly existed in Blackburn. Though neighbourhood and kinship ties were undoubtedly strong, the mill and mining communities were neither sufficiently localized nor sufficiently insulated from alternative influences to form fertile sowing ground for the seeds of deference. Subordinates may well have displayed deferential demeanour in the presence of their social superiors, either instrumentally or out of politeness, but this is very different from deference as we have defined it.

Population growth, urban expansion, transport and wider horizons

Census returns show that in the second half of the nineteenth century Burnley, Accrington, Macclesfield, Ashton and Warrington were fast-growing, progressively more populous industrial centres. Warrington's population, for example, grew from roughly 26,500 in 1861 to over 41,000 in 1881, to slightly more than 55,000 in 1891 and to over 64,000 in 1901. Social circumstances were in marked contrast to the relatively unchanging traditionalism of some of the small, scattered, rural hamlets of the period described by Newby and clearly very different from the restricted experience of life in the often isolated factory colonies of the early industrial revolution described by Pollard and by Chapman.(20) Market day attracted people from outlying hamlets into the towns and the availability of cheap railway transport facilitated inward and outward travel.

The census returns for the borough of Burnley disclose that the population more than quadrupled in the half century after 1851, rising from roughly 21,000 to about 29,000 in 1861 and to some 97,000 by 1901. The 1870s and 1880s were decades of particularly fast growth; between 1871 and 1881 numbers increased by some 18,000, and during the next ten year period (1881 to 1891) by a dramatic 28,000. In part this general population increase was the net effect of migration into and out of Burnley, but something is owed also to the conjuncture of high birth rates and falling death rates. The birth rate over the twenty-year period of rapid population increase ranged between 36 and 42 per 1,000. Before 1870 the death rate for the Burnley district hovered at about 30 per 1,000; this figure had improved to roughly 23 per 1,000 by 1884 and to 18.8 per 1,000 by the mid 1890s. The local mortality rate of 16.67 in 1895 was significantly better than the national average of 19.13.(21) The salient point to be made here is that, despite the human wastage caused by the high percentage of deaths amongst young children, Burnley had a rapidly increasing urban population.

Population growth from natural increase, augmented by net migration into Burnley from outlying rural areas, promoted building and construction and the creation of new development areas(22) in an era characterized by much speculative building activity.

Mobility within and beyond the town widened horizons. There was a great deal of new building in St Andrew's Ward, encouraged and assisted after 1882 by a passenger transport service linking the district with the town centre. Likewise, the growth and spread of local transport services both reflected and promoted building enterprise in the Padiham Road and Accrington Road districts and, with the erection of new mills, there was additional speculative investment in residential developments already underway in the Stoneyholme, Whittlefield and Oxford Road areas. The rapidity of urban expansion is reflected in statistics, quoted by Bennett, relating to the erection of new homes. Between 1851 and 1871 speculative building produced some 9,000 new houses, but the three succeeding decades produced respectively 12,000, 18,000 and 21,000 new houses. Nor was expansion confined to the domestic sphere. New construction in 1866 included in addition to 510 houses and shops, four new mills, two printing works, St James's Hall and new premises at Bank Top Station; the year 1877 saw the construction of 738 houses and shops, thirteen mills, five chapels and four public buildings; in 1888, by no means an exceptional year in a decade of vigorous expansion, the building and construction industry erected 846 houses and shops, three sheds, seven warehouses and one school. All of this undoubtedly promoted a great deal of interest, discussion, inspection and inquiry amongst townsfolk in general, not least because the last three decades of the century witnessed the official opening of several major public buildings - the Town Hall, the Grammar School and the new workhouse may have been provided 'from above' as monuments to civic pride or as institutions enabling the leaders to expedite the duties of urban management, but there are no obvious implications for the socialization or social control of the lower classes in the provision of the Market Hall and the Cooperative Buildings. Much of the construction of new premises that went on in the town in these years was simply a matter of convenience for local government or the product of independent speculative activity of business and commerce in response to market demand.

Urban expansion, a reflection of population growth, undoubtedly affected the way in which lower-class members conceptualized their position within the socio-economic structure. Mobility, permitted and promoted by local and regional developments in transportation, widened their world view and potentially made available alternative definitions of power and privilege, duty and responsibility, status and hierarchy. Warrington(23) with an increasingly diversified local economy - glassware, brewing, wiredrawing and various ancillary trades associated with shipping and shipbuilding - had important, well-established transport linkages by river, canal, road and rail in the second half of the nineteenth century. Located, as the town was, at the intersection of lines running from London, Liverpool, Manchester, Wales and the rest of Lancashire, Warrington bustled with commercial activity. More modern forms of transport simply added to the speed and volume of traffic.

Not all of the expanding towns of the North West had such a busy flow of transport and communication as Warrington but the nature of the industrial base of towns like Burnley, Macclesfield, Ashton and Accrington necessitated an inflow of fuel, industrial raw materials and marketable consumer goods and an outflow of finished and semi-finished products. Local self-subsistence had vanished long ago; few townsfolk could be completely unaware of the existence of economic links both beyond their own place of work and beyond the particular town.

During the later decades of the nineteenth century most sizeable towns in the industrial North West had their omnibus, horse-drawn wagonette and steam tramway services operating within and between towns. In Burnley(24) horse-drawn buses ran hourly between Wood Top and Barde Lane until the mid-1880s when the major routes were taken over by the tramways. By 1885 there was a regular 'through' service connecting Nelson, Burnley and Padiham. But it was the railways which annihilated isolation and distance and which, for longer journeys, soon established their superiority over the roads. The number of passenger bookings at Bank Top Station alone increased from 83,000 in 1850 to 226,000 in 1866, and thence escalated dramatically with the popularization of cheap railway travel to the coastal resorts during the summer months.

Most of the arterial lines of the national railway network were laid down during the thirty-year period 1840 to 1870; and in the North West the Lancashire and Yorkshire Railway Company was bringing the remaining industrial towns of the region on to the railway map.(25) Much of the additional track laid down in the late nineteenth century comprised branch lines or local lines, loop-lines or cut-offs. The numerous branch lines built in these years, either as feeders to the main lines, as links with outlying communities or as services for recently expanded industrial areas, were extensions of the Lancashire and Yorkshire Railway. Restrictions upon the mobility of the relatively poor were dissolved by the progressive reduction in the cost of third-class travel, particularly after the abolition in 1883 of the passenger duty. Cheap travel facilities, popular pricing and the gradual introduction in some areas of reduced fares for weekend, tourist and excursion travel encouraged movement. Falling prices were associated not only with increased freight carriage but also increased passenger traffic. As Ellis(26) has noted, two of the great virtues of railway transport were the speed and the frequency of services, including those forming the inter-urban links of Lancashire. The wider horizons provided by this relatively extensive framework for transportation are likely to have diluted the ideological potency of the leaders' creed. Other factors worked in the same general direction.

Wider horizons: trade unionism

Trade unionism was becoming progressively less localized in structure and less fragmented into autonomous units within each trade. The Trades Union Congress, uniting affiliated unions into a national organization, came into existence in 1868. Industry-wide trade unions, led by full-time paid officers and characterized by the centralization of administration and funds, brought greater strength and stability to the organizational structure. Progress was not inexorably onward and upward, of course; there were many setbacks both locally and nationally, but reversals were offset by periods of rapid growth in aggregate numbers and by the expansion of the national network of local branches affiliated to regional and national bodies. By the end of the nineteenth century it was still a minority of all male workers and an even smaller minority of all female workers who had secured membership, yet by that time the movement had assumed a settled if not altogether peaceable permanence.

The measurable growth of trade unionism, disclosed by statistics relating to membership and to the creation of new local branches, plus the appearance of both regional and national organizational frameworks, is the most obvious but not the sole indicator of the wider perspective being adopted by wage-workers. There were the intermittent, spasmodic, mass responses to the inadequacy of wages; the tradition of collective bargaining by riot had not disappeared completely. There was by now, however, greater emphasis upon institutionalized forms of combination in what Perkin has termed a 'viable class society', but there was also pressure group action organized and led by activists seeking the redress of specific grievances.

Wages were the major preoccupation of the weavers' union.(27) The mass meeting held in Burnley early in August 1878 was part of a Lancashire-wide movement to resist a ten per cent pay cut throughout the region. Further local demonstrations were held at Fulledge, followed by a great demonstration in Padiham on August 6th when the weavers were joined by the spinners. Within a few days the Burnley millowners had joined forces in the Masters' Federation along the lines adopted by cotton employers in other towns. The masters clearly viewed the problem as wider than the recurrent conflicts which could be dealt with more or less effectively at the level of the individual employing enterprise. There is little to indicate that workers conceptualized their grievances in other than economic terms, yet the identification of mutual interest was region-wide and united workers along lines which transcended the localized particularism of the individual firm.(28)

Burnley workers were in touch with events elsewhere. A mass meeting in October 1878 received news of riots in Wigan, Bacup, Preston and Stockport and, at a rally held in Marsden during the same month, leaders of the Lancashire-wide movement were pressing the necessity of solidarity among all workers throughout the county. Speakers from some of the major industrial towns urged the need for all to 'stand firm' in class-conscious rhetoric which contradicts arguments premised upon the blinkered insularity and myopic parochialism of factory-based occupational community.

The region-wide dimension of workers' evolving perception of loyalty and of attachment to fellow workers - workers acutely conscious in certain of circumstances of mutual grievances and of a shared sense of alienation, hostility and deprivation - was embodied in the objective of the East Lancashire Amalgamated Society of Power Loom Weavers. The union, formed about 1858, was demanding uniform district-wide wage rates. It had a membership amounting to as many as 12,000 within a year, and was headed by a paid secretary, Abram Pinder. It held regular committee meetings at its headquarters in Bolton, and branches were formed in most of the leading weaving towns of textile Lancashire, including Burnley, during the following year.

Some local branches of the East Lancashire weavers' union were more securely and successfully established than others. The Burnley branch, after a precarious start in 1859, broke up the following year and did not re-form until 1870, but from that time, with a growing membership recruited from mills in all parts of the town, the branch had an unbroken record of activity to the end of the century.

The conduct of industrial relations shows a keen awareness of the union's need to adopt a strong oppositional stance in certain circumstances, and of the need for firm resistance to cavalier attempts by employers to reduce wages. There were, of course, some who chose to dissociate themselves from the union movement, but an identification of mutual interests, recurrently opposed to those of the masters, united large numbers of weavers from mills throughout the town. A levy of 1d. per week was realistically affordable, but this low level of subscription was clearly unlikely to provide a sound financial basis to supply strike pay if there was frequent 'unofficial' strike action, or if industrial action occurred over a prolonged period at all the mills simultaneously. Union officers, therefore, proposed a strategic concentration upon selected premises and, with this objective in view, a Vigilance Committee was formed to take decisions about which particular mills should be targeted. It was this wide basis of support which enabled workers at one of the town's mills to maintain their strike from February 1872 to October 1873.

Strikers were not blind to the need to maintain communications beyond the immediate locality, and initiatives to disseminate information show a clear understanding of effective pressure-group strategy. There was an extensive communications network which linked up local branches. Communication with unions in other towns provided information for comparison and for evaluation of what was fair and just. The network operated also at the level of the town, linking union members employed at the numerous mills; it provided both practical and moral mutual support. In Burnley in the 1870s, for example, an inflammatory broadsheet seeking to rally workers to industrial action was circulated throughout the town and outlying districts; and a series of letters, many of which were models of rational argument likely to win the respect if not the assent of educated middle-class readers, was published in the local press. At the same time the activities of a strike committee, appointed to arrange shop-meetings, round robins and public demonstrations, served to refuel flagging enthusiasm and to boost morale during what was proving to be a prolonged strike.

The Burnley branch of the weavers' union was well aware of the need to maintain order and discipline amongst the membership; effective industrial action needed to be controlled, regulated and co-ordinated. There was much anxiety on the part of the committee about the proliferation of unofficial strikes at individual mills, strikes which achieved little for the workers concerned and which proved to be a drain upon the union's finances. Eventually a resolution was passed to the effect that no strike pay would be forthcoming to workers who went on strike without the official sanction of the local branch. Again, both strategy and ideology were premised upon links which united operatives beyond the individual firm and beyond the particular town.

Local branches which formed part of the wider interconnections of regional and national organization often had modest beginnings. An early form of combination amongst miners in the Burnley district was the traditional kind of benevolent club, the Miners' Sick and Burial Society,(29) which was in existence at the end of the 1850s; but evidence of a wider perspective dates from 1860 when a Burnley branch of the Wigan Miner's Union supported a strike of one hundred colliers at one of the Burnley mines. The formation of the Burnley Miners' Association suggests a strengthening of the will to resist and it reflects increasing organizational confidence which drew together miners at pits owned or managed by several different mining companies. Optimism was short-lived at this juncture, however; unsuccessful strikes, consequent demoralization and the exhaustion of funds were recurrent problems. But vulnerability of this kind does not signify restriction of vision. Opportunistically the miners reorganized. In 1872, when coal prices began to rise, the Burnley branch of the Amalgamated Miners' Association was formed, only to suffer virtual dissolution in the aftermath of the prolonged and ruinously costly strike of 1873-4. Nevertheless, the collective principle persisted amongst the miners, despite the vague and precarious existence of formal union organization for more than a decade after 1874. Late in 1888 organization was revived in the district with the formation of a local branch, this time attached to the regional body, the Lancashire Miners' Federation.

The details of local trade union history are less relevant in the context of the present study than the generalization that the union movement provided a wide-ranging network linking trade unions in Burnley with regional and national levels of organization in an extensive web of interconnection. Such considerations raise doubts about arguments stressing the overriding significance of narrowly localized occupational community. Even Burnley's comparatively small local association of carpenters and joiners was tied in with the national organization - the General Union of Carpenters and Joiners(30) with its headquarters in Nottingham. Central office maintained a network of communication with local secretaries, supplying information about the action planned by each branch and inviting observations and comments. It is clear that the activities of other branches were reviewed and discussed. Union logbooks record statements such as: 'Our sanction is given to the Wigan branch to request a new privilege - a tea half-hour' and 'Our sanction is given to the Nottingham officers to strike for an advance of wages . . ..'

In the sphere of industrial relations many of the wage demands made during the second half of the nineteenth century indicate that there was an often acute awareness of differences in the pay rates of workers in similar jobs. Resentment about what was regarded as unjust disparity fuelled demands for the observation of conventions governing wage-rates elsewhere. The Burnley branch of the weavers' union, for example, demanded the introduction of standard rates based on the Blackburn 'List' (allegedly 12 per cent higher than the average rates paid in Padiham and Burnley). The demand was rejected by the masters; uniform rates throughout the county were declared to be an impossibility because of local differences in production costs.(31) The significant point to be made here is that the reference points which influenced bargaining over wages were not narrowly parochial.

There is other evidence of the 'wider horizons' which characterized workers' world view. There can be little doubt of lower-class awareness of life and opportunities beyond the confines of Burnley. The chance of geographical mobility and the willingness to seek employment opportunities elsewhere may of course weaken workers' resistance during a strike or a lockout by its defeatist effect upon collective solidarity and morale; yet, in a more positive sense, the result may be an improvement in the situation of those left behind by the effect of outward migration upon slackness in local labour markets. The unions often encouraged and aided such moves. In May 1854, for example, the weavers voted to set up an emigration society to assist workers wishing to move to other towns in search of work.(32) The Burnley and Church branch of the Amalgamated Miners' Association offered similar assistance in the aftermath of the disastrous strike of 1873-4.(33) Many Burnley colliers left the town; several joined the army or found employment in other industries. In July 1874 the officials of the local union acknowledged the hopelessness of continuing resistance and issued a notice promising to pay the expenses of any striker willing to remove from Burnley. This strategy was not unique to the time or to the place. There was already a well-established emigrant tradition amongst operatives at the beginning of the century and the recessions which punctuated the later decades promoted a spate of initiatives of this kind.

Movement out was paralleled by movement into the town. Strike-breakers from Coventry were brought into Burnley during the eleven-months-long weavers' strike at the beginning of the

1860s; during the miners' strike of the early 1870s the coalowners brought in strike-breakers from as far afield as Devon and Cornwall. These are not isolated examples, as trade union histories show.

The widening of wage-workers' world view is reflected in, and was promoted by, the democratic principle underlying trade union collectivism which occasionally took the form of voting on a county-wide basis. When a key decision involving a change of strategy was to be taken the majority view was ascertained by trade union officers before new resolutions were made. The 1878 weavers' strike provides a good example. On May 25th of that year union officials conducted a ballot of all enrolled Lancashire members in order to decide whether the prolonged strike against a 10 per cent wage reduction in the industry should be continued. In the final analysis a large majority in favour of prolonging industrial action made little difference to the course of events, since the exhaustion of union funds and the consequent inability of the union to continue to provide strike pay led to a gradual return to work by weavers at a 10 per cent reduction.

It is of some relevance to the widening perspective that David Holmes,(34) one of Burnley's leading trade unionists and president of the Burnley branch of the weavers' union for thirty-five years, was also a major figure in the conduct of union affairs regionally and nationally. He was president of the Northern Counties Weavers' Amalgamation for twenty-one years, a textile representative on the Parliamentary Committee of the TUC for twelve years and a principal witness providing evidence before the various Parliamentary commissions of inquiry into the textile trades. It is a measure of the success of his organizing ability and personal charisma that, when he died in 1906, the local union branch had a membership of some 14,500, had acquired new permanent purpose-built headquarters (the Weavers' Institute) and had accumulated a financial reserve of £24,000. When the new premises were completed, the opening ceremony on August 3rd 1890 was performed by Lady Dilke, supported by William Abraham, MP for Rhondda Valley.

Patterns which evolved in Burnley were replicated elsewhere. In Ashton(35) labour affairs were dominated by three major unions during the last three decades of the nineteenth century - the weavers, the spinners and the miners but, as in most industrial towns in these years, a host of smaller unions grew up, including those for shop assistants, railwaymen, tailors, carters and municipal employees. By far the largest of Ashton's unions was the weavers' association which recruited well beyond the borough boundaries;

by the end of the 1890s it had built up a membership of some 7,000 and had an annual income of £3,833. It is also relevant from the viewpoint of outside influences and wider perspectives that there was increasing recognition of the commercial viability of newspapers for the working-class market. Operatives and their families were interested not only in the economic, social and political events of their hometown but in national and international current affairs. Men like Ashton's J. Andrews, who founded the *Cotton Factory Times* and the *Ashton-under-Lyne Herald*, were responding to market circumstances. The *Herald*, staunchly Tory in political outlook, contained progressively more detailed notes, accounts and reports of trade union activities. The town, as other industrial conurbations, was building upon the legacy of combination inherited from the past; what was acquired in the quarter-century before the First World War was trade unionism in depth and greater interest in labour affairs in general.

Evidence of the widening scale of reference is contained in the spread in most major industrial areas of Trades' Councils linking workers of different trades and, in both a practical and psychological sense, strengthening the checks and balances against masters' associations. According to the Webbs, some sixty Trades' Councils came into existence between 1860 and 1889, and a similar number between 1889 and 1891.(37) Equally important is the fact that local Trades' Councils became regionally coordinated into the Lancashire Federation of Trades' Councils in the later nineteenth century. Trades' Councils acted to broaden the potentially blinkered vision of trade union specificity. Many unions were beginning to recognize that there was not only a need for one-dimensional collective solidarity which reinforced the oppositional potency of the particular trade, but that there were compelling reasons for the separately organized trades to come together in a co-ordinated, multi-dimensional unity in which the shared objectives of class transcended but also strengthened trade particularism.

Most of the major industrial towns of the North West had Trades' Councils by the mid 1880s. These bodies undertook the vital role of co-ordinating union activity, less to promote class warfare than to act as a counterbalance to the often formidable power of employers' federations. The Ashton Trades' Council(38) was formed in 1886 and grew from a body with only ten affiliated societies representing 1,400 members to one with over seventy affiliated societies representing around 10,000 workers in 1914. But the task of co-ordinating the activities of the various unions which often possessed very different, even antithetical, interests was not straightforward. Dissent was far from uncommon. The Ashton Trades' Council, as Trades' Councils elsewhere, was incomplete. In particular, some of the older established unions professed their independence by refusing membership. In July 1888 the Council expressed its regret that the engineers, bricklayers, cabinet makers, stonemasons, spinners, and carpenters and joiners continued to show no interest in overtures offering admission. From time to time there were reversals. In 1897 the spinners' association withdrew from the Ashton Trades' Council and did not rejoin until 1912. The powerful local branch of the miners' union remained unconvinced by the rationale of the unity argument. By 1895 there were at least 2,000 colliers in Ashton and district and the trade was highly organized, but a persistent spirit of independence and aloofness characterized the union's activities. The miners maintained their separatism both from other unions in Ashton and from other miners' organizations in Lancashire.

Yet the crucial point to be made here is that the miners' separatist policy derived neither from an obscurantist conservatism nor a lack of known opportunity, but from free choice. The local branch was well aware of both the local and wider regional network but preferred to stand alone. It was, nevertheless, a qualified kind of isolation which was sought; it is noteworthy that in the 1870s and 1880s, the Ashton miners chose to remain affiliated to the Miners' National Union when most other local branches in Lancashire had become disaffiliated.

The friendly society tradition, long established amongst trade unions, is a reminder that subordinates were not entirely dependent upon welfare protection provided 'from above' by employers, the Poor Law and the voluntary charities. Experience had long ago sensitized the lower orders to the need for collective protection via self-organized mutual insurance; trial and error had long ago led to the codification of conditions governing subscriptions, benefits and eligibility. The persistence for over two centuries or more of workmen's combinations for this purpose is explained less as the triumph of blinkered hope over dismal experience than as practical proof of the effectiveness of these initiatives. Friendly societies, sick clubs, benevolent clubs, as they were variously called, were not the product of the later nineteenth century; evidence suggests that there was a long friendly society tradition as a spontaneous grass-roots response to mischance. This type of self-help organization, both in principle and in practice, was already well-established by the mid-eighteenth century. The comprehensive, formally codified rules and regulations of the scheme, dating from 1755 and run initially independently by the miners of the London (Quaker) Lead Company at Alston Moor,(39) show that these men were not fumbling in the dark with the unfamiliar but were well aware of the potential pitfalls which mutual insurance involved.(40)

As far as the worker was concerned, union-based welfare benefits were clearly desirable but not always easily affordable. Even where a more permanent trade union organizational identity increased the likelihood that insurance pledges would be honoured, there was a world of difference between the benefits which were realistically available to highly paid labour aristocrats and workers with more modest earnings.

In late nineteenth-century Burnley the engineering workers fared best.(41) The local branch of the Amalgamated Society of Engineers was formed soon after the national body came into existence in 1851. The functions, as traditionally, were social as well as economic. By 1870 the Burnley branch, which by that date had some 120 members, met on alternate Saturdays at the Sun Inn to hear officers' reports, to discuss industrial problems and to enjoy an evening of relaxation and conviviality. The union had a well-codified set of rules and regulations governing members' subscriptions and what, by the standards of the time, was a highly eligible assortment of welfare benefits. These last included unemployment pay, sickness benefit, death grants, gifts to widows, superannuation for elderly workers seeking permanent retirement from the industry, and compensation in the case of industrial accident. The society could be generous indeed when the circumstance was catastrophic. In 1868 compensation paid to a member who suffered permanent disablement through industrial accident represented nearly a quarter of the branch's total subscriptions for the year. Earnings in the industry in the 1870s - moulders at Keighley's, Sagar's and Bracewell's were earning 30s. a week, mechanics 32s. and even labourers 21s. - enabled workers to pay the subscription rates necessary to fund wide-ranging welfare facilities of this kind.

In sharp contrast was the weavers' minimalist approach to welfare.(42) In 1870 when the worker's subscription was 1d. per week, the only benefit appears to have been a death grant payable from the society's burial fund. It was not until the industry had recovered from the 1878 region-wide strike that fresh initiative was taken to re-establish the union's funds on a sounder financial basis and to provide a wider variety of benefits with an element of choice. A new scale of contributions, introduced in 1879, ranged from 1d. to 4d. per week; those choosing to pay the higher rates were insured for a more varied assortment and for higher levels of benefit. These included weekly payments during sickness absence, payment during unemployment due to the breakdown of machinery, compensation for dismissal due to victimization, payment during strikes, and also death gratuities to widows and dependents. There was recognition of the need to protect union funds from exploitation by the less scrupulous in order to ensure adequate cover for the rest. There was the risk of insolvency arising from an excessive number of claims for assistance. Unofficial strikes at individual mills were a drain upon the funds and eventually the branch officers resolved to withhold payment from strikers who acted without official sanction. Likewise, evidence in cases of alleged victimization was more thoroughly scrutinized with a view to deterring bogus claims; the dismissal of a worker, the union recognized, was not always unfair. The record of disbursements notes, for example:

> Mr X be allowed a week's victim-grant in consideration of the good work he has done the society but we do not consider him a victim in as much as he has given the master a chance to discharge him for drunkenness.(43)

The cash value of benefits themselves and the dependability of union-sponsored mechanisms for members' social welfare differed quite widely amongst the several trades. The range of choice and the sums payable were a function of the level of subscriptions which members were willing or able to pay, and these in turn depended on wage rates, weekly earnings and security of employment in the particular industry. There was always the hazard of insolvency; the prospect sometimes led to reduced benefits or to their temporary suspension, though appeals for assistance could be made to union branches in other towns. Such appeals were often greeted sympathetically.

There were constraints which circumscribed the welfare protection it was possible for the union to offer. At its most haphazard, assistance for a fellow worker in distress might consist of a 'whip-round' or impromptu collection. Nevertheless, the fact that there was a long-established and on-going tradition of mutual insurance highlights the existence of a network of what were often more acceptable welfare alternatives than those provided 'from above'. The bonds of loyalty and allegiance promoted by attention to welfare were not exclusively vertical in structure. During the troubles of 1878 emergency relief for the families of those without work did not come solely from middle-class benevolence. There was a good deal of mutual aid generated within the lower social stratum itself.(44) During the weavers' strike the Burnley branch of the weavers' union divided the town into districts and appointed 'captains' to speak at mass meetings, to organize collections, to receive donations, and to distribute relief to those in need. It is not obvious why sentiments of gratitude and respect should focus upon middle-class philanthropists rather than on trade union activists. Extraordinary relief efforts by the local middle class may have been essentially propitiatory, seeking merely to reduce tension. It is clear that expressions of gratitude to middle-class dispensers of charity sometimes masked resentment. Demeanour may have been deferential, but the sentiments of the recipient may not necessarily be defined in terms of deference. It is noteworthy that, when the Burnley standard 'List' fixing new wage rates for the local textile trade was agreed in 1873, workers' gratitude was directed towards union representatives responsible for the successful outcome of negotiations. As a press report notes: 'The union organized a monster tea-party to celebrate the occasion, and congratulations were given to all officials who had negotiated the settlement . . ..'(45)

The foregoing evidence argues that it would be erroneous to represent the response of the lower class in terms of deference - the ability of the dominant class to impose 'from above' a particular set of values judged to be appropriate to the subordinate station in life. It is equally misguided to represent 'social improvement' simply as a matter of voluntary emulation 'from below' of middle-class habits of thought and behaviour. Without doubt, as F.M.L. Thompson suggests, changes in lower-class cultural values owed something to environmental improvements in urban amenities for public health such as better housing, sanitation, clean water supply, piped gas and street paving. It is likely, too, that the principle of less eligibility, which continued to stigmatize and degrade the recipients of poor relief, was a spur to greater efforts to maintain an independent respectability - if only to avoid the workhouse. Account must be taken also of the possibility of autonomous changes in lower-class culture.

Culture and ideology are subject to neither sudden nor dramatic transformation; there is a persistent traditionalism which preserves custom and habit at grass-roots level, but ideology is not static. New problems encountered in a changing industrial and urban environment increased the propensity to adapt, irrespective of the preaching of middle-class reformers. There is little to suggest that the habits, values and modes of conduct which middle-class moralists sought to promote amongst subordinates were innovative cultural constructs devised exogenously and forced upon unwilling townsfolk who were incapable of thinking for themselves and of acting independently in their own interests in ways other than oppositional combination. It seems at least as likely that perceptive middle-class paternalists sought to foster the spread of some of the responses and aspirations which were already present amongst advanced groups of workers and which were endorsed by the middle-class as one means to social improvement. Punctuality, industriousness, sobriety, thrift and respect for people and property, law and order were virtues which the lower-class was capable of discovering without assistance; wage-workers were capable of valuing these codes of conduct in their own right as essential attributes of respectable family life. As F.M.L. Thompson argues:

> There is plenty of evidence that the respectable working classes wished to be respectable not because some middle-class pundit told them to be, but because they liked it and disapproved of shiftless and sluttish ways. Similarly, the working classes did not need to be told by the middle class that family life was important, that honest toil was better than loafing, or that saving for a rainy day was sensible.(47)

Few families, even in the most deprived areas, can have preferred the excesses of profligate spending, debauchery, and lawlessness. On the one hand, numerous prominent middle-class social reformers dispensed a great deal of time, energy and effort in promoting respectable standards of behaviour; on the other hand, the lower classes were independently capable of assessing the economic and social worth of virtues such as these. But this does little more than suggest the existence of spheres of consensus. Consensus of this kind is not a proxy for deference.

References

1. Dutton, H.I. and King, J.E., 'The Limits of Paternalism: The Cotton Tyrants of North Lancashire, 1836-54', *Social History*, VII, 1982, pp. 59-74.

2. Parkin, F., *Class Inequality and Political Order*, MacGibbon and Kee, 1971, p. 97.

3. Bennett, W., *The History of Burnley*, Burnley Corporation, 1951, iv, pp. 99-101.

4. *Accrington Observer and Times*, 26 Oct. 1893.

5. *Ashton-under-Lyne Reporter*, 4 Nov. 1911.

6. *Ibid.*, 10 Mar. 1888.

7. *Ibid.*, 12 Jan. 1895.

8. Kavanagh, D., 'The Deferential English: A Comparative Critique', *Government and Opposition*, VI, 1971, pp. 333-60. Kavanagh outlines the myriad meanings that the concept has acquired in analyses of popular political attitudes and explanations of political stability. For examples of the political application of the concept see Nordlinger, E., *The Working Class Tories: Authority, Deference and Stable Democracy*, MacGibbon and Kee, 1967, and McKenzie, R. and Silver, A., *Angels in Marble: Working Class Conservatives in Urban England*, Heinemann, 1968.

9. Bell, C. and Newby, H., 'The Sources of Variation in Agricultural Workers' Images of Society' in Bulmer, M., ed., *Working Class Images of Society*, Routledge and Kegan Paul, 1975, p. 85.

10. Parkin, F., *op. cit.*, p. 84. For definition and analytical use of the concept by sociologists see Bulmer, M., ed., *op. cit.*, particularly the contributions by Lockwood, by Bell and Newby, and by Martin and Fryer. See also Shils, E., 'Deference' in Jackson, J.A., ed., *Social Stratification*, Cambridge University Press, 1968, pp. 104-32; Goffman, E., 'The Nature of Deference and Demeanour' in Goffman, E., *Interaction Ritual*, Aldine, Chicargo, 1967, pp. 47-86; Newby, H., *The Deferential Worker*, Allen Lane, 1977, ch. 1; Newby, H., 'The Deferential Dialectic', *Comparative Studies in Society and History*, XVII, 1975, pp. 139-64.

11. Parkin, F., *op. cit.*, pp. 84-5.

12. *Ibid.*

13. Parkin notes that stability may derive from responses other than deference: *ibid.*, pp. 81-3.

14. Lockwood, D., 'Sources of Variation in Working Class Images of Society', *Sociological Review*, New Series, 14, no. 3, 1966, pp. 249-67.

15. Newby, H., *The Deferential Worker*, Allen Lane, 1977, p. 59.

16. *Ibid.*, p. 55.

17. *Ibid.*, p. 414.

18. Bennett, W., *op. cit.*, pp. 122-30.

19. *Accrington Observer and Times*, 21 and 28 Oct. 1893; *Accrington Gazette*, Oct. and Nov. issues for 1893; see also Crossley, R.S., *Accrington Chronology and Men of Mark*, Accrington, 1924.

20. Chapman, S.D., *The Early Factory Masters*, David and Charles, 1967; Pollard, S., *The Genesis of Modern Management*, Edward Arnold, 1965.

21. Bennett, W., *op. cit.*, pp. 38-40.

22. *Ibid.*, pp. 31-7.

23. Carter, G.A., *Warrington: One Hundred Years a Borough*, Garside and Jolley, 1947; Crowe, A.M., *Warrington: Ancient and Modern*, J.H. Teake and Son, 1947.

24. Bennett, W., *op. cit.*, pp. 26-9, 50-3.

25. See, for example, Dyos, H.J. and Aldcroft, D.H., *British Transport*, Leicester University Press, 1969, p. 142.

26. Cited *ibid.*, p. 151.

27. Some details in Bennett, W., *op. cit.*, pp. 117-30.

28. *Ibid.*

29. *Ibid.*, pp. 130-3

30. *Ibid.*, pp. 133-6.

31. *Ibid.*, p. 119.

32. *Ibid.*, pp. 117-30.

33. *Ibid.*, pp. 130-3.

34. *Ibid.*, pp. 123-9, 142-3; see also articles on Holmes in *Men of Burnley: Press Cuttings, 1961-3*; *Men of Burnley: Press Cuttings, 1963-5*; *Burnley Notabilities: Press Cuttings, 1971*, all held at Burnley Central Library's Local Collection.

35. For detailed study of unionism in Ashton see Hall, A.A., 'Social Control and the Working Class Challenge in Ashton-under-Lyne', unpublished M.A. dissertation, Lancaster University, 1975.

36. *Ashton-under-Lyne Reporter*, 2 July 1899.

37. Pelling, H., *A History of British Trade Unionism*, Macmillan, 1963, p. 100.

38. Hall, A.A., *op. cit.*, especially chs 4 and 5.

39. Raistrick, A., *Two Centuries of Industrial Welfare: The London (Quaker) Lead Company, 1692-1905*, Society of Friends, 1938.

40. Roll, E., *An Early Experiment in Industrial Organisation: Boulton and Watt, 1775-1805*, Longman, 1930, pp. 226-7.

41. Bennett, W., *op. cit.*, pp. 133-6.

42. Cited *ibid.*, p. 127.

43. Cited *ibid.*, p. 135.

44. Russell, A. 'The Quest for Security: The Changing Working Conditions and Status of the British Working Class', unpublished Ph.D. thesis, Lancaster University, 1982; Russell, A., 'Private Industry and the Roots of Welfare', paper presented at the ESRC Conference on Roots of Welfare, Lancaster University, 1984.

45. See press coverage in *Burnley Gazette* and *Burnley Express*, issues for 1878.

46. *Burnley Gazette*, 21 June 1873.

47. Thompson, F.M.L., 'Social Control in Victorian Britain', *Economic History Review*, 2nd Series, XXXIV, 1981, pp. 189-208.

7

Leisure and Recreation
Some Implications for Acquiescence

Introduction

Increased leisure time and a corresponding increase in recreational amenities have been underestimated as social sources of stability in the progressively more populous industrial towns of the later nineteenth century. In so far as this aspect has been investigated by historians, two main schools of thought have emerged. One places emphasis upon the provision of recreational opportunities for the masses by members of the superordinate social stratum. The intended objectives were to expedite the internalization of a new ideology, to socialize the poor in specific attitudes and aspirations, and to cultivate habits of thought and behaviour deemed desirable by the suppliers. To these socially incorporative ends healthy, educative, respectable, improving leisure pursuits were promoted. In contradiction of the integrationist argument, others have questioned the extent to which socialization was achieved, given the persistence of subcultural forms of recreation. Yet protagonists in the debate are guilty of taking a blinkered view; it is argued here that vastly increased opportunities for entertainment and relaxation *from whatever source* contributed to the stability of the period - but for reasons other than those given by the proponents of the rival conventional wisdoms.

Investigators(1) who stress the influence upon subordinates' behaviour of provision 'from above' of 'rational' forms of recreation allege that such initiatives served as rehabilitating rescue operations which disseminated what the reformist providers viewed as socially desirable virtues. Sceptics(2) question the validity of this line of argument; to demonstrate the objectives of the suppliers is not to prove success in securing the intended response from consumers who frequently displayed a perverse tendency to independence in how they chose to spend their spare time. Moreover, those who utilized the opportunities made available by the promoters of rational recreation did not necessarily adopt the normative code of the dominant class. Deference was not necessarily the end product. The latter argument is persuasive, but this checkmate move does not get us very far in explaining the compliance of the disprivileged majority in the leadership of the privileged minority. There is, admittedly, a spin-off line of argument which maintains that subcultural recreational forms, by reinforcing the separatism of 'popular culture', led to an endorsement by subordinates of their own subjection. But in practice cultural separatism in the nineteenth century, as today, was less comprehensively complete than this hypothesis suggests. The role of recreation, as *one* influence among many which promoted acquiescence, deserves closer scrutiny.

More leisure time available to wage-workers in the later nineteenth century undoubtedly led to increased interest in recreational pursuits. The progressive shortening of the length of the working day, the shorter working week with the introduction of the Saturday half-holiday, plus additions to the number of annual public holidays with the Bank Holiday Acts of 1871 and 1875, all served to increase the non-work time of the masses.(3) Rising real earnings(4) for those in work, despite other constraints of the Great Depression, meant that many families had more disposable income to devote to entertainment. If time and money were in greater supply, so also were the opportunities to expend both on leisure pursuits. Arguably the market for leisure was a mass market, and as such an unprecedented one. The appearance and rapid spread of some of the outlets for the sale of entertainment in the era are inexplicable in terms other than mass consumption; the growth of the leisure industry geared to the popular market dates from the later nineteenth century.

The important point which needs to be made here is that there were multiple choices open to the consumers of entertainment. Options were available from several different sources, and many of the alternatives were low-cost or cost-free. Price was not a major deterrent to those of relatively modest means. Some insight into the implications for social and political stability may be given by identifying and assessing the significance of the sources of provision.

The alternatives fall into four main categories. Firstly, there was provision 'from above' by members of the superordinate class in their multi-faceted leadership roles as employers, philanthropists, town councillors, the lay-leadership of churches and chapels and the governorship of educational institutions. Secondly, there were the profit-oriented, commercial agencies catering for the entertainment of the masses: the music halls, theatres and spectator sports are the most obvious examples. Thirdly, there were traditional pastimes and amusements which survived as an integral part of the subculture generated by the subordinate class itself for its own recreational purposes, and others provided 'from below' more formally by institutions such as the trade union. Fourthly, there were leisure activities, often centred on the inns and taverns in the less salubrious districts, frowned upon by respectable townsfolk and frequently associated with lawlessness and disturbance of the peace.

Provision 'from above'

Provision from above, though it does not constitute the whole explanation, cannot simply be discounted as an irrelevant factor in accounting for general acquiescence in the *status quo*. Its significance, however, does not lie in its effectiveness as a means of promoting mass deference in dominant ideology.

There is much well-documented evidence to support the contention that employers in large-scale employing enterprises undertook the promotion of healthy, 'improving', educative forms of recreation. Through the medium of an assortment of recreational initiatives employers aimed to encourage the growth of company-focused bonds of allegiance and a unifying identification of communal interests amongst all who lived, moved and had much of their being within the factory walls. Tea treats, works outings and a diversity of clubs and societies enabled employers and their families, their overseers and operatives to mingle together in a less formal, more relaxed way and to share a sense of social involvement in a dimension of life other than work. Opportunities for personal contact and social interaction of this kind played an important role in the paternalistic employer's efforts to foster a family atmosphere within the factory community - a family whose collective well-being was based upon unequal but nevertheless symbiotic duties and responsibilities. At the celebration in 1880 for the coming of age of the son of Hugh Mason, one of Ashton's leading cotton masters, the entire workforce was invited to an evening's entertainment of glee-singing and dancing.(5) Such celebratory treats were frequent occurrences - at Christmas, the marriage of a member of the employer's family, an upswing in trade, or a gratifying election result. In Ashton the Rayner brothers entertained over three thousand mill hands at a party in 1880 to mark their success in municipal elections;(6) Abram Altham held a 'tea treat' for his employees on his election to Burnley's Town Council; William Mitchell celebrated his election as Burnley's MP by entertaining his workforce to a plentiful supper followed by singing and dancing.

Employer-sponsored works trips became progressively more common in an era when an expanding railway network linked the major industrial towns of the North West with the fast-growing seaside resorts of the Lancashire coast and North Wales. At Crosfield's, a family firm producing soap and chemicals in Warrington, the works outing had become firmly established as an annual treat by the beginning of the 1870s; roughly two hundred employees and their families went to Llangollen in 1861 and in 1880 as many as one thousand went to Blackpool.(7) Works outings, which enabled employers, managers, overlookers and operatives to relax together and to enjoy fresh air and sunshine, beach games and picnics, served to promote shared enjoyment free from the constraints of workday discipline.

Shared recreational experiences performed a communal bridge-building function rather than an ideologically integrating social purpose; equally importantly, they ensured that participants' perception of the relationship between the master and his workforce was not a pervasively oppositional one based upon continuous, unabated, embittered class warfare.

There were some recreational practices which were to be actively discouraged. Celebrations at mill and factory were often strongly flavoured with the ideals of chapel-bred temperance, a virtue which featured overtly as a proxy for respectability in the moral context of the era. Temperance, widely regarded by nineteenth-century moral-reformist opinion as conducive not only to family welfare but also to physical efficiency and municipal law and order, was more explicitly fostered in Nonconformist spheres; but there is little to suggest that Anglican attitudes towards the excesses of intoxication differed dramatically. To counter the attractions of the inns and taverns employers sometimes built or subscribed to the maintenance of coffee rooms and tea rooms. In Burnley Abram Altham 'without any intention of profit' built a coffee room where the local Baptist preacher lectured regularly to young people on the cause of temperance.(8) To neutralize the magnetism of Warrington's beer shops the Quaker Crosfields built and maintained tea and coffee rooms at Bank Quay, and they sponsored a circulating library and a horticultural society. In Ashton the Masons were 'unstinting' in financial aid and organizational zeal to promote temperance and rational recreation.

Pleasurable leisure activities were to be condoned, so long as interest was directed into what the providers deemed to be desirable channels. John Crosfield's address to the crowd at one of the Bank Quay flower shows, sponsored annually by his firm, discloses a not untypical attitude; the cultivation of flowers, he asserted, had a moral tendency and was a great inducement to a man to spend his time at home with his family instead of at the public house.(9)

Not all employers subscribed quite as explicitly as the Crosfields to the cause of temperance, nor broadcast its virtues with such devotional fervour by the exemplary standards of their own conduct. The Blackburn cotton master, Harry Hornby, made no secret of his own indulgence in alcohol and was reputedly a keen betting spectator at the cockpits, but there were limits to the extent to which millhands' drinking was to be countenanced. Not even the Greenalls of Warrington's brewing trade endorsed excess of this kind.

If what were viewed as debauched pastimes, which undermined moral character and self-respect, were to be discouraged, an active interest in health-improving, physical exercise was to be nurtured. Many of the sporting activities sponsored by employers such as the Crosfields in Warrington and the Masons in Ashton required team effort; competition was promoted, success and achievement were acknowledged, applauded and rewarded. Congratulatory announcements at the works, reports in the local press and the presentation of prizes were all manifestations of approbation calculated to inspire emulation.

Even in a strongly paternalistic company such as Crosfield's, heavily influenced by the ideals of incorporative welfarism, it was not all a matter of provision exclusively from above. Involvement and a sense of community were reinforced by joint effort. Workers were encouraged to assist in the organization and financing of recreational activities. With the formation of the Works Recreation Club in the opening years of the twentieth century there came into existence the Recreation Fund. Those seeking membership were asked to subscribe one penny per week - a charge which, at operatives' request, was subsequently made compulsory for all. One of the objectives of the new club was to provide additional grounds for long-established sports: football, cricket, tennis, bowls and other outdoor games. In Burnley the larger chapels, mostly dominated by leading employers of the town's major industries, ran sports clubs and organized special sporting events intermittently. Here, too, participants were directly involved in an organizational capacity. By the 1880s all the larger centres of worship appear to have had football and cricket teams which held regular practices and matches during the playing season and which joined in local league events against other teams in the district - Blackburn, Accrington, Oldham and so on.(10)

The socio-psychological significance of competitive sports such as these lies in the fact that participation provided opportunities for success and achievement. The millhand might occupy a comparatively low socio-economic position as a wage-worker in the occupational structure of the workplace, but his physical prowess as a member of a winning team offered an alternative rank order in which his status was high with, in consequence, an increased sense of self worth and a more eligible self-perceived identity. His morale and sense of personal pride were undoubtedly boosted by the congratulations he and his fellow players received from his employer, by the pats on the back from workmates, and by a sense of company-focused pride reinforced by the wearing of team colours on the sportsground. The effect was to enhance his sense of psychological well-being; the satisfaction he felt in this dimension of his life compensated for, and made the more bearable, the comparatively lowly status he occupied in the social structure of the factory during the working day. Even when hard-fought matches were lost there was some satisfaction to be derived from the experience of team spirit and fair play under the rules of the game. Nor was the sense of pride in the company's sporting activities confined to the players; it extended to the following of partisan supporters which most company teams attracted.

There were other ways in which physical exercise functioned as a potentially stabilizing force. Exercise was a means to relaxation, an outlet from the physical tension, routinized monotony and psychological stress of the working day. Mental and physical aggression built up during working hours could be released and directed into relatively harmless channels through the challenges encountered at the gymnasium, the sportsground and the swimming baths; where the participant could 'get it out of his system' by this means, there was reduced likelihood that grievances and irritations would precipitate challenges of a more disruptive kind in the workplace. The response to those in positions of decision-making authority directly affecting his life circumstances was the more likely to range between willing compliance and philosophical acceptance. It is noteworthy that every fifteen-year-old male employee at Crosfield's was taught to swim; weekly lessons were at the firm's expense and progress was demonstrated and rewarded in an annual swimming gala. There were regular athletics and bowling competitions and the firm built a gymnasium to encourage an interest in healthy exercise, as did Hugh Mason at his Ashton works.

The recreational activities provided 'from above' were not confined to physical exercise, the works trip and celebratory get-togethers, nor were they centred exclusively on the workplace. Several of Burnley's leading employers were prominent as sponsors, patrons and directors of the town's two institutions for post-elementary education: the Mechanics' Institute and the Church Institute;(11) the Masseys, the Keighleys, J.H. Scott, James Kay, William Thompson and Abram Altham were associated with the Mechanics'; the Grants, the Thursbys and John Greenwood with the Church Institute. Both institutes spawned numerous recreational clubs and societies. The choice available at the Mechanics', for example, included the vocal union, the Mechanics' band, a debating society, a photographic club, a chess club, and for some years a 'Saturday Evening Recreational' at which the dancing was interspersed with recitations, musical items and a 'moderately priced supper'.(12)

A similar kaleidoscopic recreational spread was to be found at the chapels and churches. In Blackburn, Burnley and other towns in the region these institutions were strongly influenced by leading employers in their guise as lay-preachers, church wardens, Sunday school teachers, circuit stewards and Sunday school superintendents. Relaxation and a communal identity were fostered through the more passive medium of lantern lectures, family picnics and tea parties on special occasions. Fund-raising activities, taking such forms as bazaars, 'fayres' and 'sales of work', gave practical, shared expression to a collective sense of Christian duty and moral responsibilities as well as fulfilling the more obvious leisure purpose. Dramatic societies, choral societies and brass bands provided recreational outlets for those talented in the performing arts: discussion groups, debating clubs, young men's improvement societies and young women's counterparts offered leisure pursuits for the serious-minded in search of a challenge.

There can be little doubt that the recreational amenities provided 'from above' were welcomed and appreciated, but there is little conclusive proof that those who made use of them internalized the providers' normative code in consequence. Expressions of gratitude are not proxies for deference. Arguably, subordinates were capable of thinking for themselves, of instrumentally participating because they excelled at, or enjoyed, a particular activity, without subscribing to the world view of the dominant class.

Conjecturally, the range of choice made available by employers was not to everyone's taste; the moralizing puritanical attitudes of some of the paternalists were more likely to deter rather than attract interest. The fare dished out in Burnley by the Reverend Littlehales of Sion Chapel can hardly have been the most palatable of varieties. Described as 'prominent for his outspoken criticism of the tendencies of the times,'(13) he fulminated in the Brown Street Theatre on Sunday afternoons and in Altham's Coffee Tavern on weekdays against vice and immorality . His denunciation of the theatre and drama as 'the devil's own literature' and his condemnation of intemperance, gambling and pigeon-flying (this last a popular recreational interest amongst the male fraternity of the coalmining and cotton communities) can hardly have been welcomed by work-weary men in search of a little diversion from the daily grind of work. The brutalizing experience of employment in the pits was, unsurprisingly, paralleled by resort to some of the more brutal leisure alternatives, including those to be had in the town's inns and taverns. Members of the Crosfield family persistently lamented the social problems caused by drink. In the words of the firm's historian, summarizing sentiments repeatedly expressed in public speeches:

> . . . wages were wasted in the ale-houses and gin-palaces, families were inadequately clothed and fed, children were uneducated, immorality flourished, and the poorer quarters of the town became sinks of poverty, degradation, heathenism and crime. Drunkenness filled the workhouses, the gaols and the lunatic asylums and so increased the rates; it also led to idleness and unfitted men for steady, hard work.(14)

That deep, humanitarian concern underlay what to some wage-workers appeared all too often to be kill-joy condescension and holier-than-thou intrusiveness can have done little to render the message the more acceptable. Provision 'from above' may have been avoided by some members of the subordinate class as the least eligible of all the recreational alternatives, but this still left a wide range of choice available from other sources.

The commercial agencies

The commercialization of entertainment for the mass market began and accelerated in the later nineteenth century; the music halls, spectator sports and cheap railway excursions to the seaside are but the most obvious manifestations of new recreational habits.

The supply of amenities was profit-motivated; marketable recreational products were consciously provided in response to a perceived recreational market demand. The relationship between the supplier and the consumer of entertainment was based primarily upon the economics of a commercial transaction. Facilities of this kind were not consciously constructed to influence mass audiences and spectators in healthy, morally improving, educative ways. Beyond the objective of profit, the intention of proprietors in the fast-evolving leisure industry was simply to provide an enjoyable, entertaining market product calculated to attract numerous paying customers.

Seaside trips were becoming progressively more popular from the middle of the nineteenth century, but it was not only employers, Sunday school organizers and the middle-class proponents of temperance who offered cheap travel either at subsidized prices or at concessionary fares permitted when the organizer chartered the whole train. The railway companies themselves, quick to cash in on the new mass market, ran cheap excursions independently,(15) often on Sundays as an attraction to the less devout with a preference for beach and beer-house entertainments. During this era the increasing holiday-market demand, further boosted by the railways' own popular pricing and advertising policy during the summer months, was increasingly met by the commercial agencies. The Burnley branch of the weavers' union organized regular trips for members in the summer season, but the majority of travellers were families or groups of friends. Unsurprisingly in an era when commercialized forms of entertainment catering for the masses were beginning to spread in the major towns and cities, the excursionists' demand for holiday amusements led to a corresponding commercially-orientated proliferation of seaside stalls, booths, and fairground attractions, cheap eating houses and beach amusements. In popular resorts such as Blackpool, Morecambe and Rhyl it led also to increasingly heavily capitalized centres of entertainment.(16) Day trips, weekend and week-long visits by spend-thrift wage-workers and their families produced a specialized working-class holiday season supplementary to the existing one, particularly in those seaside resorts readily accessible by rail from the populous conurbations of the industrial North West. The holiday demand, thus generated, was sufficiently heavy to effect a major transformation both of the coastal urban economy and of the social tone of seaside resorts. Blackpool, New Brighton and Morecambe began to cater more specifically for excursionists and holiday-makers of modest means. The most spectacular large-scale holiday resort expansion occurred where the market pressures of the masses were strongest.(17)

The growth of the coastal resorts of the North West testifies to the ability and willingness of the masses to afford holidays away from home; it reflected the availability both of free time and of disposable income. In Burnley, for example, most people had two additional days of holiday following the weekend of the July fair by the mid-1850s; by 1870 an extra day had been added to these, and for textile workers the fair holiday had been lengthened to a complete week by the end of the century, plus an additional long weekend in September from 1890.(18) Textile Lancashire led the holiday trend.

In the industrial towns of the North West, with the regional concentration of cotton and coal, employment opportunities for both male and female often produced two-income families. The shortage of domestic servants, much lamented by wealthier members of the community, is partially attributable to the higher wages which women could earn in the factories. Moreover, the availability of jobs and relatively good wages for adolescents with few family responsibilities to absorb time and money, released an additional flow of spending on leisure. It seems not improbable that others, eager to keep up with the latest entertainment trends and to accompany friends, chose to forego the occasional necessity for the pleasure of self-indulgence. Frugality in household expenditure made a little modest extravagance affordable.

As Walton shows, artisan bathers from Burnley were already invading Blackpool in their hundreds in the early nineteenth century. Cheap railway travel in the later years of the century simply fuelled a development already well underway. By the 1890s whole towns had a deserted appearance at the Wakes. During the early July fair holiday in 1883 some 18,000 passengers travelled from Burnley on day-excursion trains and the number had risen to 20,000 by 1888. In 1890 thirty-five special trains carrying roughly 22,000 travellers left Burnley on the Thursday and Friday of the holiday period, and an additional 16,000 left for day excursions on the Saturday and Monday. The exodus to the seaside holiday resorts, gathering momentum in the 1870s and 1880s, owes less to the organizing zeal and integrationist strategies of paternalistic employers than to the independent quest by wage-workers for pleasure and relaxation. If, as Walton observes, the social tone of hedonistic Blackpool with its boisterous fairground, saucy beach amusements, thronged beerhouses, cheap eating places, coconut shies, fat ladies, roundabouts and crowds of raucous day trippers on pleasure bent is considered a rough guide to cultural norms, values and attitudes towards Sunday observance, there is little indication that the would-be socializers of the churches and chapels had achieved their objective. The precocious growth of the resorts is attributable less to the benevolence of paternalistic employers than to the spread of independent holiday habits amongst the masses.

The commercialization and increasingly heavy capitalization of seaside-resort entertainment was paralleled in inland areas. Here again there are important implications for social order and class consciousness. The commercial agencies were responding to and exploiting a perceived market demand in an era when the masses had more leisure time and more disposable income to spend on novel forms of entertainment. The development is one indication of the preference amongst at least some subordinates to compartmentalize their time into work and non-work components; it reflects a desire for recreation, entertainment and relaxation away from and unassociated with the workplace, for a complete break from all reminders of the routine, monotony and discipline of the working day. This is not to assume that the customers of the commercial agencies did not from time to time make instrumental use of the opportunities provided 'from above' - logically individuals and groups of friends made selective choices from the entire range of options available to them - but to conjecture that relatively few are likely to have confined their choice exclusively to the employer-sponsored variety or to the commercial alternative.

If healthy exercise offered a means to release by absorbing physical energies unutilized during the working day, audience and spectator forms of entertainment provided release in a different sense. The experience liberated the wage-worker temporarily but recurrently from the drudgery of repetitive tasks in low-status spheres of employment. Physically and psychologically the world of entertainment was escapist, somewhere else to be, a dimension of experience separate from all that reminded the individual of, or that confronted him with, the world of work. In both senses release was therapeutic.

There is little evidence that the profit-motivated commercialization of entertainment was intended to socialize consumers in dominant ideology. Provision was bound primarily by economic consideration: demand and supply criteria, market tastes and preferences, cost and retail prices, and advertising strategy. In so far as control was exercised, it was with the two-fold objective of promoting a sufficient degree of order to ensure that audience or spectator pleasure was not impaired and of protecting the value of the proprietor's business investment.(19) Disorder was likely to deter rather than attract customers. Owners and managers of commercial outlets needed to strike a balance which would permit enjoyment, fun, laughter, relaxation and pleasurable diversion, but which would maintain a sufficient degree of orderliness to protect an enterprise's commercial viability. They were anxious to avoid the kind of rowdiness which would invite the unwelcome attention of the police and of magistrates with the power to impose fines and revoke licences. Boisterous but harmless fun was often the overriding characteristic of the products demanded by the lower-class audience in search of diversion from the constraints of the working week. This, as far as the commercial proprietors of the entertainment industry were concerned, had little in common with what contemporary moralists viewed as the licentious, abandoned, drunken, brutal, futile, degenerate and even subversive forms of traditional popular amusements; and it was very different from the healthy, uplifting, educative, improving, sedate, respectable pastimes favoured by those who consciously sought to mould habits of thought and behaviour.

It is noteworthy that, despite the persistent disapproval of sanctimonious intolerants apparently anxious to suppress the traditional fairs as providing fertile sowing ground for the seeds of vice, debauchery, immorality and political subversion, the police were inclined to tolerate these gatherings on the grounds that, so long as they were reasonably well-regulated and did not cause undue disturbance, there was little justification for spoiling people's pleasure. By the 1880s when the fairs, no longer necessary for their traditional business transactions, were being transformed more specifically into a commercialized form of entertainment, the Home Office concurred that, far from constituting a threat to public order, the fairs helped to preserve the peace by keeping people amused, thereby lessening the need for them to resort to less readily supervised forms of recreation. Tolerant non-interference was justified on the grounds that the job of the police was to keep order by enforcing the law, not to apply moral sanctions.(20) The salve of tolerance was often judiciously preferred to the irritant of suppression which could lead needlessly to increased antagonism and provocation.

In the sphere of theatre entertainment, the gradual shift from predominantly temporary theatre structures to permanent often purpose-built premises, suggests a progressive increase in effective market demand. From the middle of the nineteenth century temporary pavilions had been erected by the many travelling companies visiting Burnley. There were also a few semi-permanent wooden structures, and the Public Hall was available for hire. Itinerant entertainers offered everything from grand opera to minstrel shows, from Shakespearean plays to variety performances. There were regular visits by travelling music hall companies with their jugglers, step dancers, acrobats, singers and comedians, and there were other forms of popular entertainment provided by the clairvoyants, mesmerists, phrenologists and illusionists such as Signor Bosco the Wizard and Professor Pepper.(21) Prices, usually ranging from 3d. in the gallery to 1s. in the boxes, brought the pleasure of theatre-going within the modest means of most lower-class families as a regular treat.

One of the most popular of the travelling companies with their own temporary premises was Duvall's, which visited Burnley for six to eight weeks each year during the summer season and gave shows in a 'mammoth pavilion' in the Market Square or the Cattle Market. Duvall's popularity was attributable, in part at least, to its pricing policy which aimed to attract the lower end of the market. Low admission prices were also part of sales strategy at the New Music Hall opened as early as 1863 by John Sagar, landlord of Burnley's Market Inn. This enterprise specialized in music hall entertainment; tableaux, vocalists, dancers, comedians, acrobats, jugglers and so on all featured regularly on the programmes. Tickets cost 3d. and 4d. on Saturday and Monday evenings and 2d. or 3d. on other evenings.

In Burnley several new purpose-built theatre premises were opened during the later nineteenth century offering a varied choice both of programme and of price. The Victoria Theatre or Lichfield's on the Cattle Market (sometimes used for professional billiards matches as well as variety shows and drama performances), the Gaiety Theatre and the Opera House were all newly opened in the 1880s. At Lichfield's prices ranged from 3d. to 1s. and children were admitted to the gallery on Saturday evenings for 1d. Prices at the Gaiety were similar initially but in 1888 the price range was reduced. In 1876 Howarth's mill in Brown Street was converted and opened as a theatre; and in the mid-1890s Tunstill's mill was taken over and rebuilt as the Empire Music Hall. The list of permanent theatres dating from the early 1880s in Burnley and other industrial towns of the North West could be extended without difficulty.

Another manifestation of demand for commercialized entertainment generated by the mass market - a predominantly male one - was the passion for spectator sports, particularly soccer. Despite middle-class control of the football authorities, soccer rapidly became an integral part of subcultural recreational life in what amounted to a subordinate-class takeover of the game, expedited by the creation of large football grounds, the use of paid professional players, and the expression of local partisan loyalty via the sale of caps, badges, scarves and rosettes in team colours.(22)

The nationwide commercialization of soccer in the later decades of the nineteenth century built upon, and in many cases absorbed, pre-existing local leagues. In Burnley, as in most populous industrial towns in the region, there were many long-established local football teams which played 'friendlies' in the period. Burnley was one of the original twelve clubs comprising the Football League which came into existence in 1888, but there were also local teams which played in the North East Lancashire League (later known as the Lancashire Combination), in the Lancashire League, the Burnley and District League, the Burnley Junior League and the Sunday School 'A' and 'B' Leagues. In cricket also there were several local leagues which drew extensive followings in the 1890s: the Burnley Cricket League, the North East Lancashire League, Ribblesdale and District , and the Sunday School 'A' and 'B' Leagues.

The rising popularity of organized sport had a major influence upon leisure habits, but soccer soon shed any social control significance attached to it at the outset. It is perfectly true, of course, that competitive sports and team games were loudly extolled by some moral reformers as instruments for disseminating amongst the lower-class the virtues of team spirit, fair play and observance of rules; it is equally true that many subsequently well-known league clubs began as local church or chapel teams, and that the standardization of the rules of the game was carried out by football authorities dominated by middle-class personnel. Yet, as Thompson(23) argues, the lower classes rapidly appropriated the game as an important part of their own subculture, and increasingly matches were characterized by 'blind partisanship', hooliganism, abuse of referees, and other such 'unsporting' features.

Lamentable though it was from the viewpoint of those who regarded league matches as the focal cause of raucous noise, mob rowdiness and brawling, behaviour of this kind was very much a part of recreational life in the era, and it performed a potentially stabilizing function. It also cautions against assumptions that spectator sports were 'merely passive' in the conventionally accepted sense. The release of psychological and physical aggression at the match may have been a cause for concern to football authorities anxious to suppress disorder amongst the spectators, but at least the disruption could usually be contained within, and limited to, the football ground and its immediate environs; and there was less risk that aggressions bottled up during the working day would be targeted more injuriously against the prevailing socio-political fabric of local authority.

The recreational opportunities offered by the proliferating commercial agencies which came into being in the period provided cheap affordable means to diversion, relaxation and enjoyment. The escapist gratification experienced may have been fleeting, but regular outings to look forward to and to save for undoubtedly rendered the rigours of the working week and the vicissitudes of subordinates' day-to-day urban existence the more bearable.

Subcultural leisure

Indigenous lower-class culture had its persistent qualities, demonstrated not least in the intense traditionalism of mutuality and combination as a defence against the uncertainties of life. Social organisms such as mutual insurance, trade unionism, the extended family, the neighbourhood community and the pub fraternity all contributed something to the shaping of popular culture. Logically, in the nineteenth century as in the twentieth, much of the free time available to those of modest means was spent in 'pleasurable neighbourhood and kinship social contact, physical recreation involving no resources or equipment, relaxing or pottering about, chatting or reading the newspaper, and other informal non-institutional pursuits.'(24) But in the sphere of popular culture there were manifestations of both institutional and spontaneous recreational initiatives. Trade unions, in addition to their bargaining role, undertook the dual functions of providing mutual insurance and conviviality. Traditionally, many had held their meetings at a local inn, a practice which had not disappeared, even in the late nineteenth century. As the century wore on, some local branches began to acquire purpose-built premises or rented office space. In 1872 the Burnley branch of the weavers' union rented a room at the Foresters' Frugality Lodge in Thomas Street, but the furniture - six chairs, two stools, a desk and four benches - argues that in practice only a fraction of some 2,300 enrolled members ever made use of the accommodation in their spare time. Premises such as these offered a degree of comfort which was hardly conducive to relaxation. Conjecturally, the union meeting room did not rank highly amongst the available recreational options at this stage. Two years later, however, the union had opened a news-room providing three daily papers, four weekly papers and the bi-weekly, *Sporting Life*, together with playing cards, draughts and dominoes. Other regular recreational activities included annual tea-parties and dances. At these gatherings of union members and their families beef and boiled ham, ginger beer and oranges made up part of the party fare of what were reportedly popular social occasions.(25)

There were other manifestations of an independent, subcultural recreational life of a more informal spontaneous kind. In Burnley, Pickup Croft and Wood Top were thronged on Sundays with pigeon-fanciers; every district had its school of 'pitch and toss', and hare coursing and pigeon-shooting everywhere provided opportunities for betting and gambling. On frequent occasions large crowds of spectators gathered to watch informally arranged boxing and wrestling matches between local champions, the spectacle being the more sensational because no rules were enforced and butting and kicking were permitted. The town's police force tended to keep a watchful eye on such gatherings, but to avoid direct provocative intervention so long as the boisterousness did not get out of hand. Popular traditional games such as 'knur and spell' and 'buck and stick' were countenanced by the local police as long as the players avoided setting up pitches in the vicinity of buildings where there was the risk of damage to windows. Likewise, there was little interference in the traditional bowling matches played with shaped stones as long as play did not take place on the highway.(26)

Gambling, widely condemned by middle-class moralists as a 'social evil' which dissipated wages, increased indebtedness, reduced living standards and undermined family welfare, was a persistent element in the popular leisure tradition, despite the efforts of contemporary reformers to suppress it. It thrived in the pubs and taverns, but any sporting activity provided the occasion for spectators to chance their luck. In Burnley youths formed betting schools on street corners to play 'pitch and toss'; amongst older men pigeon flying, pigeon-shooting, hare coursing and other field sports offered wide-scale opportunities for gambling. After 1870 closer surveillance by the town's police force did not so much eradicate the 'nuisance' as drive it to the peripheral districts. Gaming allegedly became such a public scandal near Royle that the landowner was obliged to close the road in an attempt to suppress the menace.

The gambling tradition was not the half-concealed furtive pastime of tight neighbourhood communities; it had a thriving, pervasive presence with busy interchange between sub-districts within and beyond the town. Burnley had a regional reputation for cockfighting; the regular meetings at Crown Point drew crowds from as far away as Skipton. In the 1890s the betting fraternity turned its attention to horseracing which the anti-libertarian lobby vociferously denounced as a source of material and moral damage to lower-class welfare. Police attempts to suppress this potential threat to public order by keeping a close watch on bookies and their runners, and efforts to break up gangs of men collecting in the streets to indulge the passion for betting, were less than successful in that they tended to produce an essentially temporary dispersal, particularly as an efficient network of scouts maintained by the informal gaming schools impeded arrest and prosecution.(27)

Gambling was not class-exclusive, of course; it featured as a long-established element in the recreational preferences of the aristocracy. The social importance of gambling by members of the subordinate class lies in the fact that it produced a sense of wellbeing by distracting the individual's awareness from the reality of his own deprivation. Hope, persistent though rarely fulfilled, of a quick and easy means to affluence has a special significance for those who are least likely to achieve high material rewards through employment. Expectant optimism about the ultimate outcome of games of chance tends to be most prevalent amongst those whose position in the occupational hierarchy give them least direct control over their economic and social environment. Efforts seeking a reversal of personal fortunes by luck, chance, fate and mysterious intervention may represent both a system of perceived deprivation and an attempt to relieve it. Habitual gamblers, placing their hopes for personal improvement in games of chance, are probably less inclined to demand a radical revision of the prevailing rules governing the allocation to rewards. Such secular beliefs, Parkin argues, 'may be more counter-revolutionary than the appeals of religion in so far as they appear to exert a strong pull on the minds on the industrial working class.'(28)

Subcultural influences of this kind tended to promote a greater inclination to accommodate to authority. In Talcott Parsons's words:

> Gambling performs important functions for large classes of the populace, very similar to those of magic, as a kind of acting out of tensions which are, symbolically at least, associated with the economic sphere . . .. It . . . is a mechanism for expressing and thus releasing strains related to the economic context which, if this outlet were

completely closed, might be diverted into more dysfunctional channels.(29)

It tends to be the least powerful groups most vulnerable to manipulative exploitation who interpret the socio-economic world as one functioning according to forces which they are unable to harness to their own ends. Advance and improvement apparently depend upon luck. Such fatalistic attitudes and the associated resort to gambling are significantly less widespread amongst lower-class groups whose occupational advantage provides some control over their material environment and social circumstances. The tendency to interpret life chances in this way provides one of the safety valves which affects socio-political stability.

Subcultural recreation: the inns and taverns

There are other spontaneous forms of leisure which were an essential part of a persistent subculture in most industrial towns in the North West and which often manifested their presence by giving rise to law breaking, rowdiness and disturbances of the peace. The pubs, important traditional centres of convivial social life, sometimes fostered forms of recreation which the superordinate class deplored as injurious to health and as a threat both to respectable family life and to law and order. Vocal anti-libertarian opinion strongly disapproved of recreational habits associated with the less salubrious taverns which were deplored as underworld centres of drunkenness, prostitution, and indecent, depraved forms of entertainment such as cockfighting, gambling, ratting, wrestling and dog-baiting. These thrived overtly until the 1872 Licensing Act brought tighter control over the granting of licences to sellers of beer, wines and spirits. Thence such activities persisted illicitly.

In Burnley drunkenness and its attendant evils appear to have formed one of the greatest problems tackled but not resolved by magistrates. By 1870 Burnley had a total of approximately three hundred places where beer and spirits could be bought, including hotels, inns, taverns, taprooms adjoining public houses and numerous off-licences. In addition to these licensed establishments there were the 'hush shops' which carried an illegal trade; these were known to have been in existence in Cop Row off Burnley Lane, at Newcastle Street, Roggerham and Coal Clough. Regular fines of fifty pounds (in one case as much as three hundred pounds) failed to deter landlords in less salubrious districts where vice and cruelty were allegedly condoned as a means of increasing custom. The Poet's Corner in Curzon Street boasted a rat-pit; tavern keepers, according to police records, countenanced gambling, endorsed prostitution, permitted after-hours drinking, and did not discourage drunkenness while the customer had money to spend. In the early 1870s there was an annual average of five hundred cases of drunkenness up before the magistrates. Most offences occurred at weekends when the combination of free time and the week's pay produced some 'unedifying sights' in the Wapping, Salford, Finsleygate, Hilltop and Pickup Croft districts of the town.(30) Yet the police appear to have avoided the kind of provocation likely to make matters worse. Clearly, they were less concerned with imposing moral sanctions than with preserving the peace by keeping a judicious watch on public order. They tended to turn a blind eye upon some of the milder, less damaging offences associated with excessive drinking such as 'sleeping on the roadway or on a midden' and 'driving a horse and cart while unable to hold the reins'.

Drinking was not necessarily excessive, of course. There was more moderate recreational indulgence amongst respectable, law-abiding drinkers who frequented the pubs in search of a convivial social environment to chat, laugh, smoke and relax in the cheerful warmth of enjoyable company.

A more serious threat to the peace as a result of inebriation was the public brawling, fighting and general rowdiness which interrupted the flow of evening traffic in the town and led to vandalism and hooliganism as a more entertaining form of recreation than the respectable alternatives. In the early 1870s the Burnley police often found it necessary to intervene in street fights where both men and women stripped to the waist fought with fists, knees, heads and clogs to the point of exhaustion, and where gangs of brawling drunks armed with knives, pokers and wooden staves mounted unprovoked assaults upon law-abiding pedestrians. If, as evidence suggests, the police were concerned with expedients to suppress disorder rather than to socialize miscreants into the cultural norms of respectability and the ethos of temperance, they were often frustrated in the successful accomplishment of their objective by sheer weight of numbers. Constrained to patrol in pairs for mutual safety, officers found it virtually impossible to carry out their duties when faced with as many as two hundred hooligans from the alleys and taverns determined to prevent an arrest or to liberate a prisoner. In such circumstances the police sometimes suffered injuries at the hands of lawbreakers who subsequently escaped with impunity.(31)

Drink was not necessarily at the root of all the public nuisances to which increased leisure time gave rise. On Sunday afternoons and at weekends in general hooliganism was alleged to be a public scandal; gangs of youths shouting raucous insults and obscenities jostled people on the footpaths or loitered at street corners. Clearly, there were some, possibly many, who had not yet been reached by socializing impulses 'from above' or who, on the basis of the recreational evidence at least, chose to reject the message of the moralist. In Burnley and other northern industrial towns it was the poorer, crowded slum districts which were a cause of much anxiety to police and magistrates.

Recreational preferences such as these, which occupied the leisure hours of a small but significant minority, cannot be dismissed simply as manifestations of petty crime. Excessive drinking and its attendant misdemeanours were an integral part of nineteenth-century recreational habits. The crimes were usually of the less serious, minor kind. Such activities are socially significant in that they enabled the perpetrators to flout established authority in all kinds of trivial ways, to challenge superordinates intermittently but recurrently in an essentially peripheral manner which offered no major threat to the established socio-political structure. Without doubt there was something very satisfying in the ability to 'cock a snook' at entrenched authority. It allowed miscreants to act out, in ways less damaging to the prevailing socio-economic order, frustrations and grievances which might otherwise have been channelled into more effective forms of protest against the current distribution of power and privilege.

Recreation, acquiescence and the rhythm of life

The recreational options available to the masses in later nineteenth century industrial towns were numerous. It is the sum of these multiple recreational choices which contributed in no small degree to the general acquiescence of the period. The sources of provision and the intentions of the providers are less relevant than the fact that opportunities for recreation proliferated. No provider was in a monopoly position, and conversely no individual is likely to have limited his or her consumer preference exclusively to what was made available from a single source.

Arguments premised upon the ability of the leaders of urban communities to promote deference via rational recreation which served to socialize subordinates into dominant ideology are unconvincing. Even in the industrial towns of the North West, where urban economies were characteristically dominated by a handful of major employers, there were many townsfolk who were not extensively exposed to direct and indirect influences 'from above'. The factory-based cotton industry may have had considerable influence in shaping the character of the occupational communities which clustered around the mills in many of the towns of textile Lancashire; it must be admitted, as Joyce(32) notes, that of the total population (including all ages and both those who were occupied and unoccupied) 34 per cent were employed in cotton in Blackburn, 30 per cent in Preston, 29 per cent in Oldham and 24 per cent in Bolton. Elsewhere there were large companies in other major industries: Crosfield's in soap and chemicals and Greenall's in brewing in Warrington, Pilkington's in glass in St. Helens, the Brocklehursts in silk in Macclesfield, Thursbys in coal in the Burnley district. Yet these urban economies also contained numerous small firms, a multitude of retail outlets, the self-employed and casual workers in a bewildering variety of trades. Nor should the role of employer-dominated centres of worship in moulding attitudes through the agency of religious, educational and recreational amenities be over-stated. The Mann Census disclosed as early as 1851 only limited attendance on Census Sunday. What needs to be stressed is that subordinates who made use of the opportunities provided 'from above' may well have appreciated employers' generosity, but they were not necessarily socialized into the ideology of submission. Acquiescence is not a proxy for deference.(33)

Employer-provided recreational amenities probably went some way socio-psychologically in promoting goodwill in the workplace and beyond it, but even this argument needs to be scaled down; not all leading employers invested time, energy, effort and hard cash in the kind of comprehensive, widely variegated recreational systems constructed by the Crosfields in Warrington and by the Masons in Ashton. Minimalist practice consisting of works trips and tea treats was even less likely to result in the internalization of superordinates' normative values.

The social and political stability of industrial towns cannot be explained away in terms of the socialization of one class by another via investment in an appropriate form of recreation. Similar claims premised upon the influence of educational and religious institutions provided by the dominant class are equally suspect. But whereas schooling affected the individual for only a few years in the whole life experience and religious observance was an option chosen by one half the population at mid-century (and conjecturally by a declining proportion in the ensuing decades), the experience of at least *some* leisure to devote to recreation was pervasive and applied to the individual's lifetime.

The modern 'leisure age' dates from the later nineteenth century. It was in this era that leisure for significantly large numbers was tending to become blended into a common rhythm of life.(34) The rhythm of urban industrial life revolved around the organization of work. In industrial societies it involved the worker being on the job at specified times and it affected people doing jobs of every description. The general effect of this regularity in the organization of work was to give rise to a common, repetitive pattern of life with periods of work and leisure occurring in much the same sequence since the lives of all members of urban industrial towns were shaped by the same industrial system. The tendency introduced a daily, weekly and yearly rhythmic cycle into the evolving relationship between work and non-work time in that leisure recurred for a majority of subordinate class members in a regular, predictable and prevalent cycle. The way in which free time came to be distributed in a common cyclical pattern is arguably one of the most distinctive features of leisure in later nineteenth century industrial society. It was this very regularity, predictability and prevalence which enabled the providers of recreational opportunities to plan and arrange what was to be made available - theatre performances, sports fixtures, seaside excursions - to coincide with the periods when it was known that the bulk of the population would be free. Most people today spend much of their non-work time at home with their families, and it is highly probable that this was also the case historically; but the later nineteenth century saw an upsurge of interest in leisure pursuits undertaken outside the home.

By general consent the day-to-day experience of work affects recreational preferences. Friedman's research(35) into the effects of job specialization in present-day factory work led him to conclude that the socio-psychologically inhibiting monotonization and routinization of work tasks give rise to distinctive kinds of hobbies and pastimes designed to make boring jobs tolerable. One means to achieving this objective is to devote spare time to creative leisure activities to give expression to skills and talents unused or frustrated in the sphere of employment. An alternative way of becoming reconciled to stultifying, monotonous work is to devote part of non-work time to recreational experiences giving momentary emotional release and amusement which can serve to repress an awareness of work-related dissatisfaction. None of this is unique to the twentieth century; arguably the working environment of the later nineteenth century gave rise to a similar recreational response - an intuitive resort to leisure pursuits which compensated for physical and psychological constraints imposed by tedious routinized work tasks in mill, mine and factory. Job dissatisfaction was offset by recreational satisfaction.

Recreational choice depends upon the dissatisfactions attached to the particular job, but it is also a function of individual talents, gender and age. In the nineteenth century arduous, physically exhausting work, particularly where older workers were involved, is likely to have promoted an inclination to some of the more passive leisure activities as a means to relaxation. Physically inhibiting work may have led to a preference, especially among the young, for energetic, participatory sports as an outlet for physical energies unused during the working day. Either way the range of recreational choices available in the era catered for both majority and minority interests.

None of the foregoing is to assume that recreation as a self-help 'welfare device' was effectively therapeutic for everyone. It is probable that some people could certainly identify their personal recreational needs and preferences but were prevented from participating - by the lack of opportunity, by not having the appropriate contacts, by diffidence or reticence which inhibited individuals from breaking into the particular social circle. Others may have failed to join in group activities, whether formally or informally organized, by a failure to identify their own needs; not all of us have an intuitive understanding of the recreational component which is missing from our lives, and in consequence remain trapped in the general malaise of 'all's wrong with the world'. In such cases frustrations find other, less socially acceptable outlets or, by remaining bottled up within the individual, produce physical or psychological debility.

The experience of work undoubtedly affects how people spend their leisure and what pastimes they choose; but conversely the experience of leisure and recreation affects behaviour and attitudes to work and, by an extension of this argument, to those in positions of authority in the workplace. Recreational pursuits, whether active or passive and from whatever originating source, have recuperative and therapeutic qualities which boost the morale and promote a general sense of wellbeing. The significance of these recuperative and therapeutic qualities should not be under-estimated.

Company-sponsored recreation allowed the individual to be associated with the workplace in a dimension other than employment and its related structure of authority, status and discipline. One potential effect was to reduce a sense of alienation so that cooperation and consent were the more likely to be willing than grudging. The blurring of the lines of demarcation between work and leisure and between the different status groups within the occupational structure served to build bridges of confidence and communication.

There are additional implications arising from recreational choices not directly or indirectly linked with the employing enterprise. It is necessary, as Roberts(36) notes, to refer to the experiences, lifestyle and attitudes developed outside the workplace in explaining the ways in which people react to work. The sort of work people are willing to do is often only comprehensible in terms of aspirations acquired outside the workplace based on the desire to spend free time and money in particular ways. Job satisfaction as conventionally defined may be non-existent, but there may be satisfaction with the job because instrumentally it provides the wherewithal to achieving non-work objectives. The later nineteenth century was an era in which leisure was fast becoming the focal element in people's lives - unsurprisingly, given the meaningless stultifying nature of many industrial work tasks. Conjecturally, in such circumstances it was leisure which imparted a meaning to work, coincidentally promoting not only accommodation to the symbols of work authority but also acquiescence in the prevailing, employer-dominated, socio-political structure.

The point which has been pressed in the foregoing argument is that recreation of whatever kind, irrespective of the originating source, acts as a safety valve for pressures built up by the experience of disprivilege and deprivation, grievance and discontent in other dimensions of urban existence. It functions as a palliative to stress, tension and frustration, whether physical or psychological. It offers the means to relaxation and recuperation, and in so doing enhances health, promotes a sense of well-being and improves the individual's general outlook on life. Small, affordable pleasures to enjoy immediately and to look forward to in the near future make the vicissitudes of subordinate existence the more bearable and help the individual to come to terms with circumstances which may, or may not, be changeable in the future. This is not to allege that the stability of the period is entirely attributable to mass participation in recreation - simplistic mono-causal explanations are unconvincing - but to claim that recreation played a more important role than is generally acknowledged in promoting acquiescence.

References

1. Cunningham, H., 'The Metropolitan Fairs: A Case Study in the Social Control of Leisure', and also Storch, R.D., 'The Problem of Working Class Leisure: Some Roots of Middle Class Moral Reform in the Industrial North, 1825-50', both in Donajgrodski, A.P., ed., *Social Control in Nineteenth Century Britain*, Croom Helm, 1977.

2. Thompson, F.M.L., 'Social Control in Victorian Britain', *Economic History Review*, 2nd Series, XXXIV, 1981, pp. 189-208; Jones, G. S., 'Class Expression versus Social Control: A Critique of Recent Trends in the Social History of Leisure', in Jones, G. S., ed., *Languages of Class*, Cambridge University Press, 1983.

3. Pimlott, J.A.R., *The Englishman's Holiday: A Social History*, 2nd edition, Harvester, 1976, ch. 8.

4. Saul, S.B., *The Myth of the Great Depression, 1873-96* , Macmillan, 1969, pp. 50-4.

5. *Ashton Reporter*, 31 Jan. 1880.

6. Joyce, P., 'The Factory Politics of Lancashire in the Later Nineteenth Century', *Historical Journal*, XVIII, 1975, pp. 225-53.

7. Musson, A.E., *Enterprise in Soap and Chemicals: The Crosfields of Warrington, 1815-1965*, Manchester University Press, 1965, ch. 10.

8. Bennett, W., *The History of Burnley*, Burnley Corporation, 1951, IV, p. 186.

9. Quoted in Musson, A.E., *op. cit.*, p. 117.

10. Many announcements and reports of results in *Burnley Gazette* and *Burnley Express* during the playing season.

11. Russell, A., 'Élites at the Local Level of Society: Social Leadership in Burnley, 1870-1900', M.A. dissertation, University of Lancaster, 1976, ch. 1, section B.

12. See, for example, advertisements in *Burnley Gazette*, 21 Oct. 1877, 26 Feb. 1879 and 2 Nov. 1880.

13. Bennett, W., *op. cit.*, p. 211.

14. Musson, A.E., *op. cit.*, p. 124.

15. Walton, J.K., 'The Demand for Working Class Seaside Holidays in Victorian England', *Economic History Review*, 2nd Series, XXXIV, 1981, pp. 249-65. Some useful insights are to be found also in Walton, J.K., *The English Seaside Resort: A Social History, 1750-1914*, Leicester University Press, 1983; Pimlott, J.A.R., *op. cit.*; Delgado, A., *The Annual Outing and Other Excursions*, Allen and Unwin, 1977.

16. Walton, J.K., 'The Demand for Working Class Seaside Holidays in Victorian England', *Economic History Review*, 2nd Series, XXXIV, 1981, pp. 249-65.

17. *Ibid.*

18. Details *ibid.*

19. Thompson, F.M.L., *op. cit.*, p. 200.

20. Cunningham, H. in Donajgrodski, A.P., ed., *op. cit.*; see also Bailey, P., *Leisure and Class in Victorian England: Rational Recreation and the Contest for Control, 1830-85*, Routledge and Kegan Paul, 1978, pp. 20-3, 85-7; Thompson, F.M.L., *op. cit.*, p. 198.

21. Bennett, W., *op. cit.*, ch. 5; see also advertisements in *Burnley Gazette* in the period as, for example, 2 Dec. 1881, 14 Dec. 1882.

22. Bailey, P., *op. cit.*, pp. 130-46; Thompson, F.M.L., *op. cit.*, p. 201; see also Walvin, J., *The People's Game: A Social History of Football*, Allen Lane, 1975.

23. *Ibid.*

24. Parker, S., *The Society of Leisure*, Allen and Unwin, 1976, pp. 111-12.

25. Bennett, W., *op. cit.*, p. 126.

26. *Ibid.*, p. 18.

27. *Ibid.*; see also frequent references in *Burnley Gazette* and *Burnley Express*, especially letters to the press.

28. Parkin, F., *op. cit.*, p. 77.

29. Parsons, T., *The Social System*, Routledge and Kegan Paul, 1951.

30. Many references to drink-related disturbances of the peace in the Burnley press; see also Bennett, W., *op. cit.*, ch. 6.

31. Bennett, W., *op. cit.*, p. 16.

32. Joyce, P., *op.cit.*, p. 529.

33. Russell, A., 'Local Élites and the Working Class Response in the North West, 1870-95: Paternalism and Deference Reconsidered', *Northern History*, XXIII, 1987, pp. 153-73; see also the general line of argument in Newby, H., *The Deferential Worker*, Allen Lane, 1977, ch. 1; Newby, H., 'The Deferential Dialectic', *Comparative Studies in Society and History*, XVII, 1975, pp. 139-64.

34. Roberts, K., *Leisure,* Longman, 1970, p. 11.

35. Friedman, G., *The Anatomy of Work: The Implications of Specialization,* Heinemann, 1961.

36. Roberts, K., *op. cit.*, p. 37.

8

Religion and Education
Some Implications for Acquiescence

Introduction

Religion and education are often represented as important social sources of stability, the more so when there are close institutional links between the two, as in the nineteenth century when educational authority was reinforced by religious authority and state subvention. One body of opinion, as we have seen, suggests that religious ideology promoted deferential endorsement of what was viewed as a divinely ordained stratification order - an endorsement rendered the more likely by Christian doctrine predicting rich rewards in the afterlife for the sufferings endured in the essentially transient existence of the present world. It is argued that members of the superordinate class, who predominated in the leadership of religious and educational institutions, were strategically placed to socialize the masses into the ideology of deferential submission. Religious values pervaded education. In both the formal and 'hidden' curricula elementary education, provided largely by the churches and chapels, promoted the virtues of humility, self-denial, obedience, piety, sobriety and respect for one's elders and betters. In consequence, religion and education rendered subordinates the less susceptible to the attractions of radicalism.

Undoubtedly, exposure to religious and educational morality produced deference in some, but arguments seeking to represent this as the general response are untenable. The experience of religion and education was far from pervasive in the period under review, and there were other counter pressures which contributed to the shaping of attitudes. There were limits to both influences, yet both contributed something to acquiescence in the prevailing socio-economic order and in the established two-party political *status quo*.

The poor electoral performance of Socialism is not to be

231

explained solely, or even primarily, in terms of the countervailing influence of Christian religion. Religion and radicalism were not necessarily alternative choices. Members of congregations were not invariably indoctrinated wholesale in Christian ideology, and there were many subordinates who had no, or only limited, direct exposure to the Christian value system. In the case of education the general response was likely to have been one of accommodation rather than deference. Firstly, to the extent that education permitted fluidity between the social strata, thus enabling the more able and ambitious to attain higher social status, the response is likely to have been one of increased acquiescence in the socio-economic order. Secondly, children whose school performance continuously confronted them with the reality of their own merely average or below average ability would arguably be encouraged by this experience to moderate their expectations of the world beyond the school gates; they would come to terms the more readily with limited life chances. Thirdly, children in the later nineteenth century experienced comparatively brief exposure to the socializing influence of the school. Their employment objectives and occupational destinations were not necessarily a function of educational attainment, therefore, but rather a matter of personal or peer group preference, family tradition and local job opportunities. If objectives, moulded by other influences, were fulfilled, a degree of satisfaction would result.

These several considerations need to be explored in greater depth.

Religion

The argument has been advanced by some sociologists and theologians that there is competition between radical political movements and religious sects for the hearts and minds of the disprivileged. One body of opinion, noted earlier, maintains that those who have been successfully socialized into attitudes such as humble acceptance of one's lot, fortitude in the face of suffering in the temporal world of the present and the assurance of compensating spiritual rewards in the eternal life hereafter are the less susceptible to the arguments of the radicals.[1] Others, however, have produced evidence to show that, where religious groups and political movements are in competition, success does not necessarily fall to the former. Niebuhr's[2] research, for example, led him to conclude that radical politics tended to exert a greater pull, because the solutions promised were both more immediate and more relevant to the deprived, and were achievable in the present world, rather than delayed until the next.(3) Far from functioning as a threat to radicalism, religious influences were likely to be undermined by the more compelling attraction of movements seeking to improve material circumstances in the here and now. Additionally, there are several surveys which support Niebuhr's contention that members of the subordinate social stratum are less likely to attend places of worship and less inclined to hold religious views than are members of the dominant stratum. The same evidence suggests that, in so far as radical movements are already well-established amongst the subordinate class, religious ideology is viewed in a considerably less eligible light. However, other studies(4) have disclosed only weak interest in radicalism in communities where religious movements are already firmly established and have a strong local tradition. Religious ideology is the more influential where radical organization is weak and its tenets unfamiliar or only vaguely understood. The extent to which both ideologies are fully available and equally competitive is also of some, possibly major, significance in the propensity of lower status groups to select either the religious or the radical solution to the problems of disprivilege and low status.

Certainly in Burnley the churches and chapels were first on the urban scene; they were already well-established by the 1860s and 1870s, and opportunities for direct and indirect contact between superordinate class leaders and lower status groups were numerous and by no means confined to Sunday services. In contrast it was not until the late 1880s and the 1890s that the campaigning efforts of Socialist activists began to be effectively organized. It may be the case that during this particular period the unequal nature of the local competition between the rival ideologies - the religious and the radical - goes some way in explaining the comparatively poor initial electoral support for Socialism. In other towns, where the electoral response was stronger, the Socialist bid may have come earlier and the competition may have been less unequal.

All of this assumes that there were only two competitors - religion and radicalism - but there were other rivals for the hearts and minds of the voting population, and arguably the ability of the Socialists to rally support was circumscribed also by the extent of satisfaction with the performance at both central and local government levels of those who represented the long established Liberal and Tory parties. It was, after all, members of these parties who presided over the extension of the Parliamentary franchise in 1867 and 1884 and who extended voting rights to both males and females in elections for municipal, parish and county councils in the same period.(5)

The assumption that those who are drawn into religious movements will necessarily eschew radical politics may be misfounded, however. The two kinds of activity are not always functional alternatives; much depends upon what motivates people into church and chapel attendance. As Parkin notes:

> Many members of the lower strata who are drawn to religion are seeking relief from the kind of personal problems which are not directly related to deprivation of a material or economic kind. Spiritual comfort and support is frequently sought by the chronically sick, the physically malformed, the elderly and lonely, as well as those suffering from various forms of emotional or mental instability. For members of lower strata who are psychically, and not simply materially, deprived religion is likely to have an especially strong appeal - and particularly those forms of belief which incorporate notions of healing by faith or which give an outlet for the uninhibited expression of emotion.(6)

Subordinate class members who fall into this category are unlikely to regard political solutions as a viable alternative. Parkin's observations were based upon his analysis of present-day society but the argument is equally relevant to the urban industrial communities of the preceding century. Sectarian religion probably provided for the 'needs of those for whom the most likely alternative would be not political radicalism but personal disintegration.'(7)

Again, the claim that religion acts as a counter to radicalism by diverting the interests and energies of potential activists away from political causes is not always borne out by the nineteenth-century evidence. As Perkin,(8) Hobsbawm(9) and Thompson(10) have all shown, many of the mid-century Chartist leaders and their supporters were also associated with the activities of sectarian religion, particularly Methodism. Religion and radicalism are not necessarily sharply antithetical. The tenets of Christianity may be interpreted in a politically radical sense by members of the subordinate social stratum; '... normative control ... by the dominant class may to some extent be limited by systematic variations in the interpretation of religious precepts.' Evidence suggests 'man's ability to compartmentalize beliefs so that what appear to be logical or intellectual inconsistencies in ideology are neither interpreted nor experienced as such.'(11) That the human species is capable of espousing apparently contradictory beliefs and values cautions against simplistic generalizations about the socio-political implications of religious behaviour.

If there is need for caution about the *nature* of religious influence, so also is there need for scepticism about its *extent*. In assessing how widespread was the influence of religion upon attitudes in any industrial town consideration must be given to the numerical strength of congregations of practising Christians, and particularly to the proportion of all members of the subordinate class who attended Sunday or weekday services, Bible classes and Sunday school gatherings. Statistical information such as this is not retrievable for the period under review, but the Mann Census of the mid-nineteenth century disclosed that only about half the population attended a place of worship on Census Sunday. Conjecturally the level of attendance declined during the ensuing decades, or at least did not rise significantly. It has been argued that in the twentieth century Sunday observance, as measured by attendance, is more common amongst members of the dominant class than of the subordinate class,(12) and it seems probable that such was the case in the later nineteenth century. Burnley, Blackburn, Oldham and other industrial towns may have had numerous places of Christian worship dominated by leading employers, but characteristically many were comparatively small buildings,(13) limited accommodation being provided because relatively small congregations were expected. Whether all such premises were regularly filled to capacity is doubtful. It seems reasonable to argue that there were probably substantial numbers who were not directly exposed to religious influences. In some cases the attitudes and activities of clerics may well have deterred rather than attracted attendance. In Burnley the killjoy condemnation of theatres by the Reverend Littlehales, the ruthless use of strike-breakers in the mines owned by the Reverend Thursby, and the expulsion of the betting fraternity by Canon Townley-Parker from his estates at Royle can have done little to increase Sunday observance amongst the irreligious.

Townsfolk whose *direct* exposure to religious ideology was of the more prolonged and extensive kind did not necessarily absorb Christian doctrine in its entirety. Members of congregations in the nineteenth century, as today, were probably selective in what they chose to ingest. It was perfectly possibly to subscribe to certain standards of Christian morality - charity, care for one's neighbour, compassion for the sick - and to repudiate what might be viewed as less eligible 'virtues' - humility, self-denial, and the dignity of poverty.

Indirect exposure to religious ideology may have been more extensive; as we have seen, numerous educational, recreational and welfare activities were undertaken by the churches and chapels in Burnley. The socially stabilizing influence of religion may well owe less to the ability of religious leaders to indoctrinate the masses in the tenets of Christianity, than to the practical social services which religious institutions provided.

Education and deference

The explicit objectives of many of those who provided education 'from above' during the first half of the nineteenth century are in no doubt. As McCann(14) has shown in his study of voluntary schooling in the Spitalfields area of London, the aim was to shape attitudes and behaviour at a stage in the child's intellectual development when the mind is most receptive. To inculcate deference would ensure that children, and therefore also the future adult population, would acquire respectful, conformist values and habits of thought and behaviour appropriate to their predestined location in the prevailing stratification order. McCann's scepticism about the outcome of these socializing initiatives is well justified, his line of argument cogently constructed. As Thompson(15) maintains, it seems logical that both parents and children were selective in what they absorbed from their contact with the self-appointed, would-be socializers; voluntarism could characterize the reactions of the recipients as well as the actions of the providers of education. It was perfectly possible to make instrumental use of instruction in basic literacy and numeracy while resisting indoctrination in dominant ideology, astutely to display deferential demeanour while retaining a degree of independence of mind and spirit, shrewdly to maintain some line of contact with a view to future advancement where character references might be useful. Subordinates were surely not incapable of thinking for themselves.

Schooling was affected by educational reforms. The voluntary societies' elementary schools in the later nineteenth century were in many ways far removed from the 'seminaries of slavery' regretted earlier by Cobbett. The gradual secularization of the content of education, noted by Goldstrom,(16) undoubtedly diluted the potency of the ideological creed postulated by the providers. The demand for 'relevance' in education led to a reduction of the time spent on religious teaching and moral character training, and a corresponding increase in the time devoted to the teaching of the 'three Rs' and other useful factual subjects. The process of change gathered momentum from the time when the government department introduced the payment-by-results system, based upon school inspection with grants linked to attendance records and children's proficiency in designated secular subjects.(17)

By the 1880s the subjects taught in addition to the usual reading, writing and arithmetic at Burnley's Red Lion Street School(18) included spelling and grammar, plus algebra, geography and history in the upper standards. At Salem Street School the curriculum appears to have been rather more ambitious. At the beginning of the 1870s children in the first standard were taught reading, writing (in sand trays), arithmetic and spelling; those in the second standard took, in addition to these basics, dictation, writing (on slates or copy books), mental arithmetic and arithmetic (on slates); in the third standard a start was made on grammar and geography; in the fourth standard additional subjects included book-keeping, mensuration, algebra, biology, geography, map drawing, and needlework for the girls. In advertisements alerting townsfolk to the school's opening, the first headmaster stated that Latin, Greek, French and German could be taught 'if desired'.(19) A notable feature of the 1890 code was that woodwork, cookery and laundry work should be introduced into the school curriculum where it was possible to acquire appropriate equipment and to renovate, adapt or extend existing premises. Both the Abel Street and Burnley Wood schools had begun cookery classes within two years of the code's publication.(20)

In 1861 there were changes in the regulations relating to government grants,(21) the effect of which was to further the secularization of the school curriculum. Up to 1861 financial aid to inspected schools had been geared to average attendance, and additional funds were available to assist with the cost of extending school premises and acquiring extra equipment. The maximum grant of 12s. per scholar under the new regulations introduced in 1861 comprised 8s. for success in annual school examinations and 4s. for satisfactory attendance. Under what retrospectively has been termed the 'payment by results' system there was a corresponding reduction in the school's grant if a child failed to pass in any of the 'three Rs' or if the individual scholar's record did not show a minimum of two hundred attendances. In addition, block grants of 1s. to 2s. per scholar were made available for satisfactory school discipline, and 1s. per pupil for those able to sing 'by note' (6d. 'by ear'). There were 'class grants' based on performance in any two subjects chosen from a list which included

English (parsing and analysis, essay writing and literature), geography, history, needlework, science and drawing, plus an extra 2s. for each pupil in upper standards for proficiency in algebra, physiology or French. The grant structure was completed by a block grant of ten shillings per school-child, available regardless of the number of attendances or measured ability.(22)

The effect, it has been claimed, was for schools to bind themselves to a curriculum designed to maximize grant income. Without doubt funds were a major consideration; yet, to the extent that diversification of the curriculum occurred, it had the effect of loosening the traditional emphasis on religion and moral character training. It was expedient for the school to concentrate upon the grant-winning subjects. Schools fortunate enough to have recruited proportionately large numbers of bright children usually made strenuous efforts to retain them because their ability to do well at the inspection earned the full grant.

The major proportion of teaching time in Burnley's elementary schools appears to have been devoted to grant-earning secular subjects. In 1885, for example, Fulledge School earned an average of £1 2s. 6d. per child, Westgate School received 18s. 10 3/4d., Red Lion School was awarded £1 0s. 2d. per child and had the distinction of gaining a higher percentage of 'passes' in the government examination than any other school in the whole of England. Not all schools were as successful as these, of course; the lowest per capita grant to a Burnley school was only 13s. 1 1/4d. Nevertheless, that the overall standard of educational attainment was high, judged on the grant evidence, suggests that the teaching emphasis was firmly on the grant-winning subjects and perhaps also that teachers were more than usually proficient at their jobs.(23)

With the secularization of the *formal* curriculum the time devoted to religious indoctrination was pruned though not completely eliminated. This leaves the *informal* or 'hidden curriculum' - the expressions of approbation and disapprobation, the interests and activities which were implicitly fostered or discouraged, the verbal and non-verbal means of promoting emulation of what was deemed to be desirable conduct, teachers' attitudes inside the classroom and their lifestyle outside it. It is probable that the 'atmosphere' (whether benign or alienating) generated by social interaction within the school contributed something to the shaping of children's future outlook on life. But this is very different from a process of socialization in the ideology of submission. Nor should it be assumed that the values of the providers and recipients of elementary education were always sharply antithetical. Logically, there was a degree of consensus in the values and standards of conduct approved both by the educationists and by the parents of school populations. Without doubt, most parents subscribed to the desirability of promoting honesty, punctuality, cleanliness, orderliness, politeness, respect for people and property, care for the less fortunate - not because some moralizing middle-class dignitary told them to do so, but because members of the subordinate class were capable of deductive thought and valued these virtues in their own right. Some standards of personal conduct were common to both the dominant and the subordinate code.

Another limitation upon the potential influence of dominant ideology was the pupil-teacher ratio and the pupil-teacher system; both, in part at least, were a function of cost. Limited financial resources - parental fees, state subvention geared to payment by results, voluntary fund-raising, gifts and bequests - dictated a policy of economy, a policy not always successfully applied. In point of fact many of the smaller chapels found it cost-effectively difficult to maintain their schools with the numbers enrolled, a problem exacerbated by what appears to have been an over-supply of school accommodation in Burnley.(24) There were closures long before competition from the non-denominational Board schools in the 1890s. Bethesda Congregational School, opened in 1851, was closed as early as 1856. The Primitive Methodists' Hammerton Street School, opened in 1870, ran for only three years. The Congregational Salem School, dating from 1863, closed in the mid-1870s. The Wesleyan School at Bartle Mills, with its first intake in 1874, remained open for only two years.

Costs were a major consideration. Economy of expenditure upon teachers' salaries resulted in large classes. The extensive use of pupil teachers - a cheap, expendable, numerically flexible form of labour - permitted school governors to prune total salary costs even further. The practice of relating the headteacher's salary to the number of children on roll was an inducement to increased recruitment; moreover, the greater the number of children, the larger the school's fee income from parents and grant income from the state. Large schools permitted economies of scale.

School governors did not always honour their pledges of course. For example, one of Burnley's headteachers who had spent fifteen years building up his school from 133 to 358 pupils, thereby raising the fee income from £70 to £325 per annum, was required to accept a cut in his salary. His resistance cost him his job.(25)

Such treatment of teaching staffs may not have been widespread, but incidents of this kind underline the fact that teachers did not necessarily feel an identification of interests with the philanthropists who supplied much of the investment capital and running expenses of schools. Teachers, as paid employees, did not inevitably share the ideological sentiments of those who appointed them, and the treatment meted out to them could be alienating.

The size of classes necessitated conformity to what often amounted to regimented classroom behaviour in order that teaching could proceed at all. But regimented physical activity and rote-learning do not signify an increased probability of success in efforts to socialize children in dominant ideology. Large classes may have permitted economies of scale but they circumscribed the teacher's ability to establish direct personal rapport with each and every child. Conformity and obedience in classroom behaviour may have been successfully imposed by strict disciplinarian teachers, but evidence of corresponding success in control of the mind is more difficult to prove. Harsh discipline was likely to produce resentful compliance or even truancy rather than an identification of interests with the authoritarians of elementary schooling. Until 1895 certificated teachers were required to manage classes of up to 139 children. Pupil-teachers (youthful trainees whose own formal education was still proceeding) taught for six hours a day for a shilling or two per week. Arguably their objectives were of the practical kind - class control and the teaching of factual knowledge rather than the socialization of their charges in a particular ideology.

It is not obvious why pupil-teachers, many of them from subordinate-class home backgrounds, should be sufficiently conversant with the normative code of the providers of education or so persuaded of its moral worth as to able or indeed willing to transmit the appropriate message effectively further down the age range of the school population. The education of pupil-teachers did not go far beyond the elementary level. An entrant to the 'profession' was usually only thirteen years of age. He or she passed the initial year as a probationer on 'candidate' status with a salary of only five pounds a year, followed by a four-year period as an indentured pupil-teacher earning less than twenty pounds a year. Attempts to represent these as missionary zealots intent on disseminating dominant ideology are somewhat unconvincing. Pupil-teachers were often employed in large numbers and were expected to take full charge of classes. In the early 1870s the usual ratio was four pupil-teachers to one certificated teacher. The Red Lion Street School in Burnley, with roughly 960 children on roll, had a teaching staff of only three trained, certificated teachers who were supported by four uncertificated teachers and thirteen pupil-teachers.(26)

If the secularization of the subjects taught, class size and the use of pupil-teachers all reduced the potency of dominant ideology, other factors worked in the same general direction. Absenteeism, truancy, the half-time system, and the number of years spent in education, which ensured only limited exposure to the influence of the socializers, all need to be taken into consideration.

The duration of school life for many children tended to be limited to a comparatively short period and one sometimes characterized by interruptions. Parents with large families and low incomes were inclined to condone absenteeism when money could not be spared for schooling. Other youngsters, with parental connivance, took time off from school intermittently as and when seasonal work was to be had, or when daughters were needed to help in the home. In the most deprived districts parents, apparently unconvinced by arguments urging the need for education, continued to resist efforts to improve attendance. There was a persistent minority who evaded the socializing influence of the educators as often and for as long as possible.(27)

The problem of securing regular attendance and of retaining pupils when other schools were accessible was an intractable one which constituted a recurrent source of vexation to headteachers. The regret of one Burnley headteacher was recorded in the school log book which states that three of his best scholars had recently transferred to another school, a particularly lamentable occurrence since each needed only three more attendances to satisfy the grant requirement. Another headteacher recorded that he had lost half his scholars to two newly-built schools so that his own was over-staffed. Problems of this order must be viewed in the context of the constant battle against wilful absenteeism. The battle continued apparently unabated, despite action taken in 1871 by the Burnley School Board during the first year of its existence to make compulsory the school attendance of all children in the borough between the ages of five and thirteen. The problem of securing regular attendance led in one school to a teacher being despatched into the streets to round up the truants. Most school log books record the occasional absence of large numbers of pupils on account of 'a good cricket match', 'a circus', 'a cattle show' or 'bad weather'. In 1871, when the Burnley School Board was constituted in the wake of the 1870 Education Act, attendance in the district was as low as 58 per cent, a situation which had not improved dramatically even by 1900 when, after three decades of threats and appeals by the School Board, attendance was still only 77 per cent.(28)

Absenteeism was exacerbated by the requirement to pay school fees. Among the most pressing of the difficulties which beset the activities of the Burnley School Board during the 1870s was the dilemma of how to reconcile the required attendance of children with parental ability or willingness to pay. The failure of some parents to meet the weekly cost was a function of family size as much as level of income. In Burnley the scale of school fees, linked to the child's age and school standard, appears to have been fairly uniform, though this is not to deny that there was some 'undercutting' in what was, after all, a competitive market. By the beginning of the 1870s the minimum and maximum fees at St Peter's School were 3d. and 7d. per week respectively; at Salem the charge ranged from 3d. at the lower end of the scale to 1s. at the upper extreme in 1863 but by the 1870s the pressure of competition in recruiting and retaining scholars necessitated a reduction to a scale of from 2d. to 6d.

The vast majority were low fee-payers at this time. Of the total of some 4,910 children in Burnley's denominational elementary schools in 1870, 291 were 'free placers', 4,135 paid between 1d. and 3 1/2d. while a minority of only 484 paid 4d. or more. It could be difficult, however, for some low-income families to find even the modest sums charged at the lower end of the scale.

The Burnley School Board's solution to this problem amounted in practice to a virtually unworkable compromise. The Board agreed to pay the relevant fees where financial hardship for the family could be proved but, since supplying the necessary proof involved parents in the deterrent experience of seeking assistance from the local Board of Guardians, very few availed themselves of the opportunity. Only forty-nine applications were made to the School Board during the first eighteen months of its existence. The School Board's attendance officers were urged as an alternative strategy to adopt a more persuasive approach, to urge parents by rational argument into compliance with the attendance requirement. In the face of persistent parental intransigence there was frequent resort to the punitive powers of the magistrates, but not even this resolved the problem totally.(29)

Exposure to the socializing intentions of the educators was also limited by the half-time system and by regulations permitting early leaving. The half-time system was sufficiently widespread in Burnley to ensure that in the early 1870s, and for many years thereafter, almost a third of all school children in the area were registered as half-timers.(30) A fairly straightforward procedure, plus requirements which it was not difficult to meet, enabled children of at least average ability between the ages of ten and thirteen to confine their school attendance to two-and-a-half days per week. The qualification the individual had to fulfil - the demonstrated ability to pass the Third Standard examination set by a Government Inspector of Schools - was not excessively demanding. It was not until the minimum working age was raised to eleven years in 1891 that the percentage of all half-timers in Burnley fell to 20 per cent and thence to a mere 7 per cent in 1901 when the age was raised further to twelve years. The half-time system as such was not abandoned until 1920.

Early leaving also served to reduce the duration of the child's school life. This practice, sanctioned in the case of any pupil aged at least ten years who was able to pass the Fifth Standard examination, permitted those who qualified to leave school to take up full-time employment - or to 'roam the streets'.(31)

The problem of absenteeism, the extensive use made of the half-time regulation and exit for at least some via the early-leaving loophole all suggest that for a sizeable proportion there was no great commitment ideologically or otherwise to the unnecessary prolongation of education. It is perfectly true that many leading employers benefited from the stream of cheap youthful labour thus released into the local employment market; members of the superordinate class gained in terms of production costs and labour recruitment, but the effect was to limit exposure to the socializing influence of the educators. Arguably both pull and push factors were involved in the propensity to leave at the first opportunity.

For youngsters the attraction of earning money in the world of work was strong, the more so where the family needed extra cash and where the educational experience had been a deterrent one suffered in an environment which was not conducive to physical comfort. Attitudes, it is generally acknowledged, are affected by environmental circumstances. This being the case, it is difficult to understand how the often overcrowded unsatisfactory school buildings (sometimes renovated rather than purpose-built structures) could encourage vertically-orientated sentiments of allegiance and loyalty. Classrooms tended to be small relative to class size. In one recorded case in Burnley 127 children spent the whole of the school day in a classroom measuring only eight yards by six-and-a-half yards. Another example quoted in an inspector's report was that of a school which consisted of a single room whose limited dimensions were further reduced by a useless gallery which took up half the floor space. The furniture was so closely crowded that movement between the rows of desks was difficult, and the teachers and the inspector were obliged constantly to change places to permit teaching to proceed. Miss Needham's, one of four uninspected schools in the area in 1871, reputedly consisted of a single room housing 148 children with Miss Needham herself as the only teacher.(32)

All of these limitations upon the effectiveness of education as an instrument of socialization in dominant ideology were compounded by the belated activities of the Burnley School Board and the 'free education issue'. Competition from other readily accessible denominational schools in the area, the resultant price war when lower fees were charged in the first purpose-built Board school, and finally the Board of Education's termination of compulsory fee paying ultimately put several chapel schools out of business. 'Free' education seriously weakened the structure of voluntary schooling in Burnley and conjecturally loosened whatever hold the religious sects had over the hearts and minds of the young.

The Burnley School Board held its first meeting in January 1871 and in April of that year issued a public notice requiring the school attendance of all children in the area between the ages of five and thirteen years. As we have seen, no Board schools were provided for several years since the existing accommodation was judged to be adequate and the Board, dominated as it was by individuals with a vested interest in maintaining the viability of the voluntary denominational schools, had free scope to exercise discretionary power in the matter.

The first Board school, located in Abel Street, was opened in the early 1890s. As the School Board planned to levy a charge of only 1d. per week for each child, the governors and managers of the voluntary schools had no alternative but reluctantly to introduce a corresponding reduction in their own charges to 1d. a week for younger children and 2d. for others. The feared closure of many of these schools in consequence of their reduced fee income was hastened by the Board of Education's directive to terminate the practice of fee paying in Board schools.

The availability of 'free' education in the Board schools caused many parents to transfer their children from the voluntary schools. Unsurprisingly, there was widespread parental discontent about the insufficiency of free places. Several petitions requesting free education were submitted to the Burnley School Board in 1894 - by the residents of Wood Top, Stoneyholme, Accrington Road, Gannow and Rose Grove. Pressures such as these forced some of the chapels to close their schools or to lease their school premises to the Board for use as free schools until more modern accommodation could be built. The Wesleyans' Rosegrove School erected in 1873 was closed in 1898, their Accrington Road School opened in 1876 was taken over by the School Board in 1895 and closed in 1904. The United Methodists' Brunswick School built in 1876 closed in 1891, their Gannow School opened in the mid-1870s closed at the end of the century, and Claremont School opened as late as 1894 closed in 1927. Of the Baptist schools, Ebenezer, opened in 1870, was acquired by the School Board in 1894 and closed in 1904, North Street, opened in 1879, was taken over in 1898 and closed in 1904 also. The Congregational Westgate School, opened in 1863 and handed over to the School Board in 1895, was closed in 1900.(33)

Schools provided by other sects, which found ways of weathering the storm of competition, survived successfully. The Church of England's schools continued to educate quite large numbers, despite what appears to have been a minimal level of financial assistance from the rates. New Anglican schools included Wood Top opened in 1873, Healey Wood opened in 1881 and St John's which had its first intake in 1890. The Roman Catholic schools also survived. The boys' and girls' schools at St Mary's and Burnley Wood remained viable and new premises were opened in association with St Thomas's in 1871 and St John's in 1893. Yet for the several reasons already discussed, education in even these more enduring denominational schools had by this time become potentially less effective as a means to disseminate dominant ideology.

Schooling and acquiescence

We have argued that there were limitations to the potential influence of education as an instrument to promote deference amongst the generality of subordinate-class children. There is need for scepticism about arguments seeking to attribute the socio-political stability of the period to the imposition of dominant ideology upon school populations but, if education did not produce deference, it went some way in promoting acquiescence.

Education acts as a filter or sorter. In the process of fostering the development of general and special abilities it performs an allocational function in channelling individuals into appropriate occupations. To the extent that this function is effectively performed, education contributes to socio-political stability in that it ensures a degree of flexibility in the stratification order.(34)

The experience of deprivation in the prevailing distribution of rewards is a potential source of social and political instability, but a degree of openness or fluidity in the class system - opportunities for at least some of the less privileged to achieve more favourable positions - serves as a safety valve to release pressures built up by a sense of grievance and alienation. In the later nineteenth century there were opportunities for some of the more able and more ambitious members of the subordinate class to achieve upward occupational mobility. This was partially attributable to the improvements in education which equipped the more able with the necessary qualifications for advancement, but in part also it was attributable to increased opportunities in white-collar employment(35) both in private business enterprises and in public bureaucracy. The expansion of the tertiary sector of the economy increased the demand for clerical personnel; technological advance affected the demand for skilled manual workers and technicians. A significant observation, made by Parkin, is the fact that higher status groups in industrializing societies do not usually reproduce themselves sufficiently to fill all the new positions. Where the demand for people to fill white-collar positions exceeds current supply, attempts are made to draw recruits from the subordinate strata. The same argument applies in the case of technical and mechanical work in that employment in skilled manual jobs provides opportunities for advancement by those lower down the socio-economic scale.

Opportunities for upward occupational mobility have obvious implications for socio-political stability. Flexibility of this kind, Parkin notes:

> . . . provides an escape route . . . for the most able and ambitious members of the underclass, thereby easing some of the tensions generated by inequality. Elevation . . . represents a *personal* solution to the problems of low status, and as such tends to weaken collectivist efforts to improve the lot of the underclass as a whole.(36)

The process of syphoning off potential discontent may well be a source of weakness to radical movements. It is perfectly true, of course, that the meritocratic process of occupational selection via educational attainment today, and arguably even more so in the later nineteenth century, is not sufficiently precise as to draw off *all* the available talent; but this is not to deny the validity of the generalization that opportunities for upward mobility serve to reduce some of the tensions inherent in a stratified system, thereby promoting acquiescence in the prevailing order. For this to be the outcome, it is not necessary that advancement should affect dramatically large numbers. It is probable that in nineteenth-century industrial towns most mobility, as today, was relatively short-range, the children of wage-workers in manual employment achieving fairly modest white-collar positions as clerks, school teachers, shop assistants and salesmen. There was undoubtedly an element of commercial self-interest in the Crosfields' sponsorship of technical education in Warrington, and in employers' active involvement in the affairs of the Mechanics' and Church Institutes in Burnley, but clearly there were also status and material gains for the more competent, strongly motivated individuals who chose to seek a personal solution to the problems of disprivilege. There were at least some opportunities for upward mobility in the industrial towns of the North West; in the nearby rail-linked commercial and trading centres of Manchester and Liverpool there were good prospects for white-collar employment.

In present-day society upward mobility of this kind is frequently associated with a political shift from 'Left' to 'Right'. In Burnley and similar towns the Socialists did not have a firmly established political presence until the 1890s. To the extent that upward occupational mobility occurred, the probable effect was not so much to de-radicalize attitudes but to inhibit the growth of interest in the new ideology.

Social mobility, even of the typically short-range variety, tends to affect the life circumstances of a minority of the subordinate class. In consequence the major proportion of those born into this class will remain in it, as will their children in the next generation. It is amongst this numerically large section, where the vicissitudes of low status are not palliated by prospects for personal advancement, that moral commitment to the prevailing socio-political order might be expected to be weakest. Consequently, it is these persistently disprivileged members of the population for whom an eligible solution might be found in an ideology seeking to change the prevailing socio-political structure with its associated inequalities of status and material rewards. But the response to the problem of low status may not take the form of a resort to radicalism.

An alternative reaction to narrowly restricted life chances may be resignation rather than active resentment. The ability to reconcile oneself to the inevitability of one's lot is an essential part of survival strategy. The construction of accommodative strategies is a marked reaction amongst the disprivilege of the present day, and it is reasonable to assume that this occurred also in the later nineteenth century. As Parkin observes:

> Those who are aware that they occupy a humble place in the hierarchy of rewards are often inclined to tailor their expectations of life to a correspondingly modest level. When expectations are low, the frustration caused by unsatisfied wants is the more easily avoided.(37)

Education is one of the mechanisms which, by shaping aspirations and ambitions, prepares the individual for the hard realities to be encountered in post-school life. But acquiescence of this kind and for this reason is far removed from deference produced by socialization in dominant ideology. A contributory factor in promoting accommodation is a lack of awareness; dissatisfaction amongst the deprived, it has been convincingly argued,(38) is often lower than might be expected, because when people make comparisons the selected reference point tends to be the life situation of those in roughly similar socio-economic circumstances rather than of those who are vastly more advantaged. As Runciman has shown, there tends to be a marked ignorance amongst some lower-status groups of the nature and degree of the several inequalities which pervade society as a whole. Members of urban industrial communities in the later nineteenth century, as we have seen, were neither insulated nor isolated from life beyond the immediate neighbourhood.

The point which needs emphasis, however, is that when the economic grievances of Burnley's weavers took on collective expression in 1873, comparison was made, not with privileged white-collar groups in Burnley, but with other weavers in the neighbouring town of Blackburn where wage-rates were reportedly higher. The fact that highly-paid groups in non-manual employment were outside the socio-economic vision of many lower status groups means that the latter did not necessarily feel deprived or resent the income differential. The objective of the 1873 weavers' strike was simply to re-establish standardized pay and conditions for all those engaged in similar work.

For a *minority*, possibly a substantial one, upward occupational mobility is likely to have promoted acquiescence in the prevailing stratification order; for a *majority*, acquiescence may well have been the result of modest expectations and aspirations. It is one of the major objectives of Socialist groups to sensitize the masses to the wide and systematic material disparities generated by a class stratified society but, as we have seen, it was only belatedly in the period that the consciousness-raising activities of the political Left began to be effectively organized.

There are several influences which encourage individuals to adapt their expectations to their position in the stratification order. Of these educational experience and performance are especially significant. Aspirations and ambitions tend to be affected during school life by the level of educational attainment, by the number and type of difficulties encountered in the learning process, and by test and examination scores which continuously confront the school pupil with the reality of above average, merely average or below average ability. Such indicators permit less able as well as bright members of school populations to work out their probable point of destination beyond school life. It has been suggested that, in so doing, education 'performs a useful and humane function in psychologically preparing future members of the underclass for the harsh realities of the world awaiting them outside the school gates' by inculcating children, whether directly or indirectly, with the 'realization that they have been earmarked for the more desirable or less desirable positions in society.'(39)

To the extent that this process fosters an anticipatory adjustment to prospective roles and rewards, it serves to perpetuate the socio-political *status quo*. The more effective the education system is in promoting accommodation of this kind, the greater the difficulties encountered by radical groups in promoting rejection by the disprivileged of the inevitability of their low status.

There were in the later nineteenth century other influences, in addition to education, which affected the social horizons of the young: the family, the neighbourhood community, and the peer group. Of these, the family is especially significant. Characteristically, as Parkin maintains, subordinate-class parents

> . . . do not foster high aspirations among their offspring, either at school or in the world of work . . . . There is a wellspring of social knowledge in any underclass which derives from the personal experience of low status, and which is buttressed by the knowledge that the majority of those born into the class will remain in it.(40)

Limited ambition, deriving as it does from a realistic appraisal of the circumstances affecting the majority of the disprivileged, is crucial to an understanding of the subordinate value system. Noteworthy also in this connection is the custom, still prevalent in later nineteenth-century industrial towns, for youngsters to follow family occupational traditions, the more so where local employment was largely dominated by one or two major industries. The individual's intended employment destination may have been conditioned, albeit to an unknown extent, by influences other than education.

Amongst the disprivileged, reactions to perceived inequalities of condition may take many forms. The response produced by religion and education was one of acquiescence rather than deference.

Acquiescence, it has been argued, was likely to have been encouraged by religion and education, but not because the end product was internalization by the masses of the dominant value system. The response is better interpreted as one of instrumental compliance rather than deferential endorsement. The churches and chapels functioned not only as centres of Christian worship, but as centres providing voluntary welfare along with pastoral, recreational and educational care - services enabling the construction of confidence bridges, channels of communication and frameworks of social interaction linking the leaders and the led. Social bonding was promoted.

The schools served both to equip their populations with basic educational skills and socio-psychologically to prepare youngsters for their futures in the labour market by encouraging them to tailor their aspirations according to their abilities. Those whose educational attainment was relatively modest were the more likely realistically to reconcile themselves to the prospect of a limited range of job options available to them; the high achiever was the more likely to strive to continue his or her education beyond the elementary stage and to gain personal satisfaction from the wider range of employment opportunities available to the more competent. In these ways both religion and education contributed in no small degree to the acquiescence of the period.

References

1. Hart, J., 'Religion and Social Control in the Mid-Nineteenth Century' in Donajgrodski, A.P., ed., *Social Control in Nineteenth-Century Britain*, Croom Helm, 1977; Halévy, E., *A History of the English People in the Nineteenth Century*, Macmillan, 1949.

2. Niebuhr, H.R., *The Social Sources of Denominationalism*, Free Press, New York, 1929.

3. Parkin, F., *Class Inequality and Political Order*, MacGibbon and Kee, 1971, p. 74.

4. *Ibid.*, pp. 74-5.

5. See, for example, Hollis, P., *Women in Public: The Women's Movement, 1850-1900*, Allen and Unwin, 1979, ch. 9.

6. Parkin, F., *op. cit.*, p. 74.

7. *Ibid.*, p. 75.

8. Perkin, H.J., *Origins of Modern English Society, 1780-1880*, Routledge and Kegan Paul, 1969, chs 6 and 7.

9. Hobsbawm, E.J., *Labouring Men*, Weidenfeld and Nicolson, 1964, ch. 3.

10. Thompson, E.P., *The Making of the English Working Class*, Gollancz, 1963, ch. 11.

11. Parkin, F., *op. cit.*, p. 76.

12. *Ibid.*

13. Bennett, W., *The History of Burnley*, Burnley, 1951, IV, ch. 9.

14. McCann, P., ed., *Popular Education and Socialization in the Nineteenth Century*, Methuen, 1977, ch. 1.

15. Thompson, F.M.L., 'Social Control in Victorian Britain', *Economic History Review*, 2nd Series, XXXIV, 1981, pp. 189-208.

16. Goldstrom, J.M., 'The Content of Education and the Socialization of the Working-Class Child', in McCann, P., *op. cit.*

17. Lawson, J. and Silver, H., *A Social History of Education in England*, Methuen, 1973, ch. 9.

18. Details in Bennett, W., *op. cit.*, ch. 10.

19. *Ibid.*, p. 172; see also Young, M., 'The Burnley School Board, 1871-91', M.Ed. dissertation, University of Manchester, 1973.

20. Bennett, W., *op. cit.*, pp. 177-8.

21. Lawson, J. and Silver, H., *op. cit.*, ch. 9.

22. Many details in Bennett, W., *op. cit.*, ch. 10.

23. *Ibid.*

24. *Ibid.*

25. *Ibid.*

26. *Ibid.*, p. 172.

27. On the problem of absenteeism and its implication for socialization see Rubenstein, D., 'Socialization and the London

School Board, 1870-1914: Aims, Methods and Public Opinion',
Marsden, W.E., 'Social Environment, School Attendance and
Educational Achievement in a Merseyside Town, 1870-1900',
Madoc-Jones, B., 'Patterns of Attendance and their Social
Significance', all in McCann, P., *op. cit.*; Ellis, A.C.O.,
'Influences on School Attendance in Victorian England', *British
Journal of Educational Studies*, XXI, 1973, pp. 313-26; Hurt,
J.S., *Elementary Schooling and the Working Class, 1860-1918*,
Routledge and Kegan Paul, 1979.

28. Bennett, W., *op. cit.*, pp. 169-96.

29. Details *ibid*.

30. *Ibid*.

31. *Ibid*.

32. *Ibid*.; see also Young, M., *op. cit.*

33. *Ibid*.

34. Parkin, F., *op. cit.*, ch. 2.

35. Anderson, G., *Victorian Clerks*, Manchester University Press,
1976.

36. Parkin, F., *op. cit.*, p. 50.

37. *Ibid*.

38. Runciman, W.G., *Relative Deprivation and Social Justice*,
Routledge and Kegan Paul, 1966.

39. Parkin, F., *op. cit.*, p. 63.

40. *Ibid*., p. 67.

Conclusion

The Victorian and Edwardian period was one of growing responsibility and increasing independence for urban government in industrial Lancashire, a trend which was accompanied by widening democratic participation. An associated change was a shift in the balance of power between rural and urban leaderships. As the towns grew they acquired more sophisticated and progressively more independent local government structures of their own, and this had the effect of pruning back the area and range of county government's power.(1)

Parliamentary elections in the towns were dominated by leaders who had made their mark in industry and commerce. Joyce's calculation for the 'North West region'(2) between 1860 and 1886 shows that, of the total of 250 candidates, ninety were from 'industrial' backgrounds, fifty-two were 'men of commerce', and only forty-seven were classified as 'landed'. Most of those who aspired to Westminster were local men or men who had long-established regional attachments. Joyce identifies 165 of his 250 as 'local' and notes the suspicion and hostility with which electorates greeted aspiring, 'carpet-bagging' newcomers; outsiders were often regarded as self-interested careerists. The ideal candidate, Walton asserts, 'was a patriarchal local figure, a substantial employer and contributor to local charities, a man of known influence and reputation.'(3) Lancashire's industrial and commercial leaders were leaders in dimensions of urban life outside the world of work, and this projected them almost inexorably into becoming 'public persons' in the political sphere. Patronage and charity were locally exercised, and the most obvious medium for the expression of social status and the acceptance of responsibility to the local community was municipal government.

Leading employers on Burnley's Town Council, as we have seen, directed their attention outwards towards the wider urban community as well as inwards towards their employees; paternalism was neither narrowly selective nor workplace-specific. Conflict in industrial relations was mollified by 'good works' performed elsewhere. The voluntary paternalistic duties and services they undertook outside the factory were more pervasively significant than those undertaken within the workplace. Voluntary effort of this kind undoubtedly increased an employer's acceptability to the voting public at large at election time. Acceptability as 'fit and proper persons' for political leadership was enhanced through the exercise of charity and benevolence which took on increasingly sophisticated and permanent forms. In Burnley voluntary initiatives 'from above' produced parks and gardens, a hospital with dispensary and ante-natal facilities, and provision for the blind, the deaf, the dumb and 'distressed women'. Private donations promoted the building of churches and chapels along with their associated denominational schools, recreational amenities and practical arrangements for social welfare and pastoral care. The leaders were visible contributors to the general wellbeing of the local community, their reputations and eligibility for municipal office being enhanced by their conduct and performance in many dimensions of urban life. Townsfolk had the opportunity to become relatively well acquainted with the leaders so that they were the better able to assess the individual's dependability, predictability and commitment, whether expressed in financial terms or through active involvement in numerous schemes to improve social welfare and the environmental quality of life in Burnley. The leaders promoted a shared sense of civic pride. Visiting, the organization of charity societies and voluntary welfare work provided outlets of the energies of middle-class wives and daughters who were deprived of an active commercial involvement by the separation of business and home and by culturally defined spheres of respectable work for ladies. Such female involvement contributed in no small degree to male reputations.

Undoubtedly, there were ignoble motives underlying some of the activities of a number of wealthy individuals. Some of the less meritorious deeds publicized in the press drew criticism and active resistance. The leaders were accountable to popular opinion; their actions, whether condoned or condemned, had implications for the fulfilment or frustration of ambitions in the sphere of political leadership. Accountability of this kind acted as a check upon freedom of action to exploit the advantages of privilege and authority; adverse publicity acted as a warning to voters of all social classes at election time. In Burnley the trade unions exercised their legal rights of complaint and appeal when employers contravened the Factory Acts; borough magistrates, many of them employers themselves, demonstrated with the imposition of fines their disapprobation of those who chose to disregard statutory codes of conduct. Amongst the employer-dominated group of leaders there was much genuine philanthropic and religious concern, and much well-intentioned effort to defuse social tension, to build confidence bridges between the classes and to bring a real measure of social amelioration to some of the most deprived sectors of society.

The field of action for municipal government was becoming progressively more extensive during the second half of the nineteenth century; the sphere of authority and responsibility moved beyond the basics of law and order to encompass street lighting, paving and maintenance, drains and sewers, gas and water, parks and libraries, building regulations and, more belatedly, municipal housing, tramways and electricity. In Walton's words:

> These responsibilities, so obviously expensive and so obviously important to the health and comfort of individuals and businesses, were believed to require the attention of substantial businessmen accustomed to economical and efficient administration on a large scale, and to the taking of important decisions.(4)

This is not to suggest that all employers were consistently successful in the way they conducted their business enterprises or that all successful businessmen made equally successful and responsible town councillors; there were some who eschewed political involvement. As Walton himself admits:

> We need more systematic evidence before we can argue confidently for or against the contention that a strong business presence made for an active, innovatory municipality . . . for business leaders themselves ran the gamut from the open-handed and socially concerned to the tight-fisted and narrowly economistic . . ..(5)

Logically, however, the fact that employer-dominated leadership lingered on for so long in municipal government argues majority acquiescence - or the absence of a preferable alternative.

The civic institutions of mid- and late-Victorian Lancashire, with their growing powers to influence the daily lives of ordinary people, were dominated by leading capitalists because such people were generally regarded as best fitted to perform the appropriate duties efficiently. Garrard's(6) occupational analysis of the membership of three Town Councils, those of Salford, Bolton and Rochdale, supports this assertion,(7) as does Howe's(8) investigation of Bolton. The pattern of 'large proprietor' dominance was not universal, of course. In Ashton in both 1847 and 1857 'large proprietors' were outnumbered by dealers and shopkeepers, and civic leadership in Accrington was mainly in the hands of shopkeepers during the closing decades of the century. For most places, however, evidence confirms the political pre-eminence of big business.(9) Moreover, the strategic influence of large proprietors was much greater than the statistical evidence suggests since such men were represented in disproportionately large numbers amongst the aldermen, committee chairmen and especially amongst successful aspirants to the mayoralty.

It was not until the 1880s that the social composition of Lancashire's borough councils began to change. The influence of big business went into a patchy but nonetheless inexorable decline, its speed and extent varying from place to place. In Blackburn 27 per cent of the Council were cotton masters in 1880 but this had reduced to 19.5 per cent by 1900; in Burnley the proportional importance of major employers declined from 40.5 per cent to 23.0 per cent during the same period. In Oldham the involvement of manufacturers fell from 58.0 per cent in 1888-9 to 29.0 per cent in 1908-9. In Bolton the presence of manufacturers (including merchants) on the Council decreased from 62.5 per cent in 1861 to 31.0 per cent in 1890.(10) In general major employers were replaced by tradesmen and professionals plus a sprinkling of salaried managers and working-class personnel. Conjecturally, there were several factors involved in the gradual withdrawal of leading employers from the arena of local politics. As Walton surmises:

> A growing patrician distaste for the rough and tumble of contested elections may have helped to deter a new generation of the wealthy, secure in their status, from entering the municipal arena, especially where new opponents were emerging in the form of articulate and angry working-class representatives. The rise of the limited company, preferred lifestyle, and the widening of the distance between home and the factory or counting house certainly played their part.(11)

Yet the noteworthy feature of the withdrawal was that the old urban governing class was giving up its post from choice rather than necessity, abdicating civic authority before there was any serious threat to its being ousted. It was a protracted process set in motion more by a failure to recruit replacements from the traditional employing class than by the premature departure of those in office, as the evidence for Burnley strongly confirms. As we noted earlier, the towns of late-Victorian and Edwardian Lancashire continued to have their share of aldermen and committee chairmen, exercising disproportionate influence, drawn from the entrepreneurial class.

The gradual abdication of major employers from the sphere of municipal government did not result in the immediate efflorescence of Socialism in industrial Lancashire. There are, of course, a few exceptions to this assertion but in general Liberal and Conservative entrepreneurs were replaced by managers, professionals and shopkeepers who perpetuated the long-established bi-partisan political pattern. In some towns - Burnley, for example - Liberalism persisted; in others, Conservatism remained predominant. In central government both parties had shown themselves willing to make concession and to compromise in favour of the poor. The Socialist parties, appearing late on the political scene, found the Liberal and Tory strongholds of the industrial towns difficult to penetrate.

Socialism was disadvantaged *vis-à-vis* the long-established political parties in that the movement was fragmented. There were three main Socialist strands: the Social Democratic Federation, the Independent Labour Party and the trade union campaign for labour representation which crystallized in the formation of the Labour Representation Committee. At times these groups were interlinked in a positive way, but they were as often locked in internecine conflict as they competed for the support of the class whose real interests each claimed to represent. Ideologically both the SDF and the ILP were strongly influenced by various Socialist doctrines, some of which the LRC viewed with caution and reserve.

The Socialist parties were late-comers to the political arena and as such were up against well-established combatants with long traditions of administration and extensive experience in government.(12) The life of the Social Democratic Federation did not begin until the mid-1880s. Its ideology, as an overtly Marxist organization explicitly seeking to muster the unemployed and to effect a revolutionary transformation of society, was unfamiliar to many and extremist in tone. There had, it is true, been many supporters of Chartism in Burnley; the reformist flame had burned brightly amongst members of Lancashire's subordinate class, but Chartism (the Physical Force minority apart) had urged the need to reform rather than to sweep away the existing political system, the changes to be effected by constitutional means. The objectives, and the means of achieving these, differed in many key respects from the intended goals of the SDF.

It was not until the mid-1890s that the SDF had established what could be described as a firm basis of support; in Lancashire, with perhaps as high a proportion as a third of the movement's national leadership, the SDF was stronger than anywhere else outside London. Burnley and Salford, it is claimed, were two of the movement's regional strongholds. In Burnley, however, whatever interest and support existed was translated into immediate electoral successes in neither the municipal nor the Parliamentary spheres. Not only was the SDF's ideology unfamiliar and its rhetoric extremist, but its exponents, as recent newcomers or temporary-stay visitors, were insufficiently well known - untried and untested as yet - whereas the Liberals and Conservatives for the most part sponsored reputationally known candidates with local or regional attachments. Candidates in municipal contests tended to be long-time residents, with business and commercial skills which were transferable to business and commercial decisions in local government. In national elections aspirants to Westminster were men of at least regional repute, and it was local men who influenced the selection process. Certainly much Socialist political campaigning was undertaken in Burnley; there were demonstrations, rallies, public lectures and visits by the movement's national leaders. The idiosyncratic businessman, H.M. Hyndman, contested the Burnley Parliamentary seat in 1895, 1906 and 1910 in both the general elections of that year, but he was beaten into third place each time. Success was achieved much later by Dan Irving in 1918 - after he had resided in the town for many years.

The Independent Labour Party, founded nationally in 1893, was an even more belated newcomer. Again, the movement appears to have gained widespread interest in the North West; at the inaugural meeting more than a quarter of the delegates (32 out of 120) came from Lancashire and Cheshire.(13) ILP Socialism had many facets and meant many things to many people. This, Walton points out, was 'both an advantage and a problem.'(14) In Lancashire, however, according to Ainsworth,(15) ILP Socialism eschewed the idea of class struggle and the revolutionary transformation of the socio-political order; it stressed instead a gradual, but inevitable, evolutionary transition.

Yet both SDF and ILP Socialism remained minority creeds in these years - exponents were often 'the butt of hecklers on Blackpool beach and in the market place' - and, as such, both parties faced an uphill struggle at the polls. To continue in Walton's words:

> The attachments of the old 'cultural politics', the divisions within the working class on religious, ethnic, occupational and workplace lines, were too deeply engrained, and the identification of the existing state of things with 'common sense' was too firmly established to allow a mass following for even the ILP's eclectic Socialisms.(17)

In the late nineteenth century Socialism failed to achieve wide electoral influence in Lancashire; even in Burnley, where the ILP was active and the SDF particularly so, success proved elusive. It was difficult to surmount the bipartisan division of pre-established political allegiance. An alternative approach (and one which both the ILP and SDF subsequently began to consider) was one based upon an appeal to the narrower solidarities of trade unionism - an alliance with those whose current priorities placed emphasis upon economic gains leading both to improvement in wage-workers' standard of living and to the promotion of trade-union interests within the existing system.

In these years some trade unionists and some non-unionized workers were Socialists - but most were not. The pursuit of labour representation in Parliament was an altogether different aspiration from one seeking the Socialist millennium. In the light of such considerations the Labour Representation Committee was established; even so, there was no sudden, dramatic rush of support. The Lancashire Miners' Federation, alone among the miners' unions nationally, registered strong interest from the beginning but it did not become officially affiliated with the LRC until 1903 - five years before the national union did so. There was interest also amongst workers in the cotton industry. A ballot of the major cotton unions in 1894 produced an indecisive result, however; the cotton unions did not affiliate with the LRC at its inception but delayed until 1902. By then the implications of the Taff Vale decision for the finances of the cotton unions as much as the railwaymen had become clear - as had the need for a Parliamentary presence to reverse the judgment.

Socialism, it is true, widened the political choices available to electorates but its image and ideology were as likely to deter as to attract wage-workers' support in the towns of industrial Lancashire. The fervent, idealistic leaders of Socialist movements undoubtedly had the best interests of the disprivileged at heart; but they had to compete with the leaders of other parties with pre-established local loyalties built gradually but securely upon past performance and reputational criteria. In contrast to these 'insiders', the 'outsider' messengers of Socialism were as yet relatively 'unknown quantities'; to the many moderate-minded working men and women, the inflammatory tone of Socialist rhetoric was discomfiting and the major objective - the reshaping of the entire socio-political structure - extremist and attainable only in a far distant future. Equally importantly, the movement was fragmented, its disunity manifest in rival, sometimes recriminatory and mutually hostile, recruiting campaigns by competing factions.

Its consciousness-raising initiatives amongst wage-workers were all too often disillusioning exercises, actively seeking to sow the seeds of dissatisfaction, grievance and discontent about circumstances where, for many workers, there appeared to be no just cause; moreover, wage-workers already had their own union representatives who fought for them, often successfully, where there appeared to be genuine economic injustice. All too often Socialism represented the prevailing socio-political order not only as systematically unequal but also as unfair, uncaring and irresponsible; it reflected in its mirror a current world view in which everything was wrong, nothing was right. But in sweeping aside the curtains which veiled some of the less attractive features upon the face of Capitalism, the critics also revealed what, for the moment at least, contemporaries perceived as the unacceptable face of Socialism.

Collectively Burnley's leaders in the period under review are better represented as a group of 'top persons' than an élite. They displayed relatively weakly Meisel's 'three Cs' of élite behaviour; consciousness, coherence and conspiracy. These characteristics were discernible in, but certainly not strongly reinforced by, factors such as interlocking business partnerships, ties of kinship and inter-marriage, a shared lifestyle, common salubrious areas of residence, and membership of socially exclusive clubs. The group was conscious of its superior social status and aware of the power it exercised over fellow members of the local community, but it was also aware of the duties and responsibilities which the affluent and advantaged owed to the less privileged. Though some of the actions of particular individuals were questioned - Alderman Scott was accused of 'council jobbing', for example - there is little to suggest that the leadership in general acted in a consistently exploitative manner to self-interested, self-preserving ends with cavalier disregard for the welfare of the community at large.

A noteworthy characteristic of municipal leadership, as we have seen, was the numerical predominance of major employers. This was potentially unifying, but in point of fact the leaders were deeply divided along lines of religious persuasion and political preference. There were divisions even within the major subgroupings. In Burnley Anglicanism was split into mutually hostile 'high' and 'low' church factions; in contrast Nonconformism was fragmented into several sects but these appeared to work together in a state relatively peaceful, even amicable, co-existence. The Roman Catholics tended to keep themselves apart; they were not strongly represented amongst the leaders on the Town Council, though space was preserved for them on the School

Board and Lady Alice O'Hagan was a major figure in the sphere of charity work. In the political sphere a split within the Tory faction appeared between the older generation, demoralized by their poor performance in municipal and general elections, and the younger generation of leaders exasperated by their elders' lack of assertion and want of spirit. On the Liberal-dominated Town Council there were differences of opinion amongst the Liberals themselves; minutes of meetings suggest that heated, often prolonged, debate preceded some of the decisions arrived at.

The Liberals' predominance is in no small measure attributable to the fact that their direct, personal contacts and communications with the rest of the community via employing enterprises and especially via the multi-functional chapels, were more extensive than those of the Conservatives. The social and residential distance between the Liberal leaders and members of the subordinate class was narrower; spheres of social interaction, channels of communication, points of direct and indirect contact, and confidence bridges were all more extensive and more efficient than those of the Conservatives. Collectively and individually the Liberals were less remote; their reliability and predictability were founded upon past performance and reputations built up over many years.

Leaders in Burnley, as in other industrial towns, were not entirely unconstrained in the exercise of authority. A framework of checks and balances of various kinds affected their decisions and the execution of plans and policies. An influential landowner was sometimes strategically well-placed to veto a proposal; General Scarlett, for example, obstructed the plan to create a town cemetery opposite Bank Hall. The guidelines constructed by an evolving body of legislation passed at central government level affected the activities of employers, school managers, the School Board, the Board of Guardians and the Town Council. Public opinion, expressed through pressure groups such as the Ratepayers' Association, had the potential to influence the course of decision making; an electorate, dissatisfied with the leaders' collective or individual performances, could vote other leaders into office. Within the Town Council it was possible for the policy of the dominant faction to be influenced by the presence of an organized opposition. The fact that in Burnley the Tories were in a minority during the later nineteenth century - and for several years had only a token presence - argues that the electorate was generally satisfied with the Liberal leaders who were seen to use their powers efficiently within the inbuilt framework of checks and balances which conditioned their activities. The Liberal-led Town Council presided over major improvements in urban amenities, steering skilfully between the Scylla and Charybdis of parsimony (which may have provoked resentment about substandard urban services) and prodigality (which may have sparked off rebellion over soaring rates). The vote-casting public could have replaced Liberal councillors with Tories, but declined to do so. What was perceived by the majority to be satisfactory service undoubtedly contributed to the prolonged predominance of the Liberals in Burnley's municipal government.

The leadership style in the many industrial towns of the region was paternalistic, as Joyce(18) ably demonstrates in his study of Blackburn. But paternalism as a form of authority was twin-faced; it had both kindly and stern countenances. In Burnley the kindly aspect (revealed in acts of philanthropy, concern for environmental welfare, education, the social work of the voluntary charities and of the religious sects) was the more pervasively and persistently visible. The stern face was not necessarily resented by the majority, nor did it necessarily inspire fear and hatred. The formal and informal codes of conduct affecting life within the factory and law and order in the wider community embodied consensual values rather than harshly imposed, alienating principles which did not receive majority assent. The need for regulatory practices and procedures was generally accepted as essential to stability, order and peace. Most townsfolk, irrespective of socio-economic class, subscribed to the principles of honesty, sobriety, and respect for law and order, people and property; the minority who flouted basic standards of conduct and behaviour were viewed as 'deviants' - and treated accordingly. Moderate, rational trade unionists deplored irresponsible, 'unofficial' strikes and running riots in the streets, while accepting the need for solidarity in the strategic use of the strike weapon when institutionalized negotation failed to produce a satisfactory settlement. Employers did not condone the conduct of those within their own ranks who did not abide by the requirements written into legislation relating to employment.

Consensus was not 'total', of course. The leaders did not always act as subordinates would have liked, and subordinates did not invariably comply with the wishes of the leaders. Often, however, the differences which occurred were resolvable by peaceable, institutionalized ways and means. Recurrent workplace dissatisfactions were negotiable by representatives of both sides, with the settlement of differences as the intended outcome; neither side preferred to live life within the factory in a state of continuous, ever-present class warfare. But the confrontation was occasionally violent when feelings of injustice ran high and there was a failure to compromise. Moreover, given changes in the balance of workplace power according to the state of trade and the state of the labour market, one side could impose its will upon the other.

Masters were capable of enforcing their will by resort to harsh, repressive strategies. The Thursbys, for example, brought strike-breakers into their mines and neutralized the power of the miners' union in order to regain control of production and industrial relations. Subordinates were not powerless, however; the potentially disruptive impact of collective action, whether by unionists or non-unionists, was fully understood. Insurrection in Burnley, though feared by those in authority, did not occur during the 'cotton famine', partly because ways and means were found to defuse social tension, and partly also because the unemployed did not attribute the crisis to the masters, who were perceived to be fellow victims rather than perpetrators of the calamity.

Wage-workers' reactions were very different during the crisis year of 1878 when grievances unresolved by the usual procedures exploded into riots, arson, destruction of property and physical injury to some of those in authority. Peace was restored with difficulty. The outcome could have been very different, but effectively organized Socialism as a unified, permanent, settled force was not yet on the political scene in Burnley. In the late 1870s and the 1880s the conceptualization of the employment relationship in oppositional, occasionally violently confrontational, terms did not prevent the two sides from subsequently re-establishing a viable working relationship which for the most part permitted production to proceed smoothly; nor did it shatter the pre-established pattern of political allegiance. The salient feature of the period was acquiescence in the prevailing socio-political order.

Education, religion and recreation, either provided or controlled from above, all contributed something to the stability of the period, but arguments alleging that social control was maintained by the ability of superordinates to socialize subordinates in dominant ideology - the ideology of submission - are unconvincing. Certainly the providers sought to exert a 'civilizing' influence - but by encouraging virtues already intuitively present and by fostering habits of thought and behaviour long ago absorbed; thrift, self-help, financial prudence, family responsibility, honesty, industriousness and even, by the 1870s and 1880s, the desirability of punctuality and good time-keeping were as much appreciated by wage-workers as by their employers. There is little to suggest that in the late nineteenth century such values were being coercively impressed upon less privileged people whose own ideas were markedly different. As we have argued, there are several ways in which recreation, religion and education helped to reduce social tension but for reasons other than the promotion of deference as we defined it.

This returns us to the problem of selecting an appropriate label to attach to the general response of the masses, a problem compounded by the somewhat contradictory strands in the evidence. Certainly the relationship between the borough leaders and their local communities contains clear evidence of recurrent friction which occasionally erupted in sporadic, often barely controlled, violence, but it would be a distortion to represent the overall perspective as one of 'continuous challenge' and a 'fluctuating but ever-present class warfare'. A radical normative code, implied in the terminology which Dutton and King adopt and inferred in the confrontational emphasis they place upon the events and circumstances they describe, would embody its own distinctive ideology. It would also promote an alternative view of society, involving a different set of principles leading to organized opposition to the structure of advantage and disadvantage embodied in dominant ideology. Reactions and responses in neither Burnley nor Preston nor other northern industrial towns covered in the present investigation suggest the emergence of a clearly identifiable radical value system drawing upon a set of precepts fundamentally opposed to those currently underlying the institutions of capitalism. As argued by Parkin,[19] the social source and generating milieu of the radical normative order is the mass political party whose power base is the subordinate class. If Burnley's borough electorate was interested in the policies of emergent Socialist groups, its ongoing preference was for Liberal representation; in so far as radical values were espoused, they were not as yet widely disseminated amongst members of the subordinate class.

If generalizations which allege the mass espousal of radical ideologies in these years are unsupportable, interpretations which, at the other extreme, appear to suggest the widespread presence of deference are equally dubious. The employers' influence, although extensive, was not total. In many spheres of urban life the operatives' response to the leaders' authority was for the most part compliant, but it cannot convincingly be construed as deferential.

Deference, as we defined it at the outset, involves the

internalization of the value system promoted by the dominant group, the dominant values in this context representing the perceptions and interests of the relatively privileged. Dominant values tend more obviously to embody the perceptions of social reality held by those in positions of authority. Those groups who occupy the most powerful positions will also tend to have strategic access to formal and informal means of legitimation. The deferential worker accepts as legitimate the dominant group's claim to leadership by virtue of its inherently superior qualities and attributes, and endorses the group's view of his own subordinate location in the social structure as morally right. Inequality in the prevailing reward system with its pattern of privilege and deprivation, power and dependency, is viewed as both inevitable and just. The persistence of the prevailing socio-economic order and its associated political structures is therefore condoned.

The dominant normative order is more likely to be internalized where the experience of subordination is a total one; this is the likely outcome where there is direct experience of the economic, social and political judgments of dominant class members as, for example, in isolated rural communities or small towns with well-established status systems based upon relatively insulated occupational community.

It has been argued that the economic and social context of Burnley, of Joyce's Blackburn, and of most sizeable industrial towns in the era fails to conform sufficiently closely to the type of environment most conducive to deferential responses. As we have shown, subordinate groups displayed certain 'deviant' behaviour characteristics in some situations which the dominant group was hard-pressed to control, even by the exercise of sheer naked power. The multi-faceted authority of leading employers was widespread but, despite any intended socializing function performed by religious and educational agencies and the more explicitly coercive social control activities of police authorities, there appear to be grounds to doubt that the internalization of dominant values occurred on a significantly wide scale.

Unionism provided an alternative frame of reference in workers' perceptions of social relationships in the workplace, reflecting and reinforcing horizontally-structured 'class' loyalties which, in the sphere of industrial relations at least, circumscribed employers' strategies to create a vertically orientated framework of allegiance and dependence. Moreover, the urban communities of the northern industrial towns covered by the present study appear to have had none of the tight completeness of the factory-based occupational neighbourhood groups with their communal identities which allegedly existed in Blackburn. Though neighbourhood and kinship ties were undoubtedly strong, the mill and mining communities were neither sufficiently localized nor sufficiently insulated from alternative influences to form fertile sowing ground for the seeds of deference.

Evidence seems to suggest that the normative bonds binding the entrepreneurial middle class and their social subordinates had been loosened but not severed. Despite the widespread influence of leading employers, the local economic and social environment permitted the growth and preservation of a strong working-class subculture. On the one hand the response of the subordinate class in Burnley and other towns cannot realistically be defined as outright endorsement of the dominant normative code, but neither can it be convincingly construed as one embodying normative opposition. The social outlook is characterized by a range of accommodative or adaptive responses to the facts of subordinate status. Accommodation may, of course, spring from a fatalistic pessimism borne of powerlessness, but events and circumstances seem to indicate that a more important element in subordinates' accommodative reaction was an instrumental collectivism conceptualized in trade union ideology. The survival of trade union organization implies that members were convinced both of the necessity for improvement and of the existence of real opportunity for change. The envisaged changes were to be won, not by sweeping away the established institutions which underpinned the stratification order, but by negotiating a greater share within what, for the time-being at least, was an implicitly acceptable pattern of general rules governing the allocation of rewards. Trade union consciousness, as an element in the subordinate code, represents what is arguably the defining characteristic of the subordinate value system: a realistic economistic compromise between radical rejection and deferential endorsement of the prevailing system. The subordinate code embodies what Parkin suggests can best be understood as a 'negotiated version'(20) of the dominant ideology, or what Rodman identifies as the 'lower class value stretch'.(21) Dominant values are neither internalized nor rejected wholesale but modified by the subordinate class as a rational survival strategy in the context of its social situation and restricted opportunities.(22)

The leadership itself was not necessarily inflexible in the policies it adopted to preserve its position of authority. The concessions in industrial relations, stressed by Dutton and King, show that the dominant group recognized the need for judicious compromise in certain circumstances; but concessions, even those apparently 'forced' from Preston employers, do not signify economic, social and political capitulation. What is striking, as Joyce's research discloses, is the employers' ability to ride out the storm and to maintain their dominance of local affairs beyond the 1850s.

The foregoing argument does not dispute the significance of paternalism and deference as sources of social stability, but emphasizes that the successful exercise of paternalistic authority in the pursuit of deferential compliance requires special circumstances which were becoming progressively more elusive in the populous industrial towns of the North West during the course of the nineteenth century. Dutton and King's investigation of early nineteenth-century Preston, and the present writer's research focusing upon the 1870s and 1880s, argue the overriding effect of general economic circumstances, of the state of trade and of the industrial base of the particular town upon the prevailing character of inter-class relationships. Not all industrial towns, even in the North West, with its urban clusters of mills and factories, were dominated by a handful of employers. Elsewhere, the economic base, industrially and occupationally, was more diversified. The working class in consequence was less homogeneous. Lower-class economic sectionalism along lines of earnings, skill, and occupation, as Foster's study(23) of South Shields discloses, leads to the kind of social fragmentation which impedes collectivist, solidaristic attachment to a class ideal, particularly where opportunities for upward mobility into the world of self-employment or small workshop production promote individualistic aspirations and action. The resultant preservation of the local *status quo* is attributable neither to paternalism nor deference.

During the last quarter of the nineteenth century the lower-class response to paternalistic middle-class authority cannot be interpreted as one of deference; nor is there convincing proof of the pervasive presence of what by strict definition can be identified as radical normative opposition. For the moment, a radical ideology, in so far as it was available, was neither widely espoused nor effectively organized so as to marshal working-class discontent into a significant political force. The response to the employers' multi-dimensional paternalistic leadership was one embodying instrumental accommodation and adaptation. This interpretation, it is suggested here, has greater credibility than the sweeping and somewhat inflexible generalizations to which reference was made at the outset. Attitudes were not static. Variations in social responses, evident in different towns at different times, undoubtedly reflect differences in access to the alternative ideologies currently available. Equally important, however, is the fact that responses were also situationally determined. Changing events and circumstances had some effect, arguably a major one, on the manner in which accommodation was accomplished, whether on terms of willing compliance, grudging reluctance, or resentful hostility. Whatever the manner, the working-class response was one firmly founded on common sense.

References

1. Walton, J.K., *Lancashire: A Social History, 1558-1939*, Manchester University Press, 1987, p. 221.

2. Outline of geographical region in *ibid.*, p. 118; see also Joyce, P., *Work, Society and Politics: The Culture of the Factory in Later Victorian England*, Harvester, 1980.

3. Walton, J.K., *op. cit.*, p. 229.

4. *Ibid.*, p. 228.

5. *Ibid.*, p. 231.

6. Garrard, J., *Leadership and Power in Victorian Industrial Towns, 1830-1880*, Manchester University Press, 1983.

7. Walton, J.K., *op. cit.*, p. 239.

8. Howe, A.C., *The Cotton Masters*, Oxford University Press, 1984, ch. 7.

9. Walton, J.K., *op. cit.*, p. 230.

10. Statistical information is given in *ibid.*, pp. 230-2.

11. *Ibid.*, p. 232.

12. For review of Socialism in Lancashire see *ibid.*, pp. 274-5; see also David Howell's excellent study of the ILP: *British Workers and the Independent Labour Party, 1888-1906*, Manchester University Press, 1983.

13. Walton, J.K., *op. cit.*, pp. 274-5.

14. *Ibid.*, p. 275.

15. Ainsworth, A., 'Aspects of Socialism at Branch Level, 1890-1900' and also Carter, S., 'The ILP in Ashton-under-Lyne, 1893-1900', both in *North-West Labour History Society Bulletin*, IV.

16. Walton, J.K., *op. cit.*, p. 275.

17. *Ibid.*

18. Joyce, P., 'The Factory Politics of Lancashire in the Later Nineteenth Century', *Historical Journal*, XVIII, 1975, pp. 225-53.

19. Parkin, F., *op. cit.*, p. 97.

20. *Ibid.*, p. 92.

21. Rodman, H.,'The Lower-Class Value Stretch', *Social Forces*, XLII, 1963, pp. 205-15.

22. Parkin, F., *op. cit.*, p. 92.

23. Foster, J., 'Nineteenth-Century Towns: A Class Dimension', in Flinn, M.W. and Smout, T.C., eds, *Essays in Social History*, Oxford University Press, 1974; see also Foster, J., *Class Struggle and the Industrial Revolution: Early Industrial Capitalism in Three English Towns*, Weidenfeld and Nicolson, 1974.

APPENDIX OF TABLES

Appendix Table I

PRELIMINARY LIST OF BURNLEY LEADERS, 1870-1900

Name	Occupation	Religion	Politics	Employer	Town Council	Alderman	Mayor	Magistrate	Poor Law Guardian	School Board	Grammar School Board	Mechanics' or Church Institute	Philanthropist	Religious Office	Political Club Official	Literary and Scientific Club	Sports Club Official	Trade Union Official	Hospital Board	Masters' Association	TOTAL SCORE
Altham A.	tea packers	Baptist	L	xx	xx	x		xx				x	xx	x		x					13
Altham J.L.	and distributors	Baptist	L	xx	xx								x								5
Armistead Wm.	cashier		L		xx	x															4
Baldwin Wm.	brush manuf.	Congregationalist	L	x	xx	x	x					x		x	x	x					7
Barnes J.	cotton manuf.	Wesleyan	L	xx	xx	x						x	x		x	x					11
Baron J.	cotton manuf.	Methodist	L	xx	xx	x	x		△	x		x	xx	x	x	x					14
Bibby Jas.	shopkeeper		L		xx	x										x					4
Berry Jas.	cotton manuf.		L	xx	xx	x			x							x					6
Bracewell Wm.	ironfounder		C	xx	xx																5
Briggs B.W.		Anglican	C					xx							x						3
Brumwell Dr	doctor		L					xx				x				x					5
Brown Dr	doctor	Wesleyan	L					xx						x		x			x		5
Bulcock H.	solicitor	Anglican	C							x						x					2
Burrows Thos.	cotton manuf.		L	xx	xx	x	x	xx	x			x	x								7
Butterworth J.	cotton manuf.	Wesleyan	C					xx	x	x					x						6
Carrington A.	solicitor		C				x	xx	x	x											6
Collinge L.	cotton manuf.	Wesleyan	L	xx	xx	x						x				x					10
Collinge Wm. } sons of	cotton manuf.	Wesleyan	L	xx	xx	x	x	xx					x	x	x	x				x	13
Collinge J.S. } Luke	and upholsterers	Wesleyan	L	xx	xx	x							x		x	x	x				9
Cooper Jas.	ironfounder		C	xx	xx	x									x	x	x				7
Coultate Dr	doctor		L		xx	x	x	xx	x m.o.						x	x					9
Dickinson Wm.	ironfounder		L	xx	xx	x		xx	x				xx	x	x	x					9
Dillon Rev.	clergyman	R. Catholic	L						x	x				x							3
Dugdale A.	cotton manuf.	Wesleyan	C	xx	xx	x	x	xx	△		x	xx	x	x	x	x	x				11
Folds J.	cotton manuf.	Anglican	C	xx	xx	x	x		x			x	xx	x	x	x					12
Fielding H.D.	cotton manuf.	Wesleyan	L	xx	xx		x		x	x		x	x	x	x	x					12
Grant W.M.	school proprietor	Anglican	C									x		x	x	x					6
Grant F.J.	school proprietor	Anglican	C					xx				x		x	x	x					4

Appendix Table I (continued)

Name	Occupation	Religion	Politics	Employer	Town Council	Alderman	Mayor	Magistrate	Poor Law Guardian	School Board	Grammar School Board	Mechanics' or Church Institute	Philanthropist	Religious Office	Political Club Official	Literary and Scientific Club	Sports Club Official	Trade Union Official	Hospital Board	Masters' Association	TOTAL SCORE
Greenwood Jas.	cotton manuf. and dealer		L	xx	xx	x	x	xx		x 1903		x			x	x	x			x	14
Greenwood John.	cotton merchant	Anglican	C	x				xx				x		x	x	x					8
Grey N.P.								xx		x						x			x		5
O'Hagan Lady	landed	R. Catholic		··						x			xx			x					5
Handsley Robt.	agent to Thursby	Anglican	C						x	x											9
Hargreaves W.C.	cotton manuf.	Baptist	L	xx	xx			xx	x	x		x	x	x	x	x					12
Haslam Geo.	cotton manuf.	Anglican	C					xx						x						x	2
Harker T.W.	tinsmith		C	x	xx	x															4
Heap Jas.	cotton manuf.		L	xx	xx				x						x					x	6
Holden R.	draper		L	x	xx	x			x							x					6
Holdsworth R.	machinery agent		L	x	xx	x															4
Holmes D.	T.U. president	Wesleyan	L	xx	xx	x	x	xx	x	x								x			7
Howorth J.	cotton manuf.		L	xx	xx	x		xx	x	x		x	x		x	x			x		15
Hurtley R.J.	cotton manuf.	Baptist	L	xx	xx					x					x	x				x	10
Kay J.	cotton manuf.	Congregationalist	L	xx	xx	x		xx			x				x	x			x	x	11
Kay-Shuttlesworth Sir J.	landed		L					xx			x		xx		x	x			x		7
Kay-Shuttlesworth Sir U.J.	landed		C					xx			x		xx						x		8
Kneeshaw J.	head teacher	Anglican						xx	△			x	xx	x	x	x					4
Keighley G.	iron and engineering	Methodist	L	xx	xx	x	x			x 1903		x	xx		x	x					13
Keighley E.	engineering	Methodist	L	xx	xx	x	x					x			x	x					10
Lomas W.	cotton manuf.	Congregationalist	L	xx	xx	x	x	xx	x						x	x					11
Lancaster Alf.	cotton manuf.	Wesleyan	L	xx	xx	x		xx				x				x					9
Lancaster Wm. (father of Alf)	cotton manuf.	Wesleyan	L	xx	xx			xx					x	x							8
Law R.	cotton manuf.			xx	xx				x	x		x	x			x					6
Lupton Wm.	cotton manuf. and dealer		L	xx	xx	x									x						6
Maclure Rev.	clergyman	Anglican								x				x					x		3

Appendix Table I (continued)

Name	Occupation	Religion	Politics	Employer	Town Council	Alderman	Mayor	Magistrate	Poor Law Guardian	School Board	Grammar School Board	Mechanics' Church Institute	Philanthropist	Religious Office	Political Club Official	Literary and Scientific Club	Sports Club Official	Trade Union Official	Hospital Board	Masters Association	TOTAL SCORE
Massey J.	textiles	Congregationalist	L	xx	xx	x	x	xx	△	x		x	xx		x	x	x				16
Massey C.J.	and	Congregationalist	L	xx				xx					x		x	x					7
Massey E.S.	brewing	Congregationalist	L	xx									xx		x	x					6
Mitchell C.	draper and silk mercer	Baptist	L	x	xx	x	x	xx							x						8
Moore B.	journalist	Wesleyan	L					xx	x	x					x	x					6
Morrissey Rev.	clergyman	R. Catholic	L						x	x				x							3
Nowell Wm.	butcher	Wesleyan	L		xx	x		xx						x	x						7
Nutter H.	cotton manuf.		L	xx	xx	x			x												6
Ogle A.	cotton manuf.		L	xx	xx	x								x	x					7
Owen Rev.	clergyman	Anglican	C							x				x	x						3
Parkinson Wm.	manuf. chemist	Wesleyan	L	x	xx	x	x	xx		x 1903			x		x	x	x		x		13
Pullon Dr.	doctor		L					xx		x						x			x		5
Rawlinson J.	solicitor	Wesleyan	L	x				xx	△	x sec		x			x	x	x sec		x sec	x sec	11
Robinson Wm.	banker	Anglican	C					xx	x	x	x	x		x	x	x					13
Roberts Jas.	cotton manuf.	Anglican	C	xx						x		x		x	x	x					7
Scarlett General	landed mine owner	Anglican	C	xx							x	x	xx		x						7
Scott J.H.	engineering co.		L	xx	xx	x	x	xx			x	x	xx		x	x					14
Slater Geo.	cotton manuf.	Anglican	C	xx	xx			xx			x				x						5
Smallpage I.	cotton manuf.	Wesleyan	L	xx	xx				x						x						6
Smirthwaite-Black Dr.	doctor	Anglican	C					xx	x			x				x					4
Starkie Colonel.	landed	Anglican	C						△			x			x	x					4
Strange Alf.		Anglican	C							x 1903						x					2
Sutcliffe Geo.	cotton manuf.	Anglican	C	xx	xx	x	x	xx		x 1903		x			x						11
Sutcliffe J.S.	solicitor	Wesleyan								x											1

Appendix Table I (continued)

Name	Occupation	Religion	Politics	Employer	Town Council	Alderman	Mayor	Magistrate	Poor Law Guardian	School Board	Grammar School Board	Mechanics' or Church Institute	Philanthropist	Religious Office	Political Club Official	Literary and Scientific Club	Sports Club Official	Trade Union Official	Hospital Board	Masters Association	TOTAL SCORE
Thompson Wm. (brother of Wm.)	cotton manuf. and dealers	Wesleyan	L	xx	xx	x	x	xx		x		x	x	x		x					13
Thompson John (son of Wm.)		Wesleyan	L	xx	xx	x			x				x		x	x					8
Thompson J.W.		Wesleyan	L	xx				xx	x				xx	x	x	x					9
Townley-Parker Canon.	landed clergyman	Anglican	C							x		x	xx	x	x	x					7
Thornber Thos.		Methodist	L	xx	xx	x	x	xx				x	xx		x	x	x				15
Thornber Caleb.	cotton	Methodist	L	xx	xx	x	x						xx		x	x			x	x	12
Thornber John.	manufacturers	Methodist	L	xx	xx				x										x	x	5
Thornber Sharp.		Methodist	L	xx	xx				x	x 1903		x							x	x	9
Thursby Rev.	landed	Anglican	C	xx							x		xx	x	x					x	8
Thursby Col. Sir. J.	mine-owners	Anglican	C	xx				xx HSL	Δ		x		xx	x	x	x			x		11
Thursby Sir. J.O.S.		Anglican	C	xx		x		xx	Δ		x		xx		x	x			x		11
Tunstill Wm.	cotton manuf.	Wesleyan	L	xx				xx	x			x	x								6
Uttley H.	cotton manuf.	R. Catholic	L	xx	xx			xx	x												9
Veevers J.S.	cotton manuf.	R. Catholic	C	xx		x			x				x								6
Whittaker J.					xx			xx	x												5
Whittaker J.H.	cotton manuf.		L	xx	xx			xx											x		7
Winfield Rev.	clergyman	Anglican	C							x				x							2

Notes

Δ	Ex-Officio Guardians
× 1903	Member of the new Local Education Authority
••	R. Handsley, agent for the Thursby coal mines
L	Liberal
C	Conservative
× sec	J. Rawlinson, secretary to various bodies
HSL	High Sheriff of Lancashire for some years

Appendix Table II

BURNLEY LEADERS, 1870-1900

(scorers of 7 points or more)

Name	Occupation										Religion							Politics		
	landed gentry	landed employer	traditional large employer	small employer	doctor	banker	solicitor	school proprietor	shopkeeper or merchant	working class	Anglican	R. Catholic	Wesleyan	Baptist	Congregation-alist	Methodist	Unknown	Liberal	Conservative	Unknown
Altham A.			x										x					x		
Baldwin W.				x										x				x		
Barnes J.			x										x					x		
Baron J.			x													x		x		
Burrows T.			x														x	x		
Carrington A.								x									x		x	
Collinge L.			x										x					x		
Collinge Wm.			x										x					x		
Collinge J.S.			x										x					x		
Cooper Jas.			x														x		x	
Coultate Dr.					x												x	x		
Dickinson Wm.			x														x	x		
Dugdale A.			x										x						x	
Fielding H.D.			x										x					x		
Folds J.			x								x								x	
Grant W.M.							x				x								x	
Greenwood Jas.			x														x	x		
Greenwood John.									x		x								x	
Handsley R.						x					x								x	
Hargreaves W.C.			x											x				x		
Holmes D.										x							x	x		
Howorth J.			x											x				x		
Hurtley R.J.			x											x				x		
Kay J.			x												x			x		
Kay-Shuttleworth Sir J.	x										x							x		
Kay-Shuttleworth Sir U.J.	x										x							x		
Keighley G.			x													x		x		
Keighley E.			x													x		x		
Lancaster Alf.			x										x					x		
Lancaster Wm.			x										x					x		
Lomas Wm.			x												x			x		
Massey J.			x												x			x		
Massey C.J.			x												x			x		
Mitchell C.				x											x			x		
Nowell Wm.									x				x					x		
Ogle A.			x														x	x		
O'Hagan (Lady)	x											x								x
Parkinson Wm.				x									x					x		
Rawlinson J.							x						x					x		
Roberts J.			x								x								x	
Robinson Wm.							x				x							x		
Scarlett (Gen.)		x									x								x	
Scott J.H.			x														x	x		
Sutcliffe Geo.			x										x						x	
Thompson Wm.			x										x					x		
Thompson John.			x										x					x		
Thompson J.W.			x										x					x		
Thornber S.			x													x		x		
Thornber Thos.			x													x		x		
Thornber Caleb.			x													x		x		
Thursby Rev. Wm.		x									x								x	
Thursby Col. Sir. J.		x									x								x	
Thursby Sir. J.O.S.		x									x								x	
Townley-Parker Canon	x										x								x	
Uttley H.			x									x						x		
Whitaker J.H.			x														x	x		
TOTAL 56	4	4	36	3	1	1	3	1	2	1	13	2	16	4	5	6	10	41	14	1
	8												31							
PERCENTAGE *	7.1	7.1	64.3	5.4	1.8	1.8	5.4	1.8	3.6	1.8	23.2	3.6	28.6	7.1	8.9	10.7	17.9	73.2	25.0	1.8
	14.2												55.3							

* Figs correct to one decimal place

NUCLEUS OF LOCAL LEADERSHIP

(scorers of 10 points or more)

Name	Occupation						Religion						Politics	
	landed employer	traditional large employer	small employer	banker	solicitor	doctor	Anglican	Baptist	Methodist	Congregationalist	Wesleyan	Unknown	Liberal	Conservative
Altham A.		x					x						x	
Barnes J.		x									x		x	
Baron J.		x							x				x	
Collinge L.		x									x		x	
Collinge W.		x									x		x	
Coultate Dr.						x						x	x	
Dugdale A.		x									x			x
Fielding H.D.		x									x		x	
Folds J.		x					x							x
Greenwood Jas.		x										x	x	
Hargreaves W.C.		x						x					x	
Howorth J.		x									x		x	
Hurtley R.J.		x						x					x	
Kay J.		x								x			x	
Keighley G.		x							x				x	
Keighley E.		x							x				x	
Lancaster Alf.		x									x		x	
Lomas W.		x								x			x	
Massey J.		x								x			x	
Parkinson W.			x								x		x	
Rawlinson J.					x						x		x	
Robinson Wm.				x			x						x	
Scott J.H.		x										x	x	
Sutcliffe G.		x					x							x
Thompson Wm.		x									x		x	
Thornber Thos.		x							x				x	
Thornber Caleb		x							x				x	
Thursby Col. Sir J.	x						x							x
Thursby Sir J.O.S.	x						x							x
TOTAL (29)	2	23	1	1	1	1	5	3	5	3	10	3	24	5
		24			3				21					
PERCENTAGE *	6.9	79.3	3.4	3.4	3.4	3.4	17.2	10.3	17.2	10.3	34.5	10.3	82.8	17.2
		82.7			10.2				72.3					

Appendix Table IV.A.

ANNUAL ELECTIONS TO BURNLEY TOWN COUNCIL, 1870-1914
Social and Political Composition

ELECTED MEMBERS: Occupational Composition

Year	18 70	71	72	73	74	75	76	77	78	79	18 80	81	82	83	84	85	86	87	88	89	18 90	91	92	93	94	95	96	97	98	99
Landed personnel																				1	1	1		1			1			
Large employers	5	5	4	5	4	5	7	4	5	4	4	3	5	4	2	2	5	3	3	7	3	5	5	1	2	3	2	1	3	
Small employers	1	2	2	1	2	2	0	2	2	0	1	1	0	2	1	2	2	2	3	4	2	1	1	1	1	2	2	3	3	3
Doctors			1			1			1		1	1				1				2	1	1	1	1	1	1	2	1	1	2
Solicitors, accountants		1			1						1	1	1					1		1	1	1	1	1	1	1	1	1	1	2
Dealers, shopkeepers	1			1	1		2	2		3	1	2	2	1	5	3	2	2	2	5	4	1	2	5	3	2	3	5	2	5
Licensed victuallers		1																		1		2			2	1			1	
Working-class, trade unionists																	1			1			1	2	1	1				
Others	1		1	1			1			1	1			1						3	1		1	1	1	1	1	2	1	
TOTAL	8	8	8	8	8	8	8	8	8	8	8	8	8	8	8	8	8	8	8	25	12	12	12	12	12	12	12	12	12	12

Appendix Table IV.A. (continued)

ELECTED MEMBERS: Occupational Composition

Year	19 00	01	02	03	04	05	06	07	08	09	19 10	11	12	13	14
Landed personnel	1			1		2	2		2	2		1	1	1	1
Large employers	2	5	1	2	4	1	3	3	3	2	3	2	1	2	2
Small employers	2	1	2	3	3	1	2	3	2	2	3	1	3	5	2
Doctors			1						1		1	2		1	2
Solicitors, accountants	1	1	2	1	1	2		1	1			1	3	1	1
Dealers, shopkeepers	5	3	4	2	2	4	2	3	1	3	2	3	3	1	3
Licensed victuallers		1													
Working-class, trade unionists		1	1	2	2	2	3	2	1	3	3	1		1	1
Others	1	1	1	1					1			1	1	1	
TOTAL	12	12	12	12	12	12	12	12	12	12	12	12	12	12	12

NOTES

The Burnley Borough Extension Act was passed in 1889. Figures for 1889 include councillors elected for the 8 existing wards, for the 4 new wards created under the Act (Burnley Express, 2 Nov. 1889), and also councillors elected in by-elections arising from the promotion of members of the Council to the newly enlarged aldermanic bench (Burnley Express, 27 Nov. 1889).

Appendix Table IV.B.(1)

ANNUAL ELECTIONS TO BURNLEY TOWN COUNCIL, 1870-1914

Social and Political Composition

Year	18 70	71	72	73	74	75	76	77	78	79	18 80	81	82	83	84	85	86	87	88	89	18 90	91	92	93	94	95	96	97	98	99
Liberal	8	5	8	7	7	7	6	8	8	6	8	8	6	7	8	7	7	5	8	20	9	11	10	9	6	12	9	11	8	9
Conservative	7	3	6	7	4	4	4			2			2	6	8	8	5	6	6	9	6	10	8	9	10	12	11	9	7	8
SDF																							2	5	6	2	2	3	3	
ILP																							1	2	1					
LEA																								1	1					
Trades' Council																									2					1
Co-op.																									1					
LRC																														
SPGB																														
TOTAL	15	8	14	14	11	11	10	8	8	8	8	8	8	13	16	15	12	11	14	29	15	21	21	26	27	26	22	23	18	18

Appendix Table IV.B.(1) (continued)

(1) CONTESTANTS: Political Composition

Year	19 00	01	02	03	04	05	06	07	08	09	19 10	11	12	13	14
Liberal	10	6	9	7	7	10	7	7	7	7	8	9	7	10	4
Conservative	10	8	8	5	6	6	8	8	6	8	7	9	8	10	8
SDF		1	2	3	2	5				3	2	3	2	2	1
ILP							1			1	1	1		1	1
LEA															
Trades' Council		2		1	3					1		1		2	
Co-op.															
LRC							11	12	12		3		3		
SPGB										2					
TOTAL	20	17	19	16	18	21	27	27	25	22	21	23	20	25	14

KEY

SDF	Social Democratic Federation
ILP	Independent Labour Party
LEA	Labour Electoral Association
LRC	Labour Representation Committee
SPGB	Socialist Party of Great Britain

NOTES

The Burnley Borough Extension Act was passed in 1889. Figures for 1889 include contestants for the 8 existing wards and also the 4 new wards created under the Act (Burnley Express, 2 Nov. 1889).

Appendix Table IV.B.(II)

ANNUAL ELECTIONS TO BURNLEY TOWN COUNCIL, 1870-1914
Social and Political Composition

(II) ELECTED MEMBERS: Political Composition

Year	18 70	71	72	73	74	75	76	77	78	79	18 80	81	82	83	84	85	86	87	88	89	18 90	91	92	93	94	95	96	97	98	99
Liberal	4	5	4	6	6	6	5	8	8	6	8	8	6	5	5	5	6	5	6	19	7	6	8	6	6	5	7	8	5	6
Conservative	4	3	4	2	2	2	3			2			2	3	3	3	2	3	2	6	5	6	4	4	6	7	5	4	7	6
SDF																								2						
ILP																														
Trades' Council																														
LRC																														
TOTAL	8	8	8	8	8	8	8	8	8	8	8	8	8	8	8	8	8	8	8	25	12	12	12	12	12	12	12	12	12	12
% Liberal	50.0	62.5	50.0	75.0	75.0	75.0	62.5	100	100	75.0	100	100	75.0	62.5	62.5	62.5	75.0	62.5	75.0	76.0	58.3	50.0	66.7	50.0	50.0	41.7	58.3	66.7	41.7	50.0
% Conservative	50.0	37.5	50.0	25.0	25.0	25.0	37.5	-	-	25.0	-	-	25.0	37.5	37.5	37.5	25.0	37.5	25.0	24.0	41.7	50.0	33.3	50.0	50.0	58.3	41.7	33.3	58.3	50.0

Appendix Table IV.B.(II) (continued)

(II) ELECTED MEMBERS: Political Composition

Year	19 00	01	02	03	04	05	06	07	08	09	19 10	11	12	13	14
Liberal	9	6	4	7	6	6	6	5	7	6	4	4	4	5	4
Conservative	3	6	6	4	5	5	4	6	5	4	7	8	7	5	8
SDF			2		1	1				1	1		1	1	
ILP							1			1				1	
Trades' Council				1											
LRC							1	1							
TOTAL	12	12	12	12	12	12	12	12	12	12	12	12	12	12	12
% Liberal	75.0	50.0	33.3	58.3	50.0	50.0	50.0	41.7	58.3	50.0	33.3	33.3	33.3	41.7	33.3
% Conservative	25.0	50.0	50.0	33.3	41.7	41.7	33.3	50.0	41.7	33.3	58.3	66.7	58.3	41.7	66.7

KEY

SDF   Social Democratic Federation
ILP   Independent Labour Party
LRC   Labour Representation Committee

NOTES

1889 was the year of Burnley's Borough Extension Act. Statistics for 1889 include elected councillors for the eight existing wards and the four new wards created under the Act (Burnley Express, 2 Nov. 1889) and also councillors elected in by-elections arising from promotions of councillors to the newly-enlarged aldermanic bench (Burnley Express, 27 Nov. 1889).

Appendix Table IV.C.

ANNUAL ELECTIONS TO BURNLEY TOWN COUNCIL, 1870-1914
Social and Political Composition

LARGE EMPLOYERS

Year	18 70	71	72	73	74	75	76	77	78	79	18 80	81	82	83	84	85	86	87	88	89	18 90	91	92	93	94	95	96	97	98	99
No. nominated	9	5	7	7	6	6	8	4	5	4	4	3	5	5	4	3	5	3	3	9	4	7	5	2	2	4	2	1	4	1
No. elected	5	5	4	5	4	5	7	4	5	4	4	3	5	4	2	2	5	3	3	7	3	5	5	1	2	3	2	1	3	0
Employers as % of total elections	62.5	62.5	50.0	62.5	50.0	62.5	87.5	50.0	62.5	50.0	50.0	37.5	62.5	50.0	25.0	25.0	62.5	37.5	37.5	28.0	25.0	41.7	41.7	8.3	16.7	25.0	16.7	8.3	25.0	-
10-year moving average*						60.0	58.8	56.3	57.5	56.3	53.8	50.0	47.5	46.3	43.8	41.6	39.1	39.5	37.4	33.2	32.4	32.4	27.8	24.9	23.6	20.8	18.3	20.0	16.7	17.5
No. elected as Liberals	4	4	2	3	3	5	4	4	5	2	4	3	4	2	1	2	3	2	3	6	2	4	4	1	2	2	2	1	2	0
No. elected as Conservatives	1	1	2	2	1	0	3	0	0	2	0	0	1	2	1	0	2	1	0	1	1	1	1	0	0	1	0	0	1	0

* See Appendix IV.D.

Appendix Table IV.C. (continued)

LARGE EMPLOYERS

Year	18 99	19 00	01	02	03	04	05	06	07	08	09	19 10	11	12	13	14
No. nominated	1	3	5	1	2	4	1	3	4	3	2	3	3	1	3	2
No. elected	0	2	5	1	2	4	1	3	3	3	2	3	2	1	2	2
Employers as % of total elections	.	16.7	41.7	8.3	16.7	33.3	8.3	25.0	25.0	25.0	16.7	25.0	16.7	8.3	16.7	16.7
10-year moving average*	19.2	17.5	18.3	20.0	20.0	21.7	22.5	20.0	20.0	20.0	18.3					
No. elected as Liberals	0	2	4	1	2	4	1	3	3	3	2	3	2	1	2	2
No. elected as Conservatives	0	0	1	0	0	0	0	0	0	0	0	0	0	0	0	0

* See Appendix IV.D.

Appendix Table IV.D.

ANNUAL ELECTIONS TO BURNLEY TOWN COUNCIL
Social and Political Composition

Large employers as a percentage of total numbers elected annually displayed as a ten-year moving average

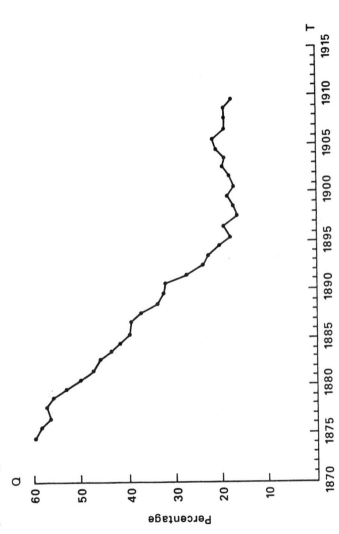

Appendix Table V

SOCIAL AND POLITICAL COMPOSITION OF BURNLEY ALDERMEN, 1870-1914

Name	Occupation	Politics	18 70	71	72	73	74	75	76	77	78	79	18 80	81	82	83	84	85	86	87	88	18 89	90	91	92	93	94	95	96	97	98	99	19 00	01	02	03	04	05	06	07	08	19 09	10	11	12	13	14	Yrs. service in period 1870-1914
Wilkinson T.T.	school master	L	x	x	x	x	x	x																																								5
Lomas Wm.	cotton manuf.	L	x	x	x	x	x	x	x																																							7
Barnes John.	cotton manuf.	L	△	△	x	x	x	∨	∨	∨																																						8
Robinson Wm.	banker	L	x	x	x	x	x	x	x	x	△	△	x																																			11
Kay J.	cotton manuf.	L	x	x	x	x	x	x	x	x	x	x	x	x																																		12
Coultate Dr.	physician		x	x	x	x	x	x	x	x	x	x	x	x																																		12
Thompson Wm.	cotton manuf. and dealer	L	x	x	x	x	x	△	△	△	x	x	x	x	x																																13
Massey L.	wool manuf.	L	x	x	x	△	△	x																																							7
Scott J.H.		L						x	x	x	x	x	x																																		6
Massey J.	textiles and brewing	L									x	x	x	x	x	x																															6
Ogle A.	cotton manuf. and waste dealer	L								x	x	x																																			3
Whittaker J.	cotton manuf. waste dealer	L											x	x	x	x																															6
Collinge L.	cotton manuf.	L											x	x	x																																3
Berry J.	cotton manuf.	L											x	x																																	2
Howorth J.	cotton manuf.(?)	L											△	x	x	x	x	x	x	x	x	x	x	x	x																						13
Fielding H.D.	cotton manuf.	L													△	△	x	x	x	x	x	△																										8
Greenwood Jas.	cotton manuf. and waste dealer	L													x	x	x	x	x	x	x	x	x	x	x	x	x	x	x	x	x	x	x	x	x	x	x											25
Thompson J.	cotton manuf. and waste dealer	L														x	x	x																														3
Altham A.	co-director wholesale tea co.	L														x	x	x	△																													3
Baron J.	cotton manuf. and waste dealer	L														x	△	△	△	x	x	x	x	x	x	x	x	x	x	x	x	x	x	x	x													15
Keighley Geo.	ironfounding and engineering	L														x	x	x	x	x	x	x	x	x	x	x	x	x	x	x	x	x	x	x	x	x												19
Sutcliffe Geo.	cotton manuf.	C																			△	x	x	x	x	x	x	x	x	x	x	x	x	x	x	x												20
Holden R.	draper	L																			x	x	x	x	x	x																						6
Nowell Wm.	butcher	L																				x	x	x	x	x	△	△	△																			8
Lancaster Alf.	cotton manuf.	L																					x	x	x	△	△	△	x	△																		6
Collinge Wm.	cotton manuf.	L																					x	x	x	x	x	x	x	x																		7
Mitchell C.	draper and silk mercer	L																						x	x	x	x	x	△	x	x	x	x	x	x	x	x	x	x	x	x	x						14
Burrows Thos.	cotton manuf.	L																x	x				△	△	x	x	x	x	x	x	x	x	x	△	△	△	x	x	x	x	x	x	x	x	x	x		16
Thornber Thos.	cotton manuf.	L																					△	△	x	x	x	x	x	x	x	x	x	x	x	x	x	x	x	x	x	x	x	x	x	x	x	24

Appendix Table V (continued)

Name	Occupation	Politics	Yrs. service in period 1870-1914
Parkinson Wm.	manuf. chemist	L	16
Lupton Wm.	cotton waste dealer	L	9
Dickenson Wm.	ironfounder	L	12
Armistead W.	cashier	L	10
Thornber Caleb	cotton manuf.	L	18
West T.	cotton manuf.	L	3
Holdsworth R.	machinery agent	L	10
Bibby Jas.	marine store dealer	L	5
Ferguson Dr	physician	L	3
Harker J.W.	tinsmith and ironmonger	C	5
Carrington A.	agent	C	5
Warburton W.	draper	L	5
Metcalfe Geo	baker	L	2
Macfarlane S.	auctioneer	L	6
Emmett H.	cotton manuf.	L	9
Nutter H.	butcher	L	5
Keighley E.	ironfounder and engineering co.	L	8
Hough W	tanner	L	7
Grey J.M.	co. director (cotton)	L	7
Hartley W.	butcher	C	5
Haworth G.	agent and auctioneer	C	6
Whitehead E.	co. director	L	4
Thornber S.	cotton manuf.	L	3
Hanson W.	builder and dealer	C	3
Walmsley T.	gentleman	C	3
Kay J.S.	solicitor	C	1
Heaton J.A.	chemist	C	1
Edmondson J.M.	newsagent	C	1
TOTAL LIBERALS		**47**	
TOTAL CONSERVATIVES		**10**	
COMBINED TOTAL		**57**	

(Columns across the table run by year from 18 70 through 19 14.)

NOTES

x = denotes serving Alderman in main part of year marked
Δ = denotes office of mayor
∇ = denotes failing health, hardly took part (John Barnes)

C = Conservative
L = Liberal

BURNLEY GENERAL ELECTION RESULTS, 1868-1924
(taken from the *Burnley Gazette*)

L = Liberal; C = Conservative; S = Socialist; L.U. = Liberal Unionist.

Nov. 17 1868	R. Shaw	L	2620
	Gen. Scarlett	C	2238
	majority 382		
Jan. 31 1874	R. Shaw	L	3066
	W.A. Lindsay	C	2490
	majority 576		
Feb. 12 1876	P. Rylands	L	3520
	W.A. Lindsay	C	3077
	majority 443		
Mar. 3 1880	P. Rylands	L	3943
	Lord Edmund Talbot	C	3217
	majority 726		
Nov. 28 1885	P. Rylands	L	4866
	H.H. Wainwright	C	4199
	majority 667		
July 3 1886	P. Rylands	L.U.	4209
	James Greenwood	L	4166
	majority 43		
Feb. 19 1887	J. Slagg	L	5026
	J.O.S. Thursby	C	4481
	majority 545		
Feb. 27 1889	J.S. Balfour	L	unopposed
July 4 1892	J.S. Balfour	L	6450
	L. Lawrence	L.U.	5035
	majority 1415		

Appendix Table VI (continued)

Feb. 6 1893	Hon. P. Stanhope	L	6199
	W.A. Lindsay	C	5566
	majority 633		
July 19 1895	Hon. P. Stanhope	L	5454
	W.A. Lindsay	C	5133
	H.M. Hyndman	S	1498
	majority 321		
1900	W. Mitchell	C	6773
	Hon. P. Stanhope	L	6173
	majority 600		
1906	Fred Maddison	L	5288
	G.A. Arbuthnot	C	4964
	H.M. Hyndman	S	4932
	majority 324		
1910 (Jan.)	G.A. Arbuthnot	C	5776
	Fred Maddison	L	5681
	H.M. Hyndman	S	4948
	majority 95		
1910 (Dec.)	P. Morrell	L	6177
	G.A. Arbuthnot	C	6004
	H.M. Hyndman	S	3810
	majority 173		
1918	D.D. Irving	S	15217
	H.C.H. Mulholland	C	12289
	J.M. Grey	L	8825
	majority 2928		
1922	D.D. Irving	S	17385
	H.E.J. Camps	C	14731
	W.T. Layton	L	12339
	majority 2654		

292

Appendix Table VI (continued)

1923	D.D. Irving	S	16848
	H.E.J. Camps	C	14197
	J. Whitehead	L	13543
	majority 2651		
1924	A. Henderson	S	24571
	H.E.J. Camps	C	17534
	majority 7037		

WESLEYAN CIRCUIT STEWARDS IN BURNLEY, 1862-98
(from B. Moore, *History of Wesleyan Methodism in Burnley and East Lancashire*)

Bold type indicates leader (see Tables I, II and III)

1862	Dr Brown, **Sam Smallpage**
1863-64	**Sam Smallpage**, Peter Phillips
1865	Peter Phillips, George Howorth
1866-67	George Howorth, **John Barnes**
1868	**John Barnes, Adam Dugdale**
1869-71	**Adam Dugdale, John Howorth**
1872	**John Howorth, William Lancaster**
1873-74	**William Lancaster, Adam Dugdale**
1875-77	**Adam Dugdale, John Butterworth**
1878-80	**John Butterworth,** John Thornton
1881-82	**John Butterworth, William Lancaster**
1883-84	**William Lancaster, H.D. Fielding**
1885	**H.D. Fielding, B. Moore**
1886	**B. Moore, William Nowell**
1887-88	**B. Moore, J.W. Thompson**
1889-90	**J.W. Thompson**, John Thornton
1891	John Thornton, E. Jones
1892-93	E. Jones, James Lancaster
1894-95	James Lancaster, **John Butterworth**
1896	**John Butterworth**, Francis Scowby
1897-98	Francis Scowby, T.P. Smith

294

Appendix Table VIII

BURNLEY STREET AND PLACE NAMES
ASSOCIATED WITH THE LEADERS,
1870-1900

Altham Street

Bracewell Street

Bulcock Street

Colbran Street

Coultate Street

Dean Street

Dugdale Street

Folds Street

Gawthorpe Road

Grant Street

Grimshaw Street

Hargreaves Street

Hartley Street

Haslam Street

Holden Road

Holmes Street

Howorth Road

Hurtley Street

The Massey Collection (in
Burnley Central Library)

The Massey Music Pavilion
(in Towneley Park)

Massey Street

Mitchell Street

Pollard Street

Pritchard Street

Rawlinson Street

Robinson Street

Sagar Street

Scarlett Street

Scott Park

Scott Park Road

Scott Street

Scott Terrace

Slater Street

Smirthwaite Street

Starkie Street

Thompson Park

Thompson Street

Thornber Gardens

Thursby Gardens

Thursby Road

Thursby Square

Towneley Park

Towneley Road

Towneley Street

Veevers Street

The William Thompson
Recreation Centre (near
Burnley Central Library

COMPOSITION OF THE
BURNLEY SCHOOL BOARD
1871-1901

Name	1871	1874	1877	1880	1883	1886	1889	1892	1895	1898	1901
Hurtley R.J.	N.C.	N.C.	N.C.	N.C.							
Massey J.	N.C.										
Baron J.	N.C.	N.C.	N.C.	N.C.							
Flanagan Rev.	R.C.										
Grant Wm.	Ch.	Ch.	Ch.	Ch.	Ch.	Ch.					
Townley-Parker Rev.	Ch.			Ch.	Ch.	Ch.	Ch.				
Roberts J.	Ch.	Ch.									
Howorth J.	N.C.	N.C.	N.C.								
Maclure Rev.	Ch.	Ch.	Ch.								
Scott J.H.		Ch.									
Cowban J.		R.C.									
Collinge L.		N.C.									
Greenwood J.			Ch.	Ch.	Ch.						
Cranwood Rev. J.			N.C.								
Robinson Wm.			Ch.	Ch.							
Dillon Rev.			R.C.	R.C.							
Owen Rev.				Ch.	Ch.	Ch.	Ch.	Vol.	Vol.		
Priestley Rev.				N.C.							
Butterworth J.					N.C.						
Holmes D.					N.S.	N.S.	N.S.	Pro.	Pro.		
Kay J.					N.C.			Pro.	Pro.		
Berry J.					N.C.						
Morrisey Rev.					R.C.	R.C.	R.C.	R.C.	R.C.	R.C.	R.C.
Barton Rev.						N.C.					
Strange A.						N.C.	N.C.				
Sutcliffe J.S.						N.C.	N.C.				
Thompson W.						N.C.	N.C.				
Hargreaves W.C.							N.C.	Pro.	Pro.	Pro.	
Grey N.P.							Ch.				
Waddington J.C.								Pro.	Pro.		
Leeming J.								Pro.	Pro.	Pro.	Pro.
Thompson J.W.								Pro.			
Hudson J.								Pro.			
Pritchard T.								Vol.	Vol.	Vol.	Vol.
Pullon Dr.								Vol.	Vol.	Vol.	
Berry H.								Vol.			
Bulcock H.								Vol.	Vol.	Vol.	
Winfield Rev.									Vol.	Vol.	Vol.
Jones G.									Pro.		

Appendix Table IX (continued)

Name	1871	1874	1877	1880	1883	1886	1889	1892	1895	1898	1901
Wells W.									Vol.		
Irving D.D.										Pro.	Pro.
O'Hagan Lady										Pro.	Pro.
Mallinson F.										Pro.	
Parry Rev.										Pro.	
Hodgson Dr.										Vol.	
Sparling J.										Pro.	Pro.
Watts J.											Pro.
Smith T.P.											Pro.
Gill G.											Pro.
Altham J.L.											Pro.
Taylor Rev.											Vol.
Cowell W.											Vol.
Creeke M.B.											Vol.
Hargreaves T.W.											Vol.

TOTALS		1871	1874	1877	1880	1883	1886	1889	1892	1895	1898	1901
	Ch.	4	4	4	5	4	3	3				
	N.C	4	4	4	3	3	4	4				
	R.C	1	1	1	1	1	1	1	1	1	1	1
	N.S					1	1	1				
	Pro.								7	6	7	8
	Vol.								5	6	5	6
COMBINED TOTALS		9	9	9	9	9	9	9	13	13	13	15

KEY

Ch. = Churchman
N.C. = Nonconformist
R.C. = Roman Catholic
N.S. = Non-Sectarian
Pro. = Progressive
Vol. = Voluntarist

The School Board was increased to
13 members in 1892 and to 15 in 1901.

In 1903 the School Board was replaced by the
Local Education Authority which contained
representatives of various interests in the
proportions below.

Representatives of the Town Council	5 Aldermen
	15 Councillors
Reps. of Church Schools	2
Reps. of R.C. Schools	1
Reps. of N.C. Schools	1
Reps. of Board Schools	1
Co-opted members with specific educational experience	5
TOTAL	30

CENTRES OF WORSHIP IN BURNLEY

Church of England
St Peter: centuries old parish church; alterations to fabric, 1853; new chancel dedicated, 1873.

Holy Trinity: church consecrated, 1873; chancel added, 1873.

St James: Sunday school opened, 1839; church consecrated, 1849; tower and spire added, 1869.

All Saints: Sunday school opened, 1842; church consecrated, 1849; church extensively rebuilt, 1862; site given by Sir James Kay-Shuttleworth.

St Paul: Sunday school opened, 1848, church consecrated, 1853; site given by the Reverend William Thursby and General Scarlett.

St Andrew: Sunday school opened, 1865; church consecrated, 1867; site given by R. T. Parker of Cuerden; funds donated by the Thursby and Hargreaves families.

St Stephen: mission opened, 1865; school chapel dedicated, 1870; church consecrated, 1879; site given by Canon Townley-Parker; funds donated by the Thursby and Hargreaves families.

St Matthew: mission school opened in Back Lane, 1835; church consecrated, 1879; north aisle added, 1895; funds donated by the Reverend William Thursby and Sir James Kay-Shuttleworth.

St John: Sunday school opened at Wood Top, 1868; church consecrated, 1880; site given by the Reverend William Thursby and Lady Scarlett; funds for the tower and reredos donated by the Thursby family.

St Catherine: church consecrated, 1897; funds donated by the Thursby and Hargreaves families.

St Margaret: church consecrated, 1898; funds donated by the Thursby and Hargreaves families.

St Cuthbert: church consecrated, 1908; funds donated by the Thursby and Hargreaves families.

Roman Catholic
St Mary: church dedicated, 1849; convent opened, 1885.

St Thomas: chapel of ease opened, 1895.

St Mary Magdelene: mission opened 1883; church dedicated, 1904.

St John the Baptist: Elm Street mission opened, 1891; Ivy Street mission opened, 1893; church dedicated, 1908.

St Augustine: mission opened, 1898; church dedicated, 1926.

Christ the King (to replace St Thomas's Church): mission opened 1929; church dedicated, 1935.

Wesleyan Methodist
Keighley Green: chapel opened, 1787.

Wesley Chapel, Hargreaves Street: chapel opened 1840.

Wesleyan Town Mission formed 1857.

Fulledge: chapel opened, 1861.

Lane Bridge: mission opened, 1865; chapel opened, 1868.

Accrington Road: chapel opened at Bartle Hills in 1849 removed to Accrington Road, 1871.

Rosehill: mission opened, 1871.

Colne Road: meeting place opened, 1863; chapel opened, 1872.

Whittlefield: mission opened, 1873; chapel opened, 1878.

Brooklands Road: mission opened, 1879; chapel opened, 1888.

Stoneyholme: mission opened, 1880; chapel opened, 1888.

Wood Top: mission opened, 1878; chapel opened, 1891.

United Methodist Free Church
Mount Pleasant: chapel opened, 1835; removed to new premises at Brunswick, 1869.

Myrtle Bank: Mount Pisgah opened, 1835; removed to Myrtle Bank, date unrecorded.

Claremont: chapel opened at Gannow, 1861; removed to Claremont, 1891.

Hanover: mission opened, 1878; chapel opened, 1893.

Lincoln Street: chapel opened, 1883.

Primitive Methodist
Curzon Street: chapel opened, 1834.

Bethel: chapel opened, 1852.

Appendix Table X (continued)

Mount Zion: mission opened at Rake Head, 1847; small chapel opened in Briarcliffe Road, 1858; new chapel opened in Colne Road, 1879.

Elim: small chapel opened in Lane Head, 1867, new chapel opened, 1895.

Rehoboth: mission opened in Springfield Road, 1858; chapel opened, 1869.

Zion: chapel opened at Gannow Top, 1869.

Rosegrove: chapel opened, 1905.

Jubilee: chapel opened in Padiham Road, 1902.

Congregationalist
Bethesda: chapel built, 1814; chapel rebuilt and re-opened, 1881.

Salem: chapel opened, 1851.

Westgate: chapel opened, 1861.

Hollingreave Road: mission opened, 1889; chapel opened, 1896.

Rosegrove: chapel opened, 1900.

Thursby Road: chapel opened, 1914.

Baptist
Ebenezer: chapel built, 1786; chapel enlarged, 1816; Sunday school built, 1850, but demolished to provide the site for a new chapel opened in 1861; Sunday schools opened, 1870.

Sion: chapel opened in Yorkshire Street, 1830; new chapel opened, 1863; Sunday school opened, 1884.

Enon: chapel opened, 1852.

Mount Pleasant: chapel bought from Methodists, 1871.

Angle Street: chapel opened, 1877; Sunday school opened, 1878.

Mount Olivet: chapel opened, 1893.

Emmanuel: chapel opened, 1895.

Unitarian
Services held in rented room in Thomas Street, 1858; removed to permanent premises in Tanner Street, 1859; chapel opened in Trafalgar Street, 1871.

Select Bibliography

ABERCROMBIE, N. and TURNER, B.S., 'The Dominant Ideology Thesis', *British Journal of Sociology*, XXIX, 1978, pp. 149-70;
The Dominant Ideology Thesis, Allen & Unwin, 1980.

ABERCROMBIE, N., HILL, S. and TURNER, B.S., *Dictionary of Sociology*, Penguin, 1984.

ANDERSON, G., *Victorian Clerks*, Manchester University Press, 1976.

AUGAR, P., 'The Cotton Famine, 1861-65', D.Phil. thesis, University of Oxford, 1979.

BAILEY, P., *Leisure and Class in Victorian England: Rational Recreation and the Contest for Control, 1830-85*, Routledge & Kegan Paul, 1978.

BELL, C. and NEWBY, H., 'The Sources of Variation in Agricultural Workers' Images of Society' in BULMER, M., ed., *Working Class Images of Society*, Routledge & Kegan Paul, 1975.

BENNETT, W., *The History of Burnley*, IV, Burnley Corporation, 1951.

BLAUNER, R., 'Industrialism and the Labor Response: The Case of the American South', *Berkeley Publications in Society and Institutions*, Summer, 1958.

BULMER, M., ed., *Working Class Images of Society*, Routledge & Kegan Paul, 1975.

BURNHAM, J., *The Managerial Revolution: What is Happening in the World?*, Putnam, New York, 1942;
The Machiavellians, John Day, New York, 1943.

CARTER, G.A., *Warrington: One Hundred Years a Borough*, Garside & Jolley, 1947.

CHAPMAN, S.D., *The Early Factory Masters*, David & Charles, 1967.

CHILD, J., 'Quaker Employers and Industrial Relations', *Sociological Review*, XII, 1964, pp. 293-315.

CLARKE, P.F., *Lancashire and the New Liberalism*, Cambridge University Press, 1971.

CORNFORD, J., 'The Transformation of Conservatism in the Late Nineteenth Century', *Victorian Studies*, VII, No. 1, 1963, pp. 35-66.

CROSSLEY, R.S., *Accrington Chronology and Men of Mark*, Accrington Corporation, 1924.

CROWE, A.M., *Warrington: Ancient and Modern*, J.H. Teake & Son, 1947.

CUNNINGHAM, H., 'The Metropolitan Fairs: A Case Study in the Social Control of Leisure' in DONAJGRODSKI, A.P., ed., *Social Control in Nineteenth Century Britain*, Croom Helm, 1977.

DANZIGER, K., *Socialization*, Penguin, 1971.

DELGADO, A., *The Annual Outing and Other Excursions*, Allen & Unwin, 1977.

DOGAN, M., ed., *The Mandarins of Western Europe*, McGraw-Hill, New York, 1975.

DONAJGRODSKI, A.P., ed., *Social Control in Nineteenth Century Britain*, Croom Helm, 1977.

DOYLE, M.B., 'Social Control in Over Darwen, 1839-78', M.A. dissertation, University of Lancaster, 1972.

DURKHEIM, E., (1912), *The Elementary Forms of Religious Life*, Allen & Unwin, 1954.

DUTTON, H.I. and KING, J.E., *Ten Per Cent and No Surrender: The Preston Strike, 1853-54*, Cambridge University Press, 1981; 'The Limits of Paternalism: The Cotton Tyrants of North Lancashire, 1836-54', *Social History*, VII, 1982, pp. 59-74.

DYOS, H.J. and ALDCROFT, D.H., *British Transport*, Leicester University Press, 1969.

ELLIS, A.C.O., 'Influences on School Attendance in Victorian England', *British Journal of Educational Studies*, XXI, 1973, pp. 313-26.

ENGELS, F., (1845), *The Condition of the Working Class in England in 1844*, reprinted by Allen & Unwin, 1968.

FIELD, G.L. and HIGLEY, *The Professional Soldier*, Glencoe, Illinois, 1980.

FOSTER, J., 'Nineteenth Century Towns: A Class Dimension' in FLINN, M.W. and SMOUT, T.C., eds, *Essays in Social History*, Oxford University Press, 1974;
Class Struggle and the Industrial Revolution: Early Industrial Capitalism in Three English Towns, Weidenfeld & Nicolson, 1974.

FRIEDMAN, G., *The Anatomy of Work: The Implications of Specialization*, Heinemann, 1961.

GARRARD, J., *Leadership and Power in Victorian Industrial Towns, 1830-1880*, Manchester University Press, 1983.

GOFFMAN, E., 'The Nature of Deference and Demeanour' in his *Interaction Ritual*, Penguin, 1972;
Strategic Interaction, Blackwell, 1970;
Encounters: Two Studies in the Sociology of Interaction, Bobbs-Merrill, Indianapolis, 1961.

GOLDSTROM, J.M., 'The Content of Education and the Socialization of the Working Class Child' in McCANN, P., ed., *Popular Education and Socialization in the Nineteenth Century*, Methuen, 1977.

GRAMSCI, A., *Selections from the Prison Notebooks*, New Left Books, reprinted 1971.

HALÉVY, E., *The Birth of Methodism in England*, translated and edited by SEMMEL, B., Aldine, Chicago, 1971.

HALL, A.H., 'Social Control and the Working Class Challenge in Ashton-under-Lyne, 1880-1914', M.A. dissertation, University of Lancaster, 1975.

HALL, H., *Lowerhouse and the Dugdales: A Study of a Lancashire Mill Community*, Burnley and District Historical Society, undated.

HART, J., 'Religion and Social Control in the Mid Nineteenth Century' in DONAJGRODSKI, A.P., ed., *Social Control in Nineteenth Century Britain*, Croom Helm, 1977.

HILL, S., *The Dockers: Class and Tradition in London*, Heinemann, 1976.

HOBSBAWM, E.J., *Labouring Men*, Weidenfeld & Nicolson, 1964.

HOGGART, R., *The Uses of Literacy*, Chatto & Windus, 1957.

HOLLIS, P., *Women in Public: The Women's Movement, 1850-1900*, Allen & Unwin, 1979.

HOWE, A.C., *The Cotton Masters*, Oxford University Press, 1984.

HOWELL, D., *British Workers and the Independent Labour Party*, Manchester University Press, 1983.

HURT, J.S., *Elementary Schooling and the Working Class, 1860-1918*, Routledge & Kegan Paul, 1979.

JONES, S.G., 'Class Expression versus Social Control: A Critique of Recent Trends in the Social History of Leisure' in JONES, S.G., ed., *Languages of Class*, Cambridge University Press, 1983.

JOYCE, P., 'The Factory Politics of Lancashire in the Later Nineteenth Century', *Historical Journal*, XVIII, 1975, pp. 525-53; *Work, Society and Politics: The Culture of the Factory in Later Victorian England*, Harvester, 1980.

KAVANAGH, D., 'The Deferential English: A Comparative Critique', *Government and Opposition*, VI, 1971, pp. 333-60.

KING, J.E., ' "We Could Eat the Police:" Popular Violence in the North Lancashire Cotton Strike of 1878', *Victorian Studies*, XXVIII, No. 3, 1985, pp. 439-71.

KNEESHAW, J., *Burnley in the Nineteenth Century*, Burnley Corporation, 1921.

KUPER, A. and J., eds, *The Social Sciences Encyclopedia*, Routledge & Kegan Paul, 1985.

LAWSON, J. and SILVER, H., *A Social History of Education in England*, Methuen, 1973.

LOCKWOOD, D., 'Sources of Variation in Working Class Images of Society', *Sociological Review*, New Series, XIV, No. 3, 1966, pp. 249-67.

MADOC-JONES, B., 'Patterns of Attendance and their Social Significance' in McCANN, P., ed., *Popular Education and Socialization in the Nineteenth Century*, Methuen, 1977.

MANN, M., *Consciousness and Action among the Western Working Class*, Macmillan, 1973.

MARSDEN, W.E., 'Social Environment, School Attendance and Educational Achievement in a Merseyside Town, 1870-1900' in McCANN, P., ed., *Popular Education and Socialization in the Nineteenth Century*, Methuen, 1977.

MARVICK, D., 'Élites' in KUPER, A. and J., eds, *The Social Sciences Encyclopaedia*, Routledge & Kegan Paul, 1985.

MARX, K. and ENGELS, F. (1845), *The German Ideology*, Lawrence & Wishart, 1965.

McCANN, P., ed., *Popular Education and Socialization in the Nineteenth Century*, Methuen, 1977.

McKENZIE, R. and SILVER, A., *Angels in Marble: Working Class Conservatives in Urban England*, Heinemann, 1968.

McLEOD, H., *Religion and the Working Class in Nineteenth Century Britain*, Macmillan, 1984.

MEISEL, J.H., *The Myth of the Ruling Class: Gaetano Mosca and the Élite*, Ann Arbor, Michigan, 1962;
ed., *Pareto and Mosca*, Prentice-Hall, New Jersey, 1965.

MICHELS, R. (1911), *Political Parties: A Sociological Study of Oligarchical Tendencies in Modern Democracy*, Free Press, New York, 1962.

MILIBAND, R., 'The Capitalist State: Reply to Nicol Poulantzas', *New Left Review*, No. 59, 1970, pp. 53-60;
The State in Capitalist Society, Weidenfeld & Nicolson, 1969.

MILLS, C.W., *The Power Élite*, Simon & Schuster, New York, 1956.

MOSCA, G. (1896), *The Ruling Class*, McGraw-Hill, New York, 1939.

MOUFFE, C., ed., *Gramsci and Marxist Theory*, Routledge & Kegan Paul, 1979.

MUSSON, A.E., *Enterprise in Soap and Chemicals: The Crosfields of Warrington, 1815-1965*, Manchester University Press, 1965.

NEWBY, H., *Property, Paternalism and Power: Class and Control in Rural England*, Hutchinson, 1978;
'Paternalism and Capitalism' in SCASE, R., ed., *Industrial Society: Class Cleavage and Control*, Allen & Unwin, 1977;
'The Deferential Dialectic', *Comparative Studies in Society and History*, XVII, 1975, pp. 139-64;
The Deferential Worker, Allen Lane, 1977.

NICHOLS, T. and ARMSTRONG, P., *Workers Divided*, Fontana, 1976.

NIEBBUHR, H.R., *The Social Sources of Denominationalism*, Free Press, New York, 1929.

NORDLINGER, E., *The Working Class Tories: Authority, Deference and Stable Democracy*, MacGibbon & Kee, 1967.

ODDY, D.J., 'Urban Famine in Nineteenth Century Britain', *Economic History Review*, 2nd Series, XXXVI, No. 1, 1983, pp. 68-86.

PARETO, V. (1916), *The Mind and Society: A Treatise on General Sociology*, Harcourt-Brace, New York, 1935.

PARKER, S., *The Society of Leisure*, Allen & Unwin, 1976.

PARKIN, F., *Class Inequality and Political Order*, MacGibbon & Kee, 1971.

PARRY, G., *Political Élites*, Allen & Unwin, 1969.

PARSONS, T., *The Social System*, Routledge & Kegan Paul, 1951.

PELLING, H., *A History of British Trade Unionism*, Macmillan, 1963.

PERKIN, H.J., *Origins of Modern English Society, 1780-1880*, Routledge & Kegan Paul, 1969.

PIMLOTT, J.A.R., *The Englishman's Holiday: A Social History*, 2nd edition, Harvester, 1977.

POLLARD, S., *The Genesis of Modern Management*, Edward Arnold, 1965;
'Factory Discipline in the Industrial Revolution', *Economic History Review*, 2nd Series, XVI, 1963, pp. 254-71.

RAISTRICK, A., *Two Centuries of Industrial Welfare: The London (Quaker) Lead Company, 1692-1905*, Society of Friends, 1938.

ROBERTS, D., *Paternalism in Early Victorian England*, Croom Helm, 1979.

ROBERTS, K., *Leisure*, Longman, 1970.

RODMAN, H., 'The Lower Class Value Stretch', *Social Forces*, XLII, 1963, pp. 205-15.

ROLL, E., *An Early Experiment in Industrial Organization: Boulton and Watt, 1775-1805*, Longman, 1930.

RUBENSTEIN, D., 'Socialization and the London School Board, 1870-1914: Aims, Methods and Opinion' in McCANN, P. ed., *Popular Education and Socialization in the Nineteenth Century*, Methuen, 1977.

RUNCIMAN, W.G., *Relative Deprivation and Social Justice*, Routledge & Kegan Paul, 1966.

RUSSELL, A., 'Élites at the Local Level of Society: Social Leadership in Burnley, 1870-1900', M.A. dissertation, University of Lancaster, 1976;
'The Quest for Security: The Changing Working Conditions and Status of the British Working Class', Ph.D. thesis, University of Lancaster, 1982;
'Private Industry and the Roots of Welfare', paper presented to an ESRC conference on Roots of Welfare, University of Lancaster, 1983;
'Local Élites and the Working Class Response in the North West, 1870-1895: Paternalism and Deference Reconsidered', *Northern History*, XXIII, 1987, pp. 153-73.

SAUL, S.B., *The Myth of the Great Depression, 1873-96*, Macmillan, 1969.

SENNETT, R., *Authority*, Secker & Warburg, 1980.

SHILS, E., 'Deference' in Jackson, J.A., ed., *Social Stratification*, Cambridge University Press, 1968.

STORCH, R.D., 'The Problem of Working Class Leisure: Some Roots of Middle Class Moral Reform in the Industrial North, 1825-1850' in DONAJGRODSKI, A.P., ed., *Social Control in Nineteenth Century Britain*, Croom Helm, 1977.

THOMIS, M.I., *The Town Labourer and the Industrial Revolution*, Batsford, 1974.

THOMPSON, E.P., *The Making of the English Working Class*, Gollancz, 1963.

THOMPSON, F.M.L., 'Social Control in Victorian Britain', *Economic History Review*, 2nd Series, XXXIV, 1981, pp. 189-208.

TRODD, G., 'Political Change and the Working Class in Blackburn and Burnley, 1880-1914', Ph.D. thesis, University of Lancaster, 1978.

TURNER, H.A., *Trade Union Growth, Structure and Policy*, Allen & Unwin, 1962.

WALE, D.A., 'Politics and Society in Accrington, 1880-1939', M.A. dissertation, University of Lancaster, 1976.

WALTON, J.K., *Lancashire: A Social History, 1558-1939*, Manchester University Press, 1987;
'The Demand for Working Class Seaside Holidays in Victorian England', *Economic History Review*, 2nd Series, XXXIV, 1981, pp. 249-65;
The English Seaside Resort: A Social History, 1750-1914, Leicester University Press, 1983.

WALVIN, J., *The People's Game: A Social History of Football*, Allen Lane, 1975.

WATSON, M.I., 'The Cotton Trade Unions and Labour Representation in the Late Nineteenth Century', *Northern History*, XX, 1984, pp. 207-16.

WILSON, B., *Sects and Society*, Heinemann, 1961.

WINDSOR, D., *The Quaker Enterprise: Friends in Business*, Muller, 1980.

YOUNG, M.E., 'The Burnley School Board, 1871-1891', M.Ed. dissertation, University of Manchester, 1973.

INDEX